"My God and My All"

A PRAYER
For Those Who Live Alone

I live alone, dear Lord,
Stay by my side,
In all my daily needs
Be Thou my guide.
Grant me good health,
For that indeed, I pray,
To carry on my work
from day to day.
Keep pure my mind,
My thoughts, my every deed,
Let me be kind, unselfish
In my neighbor's need.
Spare me from fire, from flood,
Malicious tongues,
From thieves, from fear,
And evil ones.
If sickness or an accident befall,
Then humbly, Lord, I pray,
Hear Thou my call.
And when I'm feeling low,
Or in despair,
Lift up my heart
And help me in my prayer.
I live alone, dear Lord,
Yet have no fear,
Because I feel Your Presence
Ever near. Amen.

Joe Kotcka

With Ecclesiastical Approval

Before the Lamps Went Out

Winston Churchill and Admiral Lord Fisher
leaving the Committee of Imperial Defence

Before the Lamps Went Out

BY

GEOFFREY MARCUS

An Atlantic Monthly Press Book

LITTLE, BROWN AND COMPANY

BOSTON — TORONTO

Library of Congress Catalog Card No. 64-17482

© *George Allen & Unwin Ltd* 1965

ATLANTIC-LITTLE, BROWN BOOKS
ARE PUBLISHED BY
LITTLE, BROWN AND COMPANY
IN ASSOCIATION WITH
THE ATLANTIC MONTHLY PRESS

PRINTED IN GREAT BRITAIN

To the memory of my father

CONTENTS

ILLUSTRATIONS

ACKNOWLEDGEMENTS

Thanks are due to the Editor of the *Journal of the Royal United Service Institution* for allowing me to reproduce some of the Naval material which appeared in the *Journal* on the fiftieth anniversary of the war of 1914-18.

Thanks are also due to all those who contributed interesting details concerning the events narrated in this book of which they were eye-witnesses. It was much to be regretted that, for reasons of space, it was not possible to mention them by name. Nor was it possible to include the detailed documentation; copies of which, however, will in due course be deposited in the British Museum and Library of Congress.

For permission to reproduce the illustrations I wish to thank the following:

Central Library, Eastbourne, for Pl. 9b

Daily Mirror, for Pl. 7a

Mr William G. Davis, for Pls. 4a, b, c, 6a, b

Fishermen's Museum, Hastings, for Pl. 10c

Mr G. G. Garland, for Pls. 2, 3a, b, 8a

Mr John Goring, for Pl. 1

Illustrated London News, for Pls. 11a, b, c, 12a, 14a

Imperial War Museum, for Pl. 13

Messrs Judges Ltd., for Pl. 10d

Mr Edgar J. March, for Pl. 10a

National Museum of Ireland, for Pl. 12b

Punch, for Pls. 6c, d

Raymond Mander & Joe Mitchenson Theatre Collection, for Pl. 5b

Radio Times Hulton Picture Library, for Frontispiece, Pls. 5a, 7b, 8b, 14b, c

Fig. 9a is a photograph by the late Mr F. Douglas Miller; the cartoons on pages 80 and 163 are from the *Reynolds Newspaper* and the *Pall Mall Gazette* respectively, and are reproduced by courtesy of the *Daily Mail*; and the cartoon on page 306 is reproduced by courtesy of *Punch.*

CHAPTER 1

'On Christmas Day in the Morning'

December 25, 1913. Six o'clock of a sharp frosty morning.

One by one the bell-ringers assembled at the old church under the South Downs, stamping and blowing on their numbed fingers. They stood in a circle with the ropes in their hands, intoning the ancient ritual words, 'Here goes one'; and the joyful chimes rang out across the sleeping countryside.

Some hours earlier little groups of people might have been seen trudging across the darkened fields, a few miles off, on their way to midnight Mass; for here and there throughout Sussex the old Faith still survived. The manger in the little Crib was empty; but, presently, the priest came in bearing the figure of the Babe, which, as the people sang the opening carol, he laid gently in the hay. The gospel for that first Mass on Christmas Day told of a certain morning, at Bethlehem in 'the land of Judah', more than nineteen centuries ago.

' . . . And Joseph also went up from Galilee out of the city of Nazareth into Judea, to the city of David, which is called Bethlehem: because he was of the house and family of David, to be enrolled with Mary, his espoused wife, who was with child. And it came to pass, that when they were there, her days were accomplished, that she should be delivered. And she brought forth her first born son, and wrapped Him up in swaddling clothes, and laid Him in a manger, because there was no room for them in the inn. And there were there in the same country shepherds watching, and keeping the night-watches over their flock. And behold, an angel of the Lord stood by them, and the brightness of God shone round about them, and they feared with a great fear. And the Angel said to them: Fear not; for behold, I bring you good tidings of great joy, that shall be to all the

15

people; for this day is born to you a SAVIOUR, who is Christ the Lord, in the city of David. And this shall be a sign unto you; you shall find the infant wrapped in swaddling clothes, and laid in a manger. And suddenly there was with the angel a multitude of the heavenly army praising God, and saying: Glory be to God in the highest, and on earth peace to men of good will.'

This, broadly speaking, was the accepted belief of the great mass of the English people—more especially of the country folk. It was the fixed, final, and certain explanation of the mystery of the universe, and of the destiny of man. It was shared by all classes of the population, from the oldest to the youngest, and formed one of the principal bonds of union among them. *Et Verbum caro factum est*—'And the Word was made flesh'. That, in a word, was the meaning of Christmas. The custom of regular church-going had declined since the Victorian heyday, at any rate in the towns; but not a few of the people who did not usually go to church went there as a matter of course on the two great festivals of the Christian year, Christmas and Easter.

St Mary's Church at Wiston, in Sussex, lay hard by the fine Tudor mansion under Chanctonbury Hill. From all around the people came across the frosty fields and meadows in the bright December sunshine to the eleven o'clock service. That morning there was scarcely an empty place in the church, where their ancestors had worshipped for so many centuries. The congregation was disposed in the customary manner — the men sitting in one block of pews and the women in another. The schoolchildren were accommodated in special small pews of their own on the north side of the main aisle. The Squire and his family sat in high-backed stalls at the back of the church—the Squire on the men's side, and his wife on the women's. Immediately below were the butler, coachman, housekeeper, lady's maid, and other upper servants; after that came several rows of pews filled by the footmen, grooms, and gardeners, and the house-, kitchen-, and laundry-maids. (The indoor and outdoor staff at Wiston House numbered from thirty to forty persons.) All the men-servants were in livery, and all the women wore black hats. Over near the altar was the fine brass above the tomb of Sir John de Braose, the last of a line who had held these lands since the Norman Conquest. The little church was decorated in honour of the Christmas feast with quantities of red-berried holly, ivy, and other evergreens.

Many of the time-honoured Christmas customs were gradually falling into abeyance. The ancient ceremony of bringing in the Yule log had long since died out in Sussex, though it was still kept up in certain parts of Cornwall, Northumberland, and other distant regions. But the old custom of 'wassailing', or carol-singing, still survived. Parties of men and boys would go round the parish, calling at the larger houses, chanting carols and other traditional airs like 'The Bailiff's Daughter of Fair Islington', 'A Sweet Country Life', and 'The Blind Beggar's Daughter of Bethnal Green'. Some of these songs, and the loveliest, were of very ancient origin.

> Here we come a-wassailing
> Among the leaves so green;
> Here we come a-wassailing
> All fair to be seen.
> Love and joy come to you,
> And to you your wassail too,
> And God bless you and send you
> A happy New Year.

It was customary for the Squire to distribute coal and various foodstuffs among the poorer families of the parish. The annual Christmas party for the school children would be held either in the manor-house or in one of the larger farmhouses. Sometimes there would be a magic-lantern show or some other entertainment on these occasions, and there was invariably a Christmas tree. At Wiston the annual children's party used to be held in the Great Hall, with a huge Christmas tree set up in a tub by the high mullioned windows and the musicians' gallery hung with boughs of scarlet-berried holly. The traditional games were played—'Ring-a-roses', 'Poor Jenny is a-weeping', 'Here we come gathering nuts in May', 'Oranges and lemons', 'Blind man's buff', 'Puss in the corner', and the rest. There were *tableaux vivants*, and singing, and dancing; and at the appointed hour Father Christmas would emerge from the great open hearth with a bulging sack over his shoulder, to the immense delight of the younger children.

Twelfth Night saw the time-honoured gambols of the strolling players, variously known as Tipteers in Sussex, Mummers in

Berkshire, Guisers in Staffordshire, and Geese-dancers in Cornwall. The Mummers' play centred around the old story of St
George, the Turk, and the Seven Champions of Christendom;
but it had come down through so many generations that the
plot—and a good many of the lines as well—were now almost
unintelligible. The play varied considerably from county to
county, and even from village to village, and sometimes
incorporated various other stories and legends. (In the Dorset
version of the Mummers' play, the dialogue between Captain
Hardy and the dying Nelson in the cockpit of the *Victory* was
introduced at some date after Trafalgar.) There were certain
recognized characters in the play like Father Christmas ('Here
comes old Father Christmas, Cold or hot. Am I welcome, Or
am I not?'), St George, the Turkish Knight, and the Doctor,
with occasionally Beau Slasher, Beelzebub, and Little Devil
Doubt. The players, who were often farmers' sons, were weirdly
and wonderfully attired, and sometimes had their faces
blackened or wore masks of sheepskin. There was a good deal
of horseplay and rough knockabout humour. The proceedings
terminated with the 'Mummers' Carol' sung by all the players.

Half a century ago, a considerable portion of this island was
rural through and through. The balance between town and
country had not been destroyed. The countryman was essentially
a countryman. The civilization of the town had not yet sup-
planted the rural dialect and the rural outlook. Nearly every
county in the kingdom had its own distinctive speech, which
not infrequently was almost unintelligible to outsiders. The outlook of a large proportion of the population tended to revolve round
the parish pump. What the late Dr Blaker wrote of his native
Sussex was equally true of farm workers throughout the land:

'It was not an usual thing for men to work all their lives on
one farm, and in it and all that belonged to it they took the
deepest interest, regarding it almost as their own property and
speaking always of "our" cows, "our" sheep, "our" wheat; and
their great object and ambition was to do their work, ploughing,
mowing, etc., well, and to have their own crops and animals

under their care to look a little better than their neighbours'.'[1]

Such changes as had occurred were of a slow and gradual nature. The spread of the railways had produced nothing like so profound a revolution in country life as the advent of the motor-bus and electricity was later to achieve. It was the last phase of an era—a phase, as Hilaire Belloc once observed, 'whose complete literary expression is to be found in Gray's Elegy'. The old rural crafts still flourished. In practically every village of any size there lived a blacksmith, a thatcher, a shoemaker, and a rat-catcher, and somewhere in the neighbourhood there was a wheelwright, a saddle- and harness-maker, a miller, and a carpenter. Girls and boys usually left school about the age of thirteen, and then went into service and started work on the land respectively. Certain of the rural vocations were almost hereditary—they tended to run in particular families. The son of a shepherd frequently followed in his father's footsteps—as did also that of an ox-herd, carter, or gamekeeper. The lives of all were regulated by the slow passage of the seasons, and they paid little heed to what was happening in the outside world. As in the days of Thomas Gray—

> Along the cool sequester'd vale of life
> They kept the noiseless tenor of their way.

In the more out-of-the-way parts of the country one might still behold the corn reaped with sickles in the ancient way; and, yet more remarkable, one might still see wagons and ploughs drawn by two or three couples of huge, slow-pacing, long-horned black oxen.

Old beliefs and superstitions still lingered on in the age of motor-cars and wireless telegraphy. The services of the dowser were often resorted to with success when more scientific methods had failed. The custom of 'telling the bees' survived in many places. There were endless superstitions about magpies and other birds. Children were warned not to make faces for fear that the wind should suddenly change and they 'would be struck like it'; and they were sometimes taken to the local wise woman to have their warts charmed away. Within living memory stories about the fairies (or 'farisees' as they used to be called in Sussex)

[1] N. P. Blaker, *Sussex in Bygone Days* (1919), pp. 4-5.

were still current. About the same time it had been the custom, on the death of a shepherd, to put a lock of wool into his coffin by way of excuse for the dead man's unavoidable absence from Sunday morning church.

The Sussex farm labourers of half a century ago were a shrewd, strong, hardy, industrious, truthful, honest, patient, cheerful, and contented set of men; tenacious of their rights— *'wun't be druv'* might be said to have been their watchword; generous to their friends and neighbours in time of need; intensely individualistic and conservative; stubborn, cautious, and slow of speech. As a rule they were known, not by their Christian names, but by some more or less picturesque nickname. Their life was one of hard, continuous, though to some extent leisurely, toil. They worked well and for long hours; but always at their own pace, and in accordance with a shrewd and reasonable philosophy.

'Look'ee 'ere, me boy,' observed an old man to a youngster who was assisting him, 'dunn'ee go too fast an' dunn'ee go too slow; a middlin' pace is what I wants; an' yer'l find as yer goes through life that be the best pace ter work; too farst means a bad job, too slow means not 'nuff done; but middlin', yer ken keep on all day an' do it well.'[1]

The shepherd, the cowman, and the carter were all master men — the aristocrats of the farm workers. They were highly esteemed by their employers, and they were well aware that they were highly esteemed.

'We old 'uns was poor,' one of them related long afterwards, 'but things was different, an' a shepherd was a *somebody* then; but now us be nobody at all.'[2]

There were also the skilled craftsmen who were on 'piece work': the thatcher, who went from farm to farm thatching the hay and corn ricks, and the farm buildings, barns, and cottages; the rat-catcher, whose services, in one capacity or another, were in demand all the year round; and the sheep-shearers, who in companies of half a dozen or more went from flock to flock during the early summer — in winter they often worked in the woods. All these men earned wages which were usually well above those of the ordinary farm worker.

[1] F. F. Wood, *Sport and Nature in Sussex* (1928), p. 115.
[2] Barclay Wills, *Downland Treasure*, p.11.

The generality of the labourers lived simply and frugally and brought up large families on a small wage. Many of them seldom left their native village, and quite a number had never been in a railway train. For the most part they made their own amusements; and, so far as can be ascertained, got considerably more out of life than their much better paid successors.

'Them was 'appy days,' is a fairly general testimony of life as it used to be in the early years of the present century. Village life was busier and fuller than it is today. For the men there was their garden or allotment and the congenial company of their fellows in the village inn—especially the good songs and the good talk there on 'Saddaday nightses'. For the women there was gossiping at the garden gate and over the tea-cups. In the happy summer time there was cricket for the men and boys, and stool-ball — an old Sussex game sometimes called 'bittle-battle' — for the women and girls; and the surrounding meadows and woods became one large, entrancing playground for the younger children. They showed their whole-hearted enjoyment of such traditional festivities as the annual ploughing match, the sheep-shearing supper, the local Club Day, the flower show, and, at the close of the farming year, the harvest supper.

For centuries the country house had been a vital and integral part of our civilization. Almost to within living memory it had been largely self-sufficient, producing almost everything that was needed by its occupants. Nearly every county in England possessed a score or so of country houses built on so grand a scale that they might well have been reckoned as palaces, as well as a large number of smaller places which in some cases were masterpieces of architecture and landscape gardening. With their finely timbered parks, their beautiful old gardens, and their aura of immemorial peace and beauty, the country house, since the passing of the Middle Ages, had formed the setting and background for the spacious life of the English landed gentry—unquestionably one of the strongest, ablest, and most successful ruling classes that the world had ever seen. The debt owed by architecture, sculpture, painting, and literature, no less than by the art of governance, conversation, manners, and taste to these

country houses is almost incalculable. To quote an eminent
authority:

'Many country houses would hardly have seemed complete unless they kindly sheltered some artist or writer, struggling for
fame or already wearied with Parnassus. One thinks of Turner
at Petworth and Pope hobbling among the groves of Cirencester;
or the mingling of culture with government and government
with wit at Stowe and Wilton; of what for a brief time Newstead
meant to Byron and his friends. Whatever the motive, there can
be no doubt much English talent could never have found
maturity without the patronage and leisure that was the gift of
the country house.'[1]

The early years of the present century had seen many of the
old manor houses throughout the country restored to their
former glory — few of them, as yet, had become derelict. The
long predominance of the landed gentry was approaching its
end; but the squire was still able to keep open house, entertain
his friends, and fill his accustomed role in local and national
affairs. For another decade or so the country house remained the
social and political focus of the neighbourhood; the traditional
village group of the manor house, church, and encircling cottages was still intact.

At Wiston, as at many another English manor, life had gone
on, year after year, generation after generation, with virtually
no sudden innovation, and with only minor concessions to the
changing times. Some nine years before the long reign of the
'Old Reverend' (the Rev. John Goring) had ended and 'Master
Charles' ruled in his place. But, to many of the older people on
the estate at least, it still seemed but yesterday that they had
seen the old Squire, with his stern, aquiline features and mantle
of snow-white hair, going his rounds in his pony chaise, apprais-
ing the crops and livestock, and admiring his new poplars (the
'Old Reverend' was a notable judge of timber); lingering, like
Sir Roger de Coverley in his day, to chat with a few of them at
the church door after service, and rising to deliver a brief address
at the harvest supper, flower show, or other local festivity

[1] Ralph Dutton, *The Country House* (1935), p. 6.

(neither the 'Old Reverend' nor 'Master Charles' was ever much of a hand at speech-making).

From the terrace of the House the rolling grassland of the park, with its old spreading oaks and dark Scotch firs, stretched away to the Steyning road. Through the leafless winter woods there were glimpses of the mellow tiled roofs of small farm-houses and of villages that were old when Domesday Book was written. High on the summit of the hill above the House was the clump of lofty beeches known as Chanctonbury Ring. More than a century and a half before, an earlier Charles Goring — who was 'Master Charles's grandfather — as a boy had trudged each day up the steep bostal leading to the ridge of the Downs and had planted the first seedlings in the turf of the bare hill-top which, in the course of time, grew into the tall beech-trees of Chanctonbury Ring. That noble grove of beeches crowning the heights above Wiston Park had been familiar to all the people of the neighbouring villages from their earliest years, and was the great landmark of central Sussex. It also served as a useful weather sign.

> When old Mother Goring wears a cap
> We in the valley gets a drap.

The social and political authority of the squires was not, in 1914, what it had been in the last century. Nevertheless, it was still considerable. The county families, with their numerous tenantry, ample retinues of servants,[1] and extensive territorial influence generally, represented one of the great conservative forces of the kingdom. They also carried on some of its finest traditions of public service. A squire would usually reside for the greater part of the year on his estate, and would be known to every farmer and farm labourer for miles around from his infancy. A fair proportion of the English landed gentry had held their estates for generations, sometimes for centuries. As an

---

[1] It is always to be remembered that these country houses, as well as the smaller but comfortable and well-appointed establishments of the upper middle class—the homes of retired admirals and generals, leading professional men and well-to-do merchants and industrialists; also the more modest residences of the rural clergy, doctors, and lawyers, depended upon an ample and unfailing supply of inexpensive, willing, and efficient servants. Before the social and economic revolution of the last half-century, this supply was never in doubt.

example of this, it might be observed that about this time there was a pageant got up in Norfolk in which one of the scenes portrayed the homage paid to Mary Tudor by twenty-two of the gentlemen of that county. 'The men who played those parts,' declared an eye-witness, 'bore the same names and held the same land as their ancestors, showing the same unbroken continuity of our landed gentry.'[1]

The majority—though by no means all—of the squirearchy were bitterly opposed to the present Government. The heavy death duties imposed in recent Budgets imperilled the very existence of the landed class. They dreaded the spread of demo-cratic tenets, and the ever-growing threat to the existing order of things. Few of them had any desire for a new scientific age. England as it was was good enough for them. In their heart of hearts they profoundly mistrusted change of every kind; con-signed all radicals (especially Lloyd George) to the devil and longed to see the Tories back in office again; doggedly opposed Irish separatism, swore by the British Empire, and put their trust in a strong Navy.

[1] Philip Gibbs, *The Pageant of the Years*, p. 123.

CHAPTER 2

The industrial regions

The great industries from which this country drew the wealth which sustained her ever-increasing population and enabled her to maintain the most powerful Fleet in the history of the sea were situated far from the quiet countryside of southern England.

By the second decade of the twentieth century, Great Britain could scarcely aspire to her former appelation of the 'workshop of the world.' The truth is, she had been unable to maintain the unique industrial leadership which had been hers in the Victorian heyday. The demand for British textiles was noticeably slackening; it was the cotton manufactures which were principally affected—woollens fared better. In the same way the British iron and steel industry was clearly unable to maintain its former standing in the world. Though the British exports of pig iron were still larger than those of any other country and our production of wrought iron was actually increasing down to 1913, both the United States and Germany were far larger producers of steel than this country.

This is partly explained by the fact that in Great Britain the heavy industries were all too often wedded to the outlook and technique of the nineteenth century. Just as in our coal-fields were located some of the most antiquated pits in Europe, so in our factories and mills one often came upon machinery still in use which should long ago have been relegated to a science museum. No serious effort had been made to bring these industries up to date. The spirit of progress, indeed, had languished during the last two or three decades. In some branches of industry there was not only obsolete equipment, but also obsolete organisation.

Moreover, the sons and even more the grandsons of many a well-known family firm had gradually become accustomed to a

25

comfortable life in which money came easily, and were disinclined to sacrifice their leisure to their business interests. Thus the week-end had been extended to Saturday morning, and later to Monday morning as well. It is significant that the long week-end coincided with the advent of increasingly formidable foreign competition.

'In Germany', declared the *Iron and Coal Traders' Review* in August 1912, 'the idea of world-wide trade domination seems to arouse almost as much enthusiasm as the naval and military aspirations of the Government, and efforts to achieve new trade conquests are backed energetically by the State and by all that science, organisation, and highly-trained intelligence can do.'

Yet the recent gigantic expansion of the German steel industry was not by any means pure gain for Germany and pure loss for this country; for much of the steel we bought cheaply from the Germans was in fact used for making machinery and for building ships, which was greatly to the economic advantage of Great Britain. Furthermore, when all was said and done, the German people were still, class for class, nothing like so wealthy as the British.

Despite the rising tide of foreign competition, Great Britain still led the world in the volume and value of her manufactures and commerce. The cotton and woollen towns of Lancashire and Yorkshire were exceptionally busy throughout these last years of peace. Though our textiles no longer occupied the predominant position which they had held in the middle of the previous century, they still accounted for roughly one-third of British exports. Moreover, Great Britain maintained her position as the common carrier and the universal shipwright. On the verge of the First World War the tonnage of the British Empire amounted to more than forty-five per cent of the world's steam tonnage. Rather more than one-half of the world's total seaborne commerce was being transported in British bottoms. Similarly she retained her unique lead in the lucrative shipbuilding industry.

For most of our industries, indeed, 1913 had been a year of unexampled prosperity. Our shipyards turned out a maximum of 1,200,000 net tons. The export of machinery totalled £37,000,000. The mining industries also prospered exceedingly. The large iron exports have already been noted. With the recent expansion of the coalfields — especially the rich South Wales field, and also those of Yorkshire and Kent—the miners totalled well over one million. Our coal exports in 1913 amounted to more than one-tenth of all the exports of the United Kingdom. At the same time the prosperity of the coal industry greatly benefited our shipping — for, by taking the place of profitless ballast, all these immense exports of coal made it possible for British freighters to operate at comparatively low rates. In 1913 imports rose by £25 millions and exports by £40 millions.

'A wonderful year', declared the *Daily News*. 'What is astonishing is that the boom should have been so long maintained at such an amazing height; there is no parallel to it in history.'

The prosperity born of our thriving trade and industry was widely diffused. By the beginning of 1914, by and large, rising wages had overtaken rising prices; and thereafter wages continued to rise.

The juxtaposition of ample coal and iron deposits, and the proximity of both to the ports, had in the past given Great Britain a decisive advantage over all rivals. In Lanarkshire, Northumberland, Durham, Lancashire, Yorkshire, Staffordshire, and South Wales extensive iron and steel works had sprung up; and in the vicinity of the principal coalfields other great industries had been established.

The Clyde was the greatest centre of shipbuilding in the world, its busy yards succeeding one another for miles below Glasgow. For generations immense efforts had been made to deepen the river which was the city's lifeline; first, by the scour of the current controlled by a system of jetties, and, in more recent years, by the constant use of steam-dredgers. These efforts culminated in a series of magnificent docks and no less than eleven miles of quays.

But the strength of British shipbuilding rested almost as much on the prolific and economical construction of tramp steamers in the Tyne, Wear, and Tees as it did on the more costly, elaborate, and specialised products of the Clyde. Here on the north-east coast of England the proximity to the sea of great

steel works and an admirable railway system made it possible
to bring together easily and cheaply all the materials needed for
modern shipbuilding; here, too, as on the shores of the Clyde,
was assembled a numerous and highly skilled labour force which
was able to transform the raw materials into vessels and engines
which had no equals anywhere in the world. From all these busy
shipyards which lined the Tyne, Wear, and Tees came the
ubiquitous British tramp (said to be 'built by the yard and sold
by the fathom') which, decade after decade, had become a
familiar visitor in the furthermost parts of the earth. These
tramps in 1914 comprised about sixty per cent of the total tonnage of the United Kingdom and had largely ousted the sailing
vessel from its position as the carrier of bulk cargoes.

On Tyneside, the famous high-level bridge constructed by
Robert Stephenson at Newcastle afforded an impressive vista of
slipways, docks, wharves, cranes, warehouses, factories, engineering works, coal-yards, sidings, timber-yards, and rope-
works, that extended, on both sides of the river, all the way
down past Gateshead, Wallsend, Hebburn, and Jarrow to North
and South Shields and, also, for several miles above Newcastle
—itself a great workshop of a town, pulsating with energy and
activity. Coal was the leading export, and there were large glass
and chemical works. But the principal occupation of Tyneside
was shipbuilding. Here were miles of lofty scaffolding, enclosing
the hulls of vessels in all stages of construction. Here were the
great yards where they built the *Mauretania* and, more recently,
the super-dreadnought *King George* V. Here, too, were the more
modest establishments that produced the tramps on which the
prosperity of the district really depended. The deep, murky river
resounded with a perpetual racket of riveting, with the muffled
roar of machinery in its shipyards, factories, and foundries, and
with the ceaseless hooting of sirens, as steamer after steamer
passed up and down the crowded waterway, while alongside the
yards on either side innumerable ships were fitting and refitting.

In the centre of Newcastle were fine broad business thoroughfares with imposing blocks of offices, banks, departmental stores,
hotels, and restaurants. Here were the municipal buildings, and
the Theatre Royal (*Goody Two Shoes* was the pantomime that
Christmas). The substantial business and professional class, who
would foregather at the Commercial Exchange and the Station

Hotel, lived out in prosperous suburbs like Gosforth and Jesmond, up the river in Hexham, or in neighbouring coastal resorts like Whitley Bay. Housing conditions in Newcastle itself were poor. Even in the middle-class districts the houses were small, and their gardens more like backyards; while the housing of the working-class must have been about the worst in the country. Row after row, street after street, the little, drab, red-brick houses extended by the mile. A wilderness of sooty roof-tops and smoking chimney-pots stretched away to the far horizon, studded with groves of tall belching shafts which, day in, day out, added their quota of smoke to the general output. That was part of the price which the industrial North had to pay for the commercial pre-eminence and prosperity of Great Britain.

Though the exteriors of the houses were drab and dingy, internally it was another matter. 'If cleanliness is next to godliness,' declared an eye-witness, 'then the women of Durham and Northumberland are close neighbours with the Almighty. Long practice and tradition have made these women so perfect in the art of making a commonplace house beautiful that one must see it to believe what good taste and industry can accomplish.'[1]

In any case the majority of the population appeared to regard their grim surroundings with equanimity, if not with positive affection. Business was good and wages were rising. The Tyne-siders were reasonably content with their lot. They did not share the Mancunians' enthusiasm for long bicycle rides in the country, but they were passionately devoted to whippet- and pigeon-racing (the Geordies were famous pigeon-fanciers), packed the football grounds of a Saturday afternoon, and flocked to Paddy's Market of a Sunday morning. They also participated in a curious local pastime known as knurr-and-spell and in brass-band festivals.

Sunderland, situated on the Wear, possessed a vigorous and progressive shipbuilding industry which came near to rivalling that of the Tyne; and some miles beyond, on the Tees, lay the huge, smoking mass of Middlesbrough — another major ship-building centre.

[1] Jack Lawson, A Man's Life (1944), p. 38.

To the south lay the extensive coalfields of Yorkshire and Lancashire, where the iron and steel industry had developed in close proximity to the collieries. Leeds, one of the chief seats of the industry, was engaged in the manufacture of heavy iron and steel goods, including locomotives and machinery. Yorkshire coal also energised the iron and steel industry of Sheffield. With plentiful supplies of coal, iron, and grindstones in the vicinity, Sheffield had long been noted for its cutlery. It was now the largest city in Yorkshire, with a population approaching half a million. Sheffield was the principal centre of steel manufactures in Great Britain, including all kinds of steel castings and forgings, turning out a vast range of steel products from drills, saws, and rails to ordnance and armour plate for battleships.

Yorkshire and Lancashire also contained the principal seats of the textile industry—for centuries the mainstay of our national economy. The sister textile trades were located, the one on the eastern, and the other on the western, side of the Pennine watershed.

The centre of the whole woollen industry was Leeds, the other leading woollen towns being Blackburn, Bradford, Halifax, Huddersfield, Rochdale, and Wakefield. The busy manufactories and the dwelling-places of the work people who toiled in them had spread into the upper Pennine valleys. Here three great textile towns — Bradford, Halifax, and Huddersfield — were situated. The dark rugged hillsides once covered with heather and bilberries, where there had been only a few lonely farmsteads and scattered cottages, were now a smoking wilderness of small, dingy, back-to-back houses, blocks of gaunt mills, box-like factories and warehouses, and groves of tall black chimneys perpetually belching forth smoke.

Situated alongside, and to some degree actually overlapping the region devoted to the manufacture of woollens, were the principal centres of the cotton industry: Accrington, Bacup, Blackburn, Bolton, Burnley, Bury, Nelson, Oldham, Preston, Stalybridge, and Wigan. These towns, with a large number of smaller places, formed an almost continuous series of industrial communities engaged in the various processes of manufacture, while Manchester, the capital of the whole region, was the great metropolis, warehouse, and distributing centre of the cotton industry. One might travel by tramcar for hours on end in this part of Lancashire and never once really emerge from the confines of this vast sprawling industrial city.

'From Manchester to Bolton or to Rochdale it is all of a piece and towns are carried into another by gas-lamps and pavements without the interval of as much as a hedge or ditch. From Manchester to Oldham it is one street, and very nearly one row or one terrace — the continuation of the same idea along seven paved and sewered miles. This community of south-east Lancashire is the closest compression of industrial humanity in the world.'[1]

The omnipresent hills and mounds of slag, together with the winding machinery and screening and loading sheds at the pit-heads, gave testimony of the wide Lancashire coalfield which energised all these busy manufactories. Clouds of white and black smoke rose above works and mills. Around the whole horizon tall chimneys stood gaunt against the grey sky. Strings of barges moved slowly along the murky canals. Between the towns lumbered wagons piled high with bales of cotton. Trucks loaded with coal stood in sidings. Over the whole scene there hung an almost perpetual pall of smoke. And, even in the more or less rural areas, the landscape never seemed to be really fresh and green—nor was the air ever really pure.

At six o'clock in the morning each town resounded with the hooting of factory sirens and the clatter of myriads of wooden clogs on the stone setts as huge crowds of men and women, and boys and girls, poured through the drab streets in the raw wintry darkness on their way to commence another day's toil. The evening saw them returning, swarming out of the gates of mills, works, and factories in their hundreds, to their homes.

In her autobiography, Gracie Fields has graphically recorded the start of the day's work in her native Rochdale:

'We used to get up at five a.m. for the mills when Old Amy, the knocker-up woman, came and rapped on our bedroom windows with her pole. Each family paid Old Amy tuppence a week to be awakened, and it was no use shouting "Righto! Amy," when you heard her tap-tap in the darkness, she just kept

[1] H. M. McKechnie, *Manchester in 1915*, p. 11.

rapping till she saw your face at the window; then she knew you
were out of bed and went on to her next customer. As Amy
trudged down the street the candles and oil-lamps lit behind her
in each little window, and in each house the kettle would go on
for the tea. Outside you could hear the clogs of the early mill
workers, the men who had to get there first to tend the furnace
fires. When the mill wanted the rest of us, half an hour later, it
whistled. The buzzer we called it. "Quick, Grace, t'buzzer's
gone." Five minutes afterwards the big gates were shut and if
you were not inside you lost a day's work.'[1]

The average northerner lived hard, and played hard. Some of
his sports were rough and cruel: cock-fighting and dog-fighting
were by no means extinct in the northern shires. He was
strongly attracted to the full-blooded melodrama of the *Murder
in the Red Barn* variety; and some of the newly established
picture palaces, or cinemas, as they were sometimes called, put
on similar pieces, with lurid titles such as *Snatched from Death,
The Black Thirteen, A Fallen Angel*, etc. Above all, there was
the music hall, an immensely popular institution in the North.
Vesta Tilley, George Robey, Little Tich, and Hayden Coffin had
been playing to crowded houses in Manchester shortly before
Christmas. Gracie Fields was touring the northern halls with
Charburn's Young Stars. In his earlier years Charlie Chaplin had
belonged to a young group of players known as Jackson's Eight
Lancashire Lads.

Once a year came Wakes Week—a halcyon time when whole
towns and districts even would stop work and go off on holiday
en masse. Every mill in the place would close down for a complete week. Many of the streets were then almost deserted, for a
large proportion of the populace had departed in a body to Blackpool. A good many people would start saving up for the annual
holiday months before; and much of the pleasure consisted in
remembering the joys of Blackpool the previous year, and in
looking forward to the next Wakes Week.

For the rest, they made their own fun, and made it very successfully. There were convivial Saturday nights in the singing-
rooms at the local 'pub' (many a celebrated music-hall artist had
made his or her *début* in one of these singing-rooms); clog-

[1] Gracie Fields, *Sing As We Go* (1960), p. 28.

dancing; pigeon- and whippet-racing; gardening, cycling, bee-keeping, and occasional socials and outings. The various local coteries — the pigeon fanciers, gardeners, racing men, trade unionists, and so on—would foregather at their own particular hostelry, which was, in fact, far more a social club than just a 'boozer'.

The manners and speech of the northerner were noticeably rougher and readier than those of the folk who lived in our southern counties. The northerner did not stand on ceremony—if he wanted to get past his neighbour he just shoved, and in a crowd would use his elbows without compunction. In the same way he was blunt and forthright in his communications with others. He possessed a strong sense of humour. His ideas of interior decoration were crude, and the hideous architecture all around him did not seem to cause him any concern: but he knew and appreciated good music. The Hallé Orchestra of Manchester was renowned throughout Europe. The Leeds Festival was one of the great musical events of the year (1913 had seen the first performance there of Butterworth's fantasy, *A Shropshire Lad*).

Though most of the actual cotton manufacturing was carried on in the satellite towns in the vicinity, all the more important firms there were represented either by a warehouse and offices, or else by an agent, in Manchester. In the central parts of the city there were great blocks of offices bearing the names of firms which were household words throughout the civilised world. Thus Manchester had grown into the metropolis of a densely populated manufacturing region. 'Take Manchester away,' the *Times* declared, 'and the Lancashire industry would fall into chaos. No other country has its Manchester.' To the Royal Exchange — the largest commercial chamber in the world — would come, on Tuesdays and Fridays, representatives of the cotton industry from all over Lancashire and beyond. In the main this immense assembly was occupied with one department or another of the foreign trade. The regulars knew exactly where they could find the yarn agents, the Bolton cotton spinners, the India or China merchants, the Blackburn or Bury cotton manufacturers, the bleachers, or the cotton brokers. The scene on the vast floor of the Royal Exchange, where, between two and three o'clock in the afternoon, which was the hour of 'High 'Change',

B

there were occasionally something like 7,000 members, for the most part assembled in stationary or slowly drifting groups, was a spectacle unique in Europe.

It was not only in the Royal Exchange, but also in the Midland Hotel and other hostelries, and in crowded underground cafés all over the centre of Manchester that everyone who was 'in cotton' would meet to do business and to exchange good stories in an atmosphere hazy with tobacco smoke. These cafés were really cotton exchanges in miniature—each establishment being frequented by members of a particular branch of the industry. Thus the spinners would meet at one café, the bleachers at another, the representatives of the finishing trades at a third, the brokers at a fourth, and so on. Sometimes they would sit for hours over their coffee. Every now and then notebooks would be pulled out of pockets, pencils produced, and figures hurriedly entered; for all this story-telling and general bonhomie in no way impeded the smooth transaction of business. As a background to the low hum of conversation was heard the characteristic sounds of Manchester—the sharp clatter of hooves on the whinstones above as carts loaded with cotton rumbled by, the periodic hoot of factory sirens, and the endless screech of trams.

Apart from its importance as the metropolis of cotton Manchester also possessed very considerable engineering resources. The opening of the Manchester Ship Canal in 1907, as a result of which the city became an important sea-port, and the completion of an extensive system of inland docks had 'made' Trafford Park. This new industrial quarter was soon a great manufacturing centre in its own right, containing some of the largest engineering works in the country. 1913 had been an exceptionally busy year for the Ship Canal.

Liverpool, which had prospered exceedingly with the growth of the Atlantic trade and the rapid development of the industrial North, still retained its place as the second port in the kingdom. At the beginning of the present century the dock accommodation of Liverpool was perhaps the finest in the world, the total length of quayage amounting to over twenty-five miles. It 'fronts the river in a vast sea wall,' says Ramsay Muir, 'as solid and enduring as the Pyramids, the most stupendous work of its kind that the will and power of men have ever created.' A few years later the shipping owned by this port actually exceeded, by half a million tons, the tonnage of the whole German Empire. Liverpool was the greatest export centre in the kingdom. It was the natural outlet for the Lancashire manufacturing region, as well as the principal import centre for the essential raw material, cotton, and for a great part of the foodstuffs of its teeming population.

From early morning till late at night one continuous procession of heavily laden carts and wagons drawn by great Clydesdale horses jolted slowly over the setts along the Great Dock Road behind the cranes and warehouses. They were loaded with produce from all over the world — cotton for Lancashire, wool for the Yorkshire manufactories, metals for Birmingham and Wolverhampton, tobacco for Nottingham. All day long this procession continued. At the same time a similar line of empty carts and wagons was proceeding, in the opposite direction, to take in fresh cargoes. About one-third of our imports, and one-quarter of our exports, passed through Liverpool.

Across the Mersey was Birkenhead—another great shipbuilding centre.

The northerner took a keen and intelligent interest in politics. (A Rochdale mill-hand was far better informed, politically, than a southern farm labourer or factory worker; and it has been reckoned that at least one-tenth of the readers of the *Manchester Guardian* belonged to the superior artisan class). The majority were Liberals, of one shade or another. If Liberalism was strong in the North, and faith in the twin principles of peace and free trade was still undimmed, it was scarcely to be wondered at: for upon peaceful relations between the nations and free access to the markets of the world the present prosperity of Lancashire in the main depended. Here in the North they watched with hostile and suspicious eye the soaring expenditure on naval armaments; frowned and shook their heads over the extremist tactics of the Dublin trade unions; and discounted, with an incredulous chuckle, the menacing pronouncements of the Leader of the Opposition and his colleagues.

The Tories were proper 'rattled', by all accounts. Still, not much they could do about it, was there? No more trouble from

the old House of Lords—which had always favoured the Tories
—now that the Parliament Act was safely on the Statute Book.

In some of these populous industrial areas a new spirit was
stirring. The youthful J. B. Priestley, who was then starting
work in his birthplace, Bradford, was many years afterwards to
give some account of the strivings and aspirations of his con-
temporaries in a novel entitled, *The Bright Day*, which records
the experiences of an impressionable youngster employed at one
of the wool firms in 'Bruddersford'.

'Workin' for John Alington at Hawes, aren't you, lad? Thought
I 'eard somebody say so. Well, John's all right. I wouldn't call
'im a fighter—he's not—an' perhaps a bit too much of the
Liberal about 'im—but he's a grand chap, John is, and there's
not many better. He runs his business an' doesn't let it run 'im,
as some of 'em do. Knows 'ow to enjoy life the right way. An'
that's all we ask just for a chance for workin' folk to enjoy life
the right way—to see their families growin' up, fine and strong
—to meet their friends and 'ave a talk and a laugh together—to
walk over the moors at the week end—to read some books worth
reading—to go to a theatre or to listen to some music. . . . Yes,
that's all we ask—just for a decent chance for the folk that do
most of the work, so that they don't 'ave to spend all their lives
goin' in and out o' mills and mucky back streets an' pubs. It
isn't a lot to ask. Every ruling class there's ever been asked for a
hundred times as much for doin' a dam' sight less. And
Socialism's coming, lad. You mark my words. There's no stoppin'
it, though some o' the Tories 'ud go to any length to try and
stop it—you'll see—an' if they're not careful, just bein' obstruc-
tive, they'll land themselves in a 'ell of a mess. It's one road or
the other, from now on, lad. You just take notice o' what I'm
saying and remember it.'

Time was when the miners and factory hands had accepted
their lot with apathy or resignation. The older generation were
usually not class-conscious, in the political sense. Many a Labour
leader has testified how hard it was to persuade the workers that
they were the victims of exploitation and injustice. But after
forty years of compulsory education, and browsing over newspapers and pamphlets, there was an increasing awareness of

other things in life besides eating and drinking and dog-fighting. To this growing awareness (and to the steady decline in the purchasing power of wages) may largely be attributed the prevailing spirit of discontent and unrest.

'The outlook of the workman has passed beyond the works and his beer and his dog. He has become—or, rather, he has been replaced by—a being of eyes, however imperfect, and of criticism, however hasty and unjust. . . . The working man questions a thousand things his father accepted as in the very nature of the world, and many others he begins to ask with the utmost alertness and persistence why it is that he in particular is expected to toil. . . . He looks far beyond the older conflict of interests between employers and employed. He criticizes the good intentions of the whole system of governing and influential people, and not only their good intentions, but their ability.'[1]

It was not only the cities and large towns of the North, but also many small places and villages, which were citadels of Nonconformity and Radicalism. One of the ablest of the Labour members in the House of Commons, Philip Snowden, had been born in a two-room cottage in a moorland hamlet near Keighley, in the West Riding of Yorkshire. In the same hamlet were born two other Labour members who sat with him in Parliament. J. R. Clynes, another prominent Labour member, who was Secretary of the Lancashire Gasworkers' and General Labourers' Union, had been born in the back streets of Oldham. (Clynes was the 'John Smith of Oldham' to whom Robert Blatchford addressed his arguments in *Merrie England*). The tide of Socialism had been running strongly in Lancashire and other regions of the North since the 'nineties.

For twenty years and more Clynes had laboured to improve the lot of the working class, first by trade-union and later by parliamentary action. In his memoirs he relates in a mordant passage how, in order to attend a trade-union conference at Plymouth, he made his first long journey away from Oldham.

'That was a wonderful journey for me, who had never before been out of the Lancashire murk. To look through the carriage

[1] H. G. Wells, *An Englishman looks at the World* (1914), pp. 45-5.

windows and see grass and bushes that were really green instead
of olive, trees that reached confidently up to the sun instead of
our stunted things, houses that were mellow red and white and
yellow, with warm red roofs, instead of the Lancashire soot and
slates, and stretches of landscape in which the eye could not find
a single factory chimney belching—this was sheer magic. . . .
And more and more strongly as I gazed, I felt a sense of indignation that the world should be so generous and so lovely, and yet
that men, women, and children should be cooped up in black
and exhausted industrial areas like Oldham, merely that richer
men could own thousands of acres of sunlit country-side of
whose existence many of the mill-workers hardly even
dreamed.'[1]

In the coming year, at Easter, the Independent Labour Party
was to celebrate its twenty-first anniversary at Bradford, the
place of its birth. Its chairman, James Keir Hardie, perhaps the
best-hated, best-loved political figure of his day, had in his earlier
years done much to organize the miners, and later had become
one of the founding fathers of British Socialism. He had
gradually gathered round him a group of able and devoted supporters, including J. Ramsay MacDonald, Philip Snowden, Margaret Bondfield, Bruce Glasier, and James Maxton. The I.L.P.
was now a power in the land. Its influence was steadily increasing, not only in Parliament, but also in local government. The
general feeling at Bradford that Easter was one of well-justified
confidence and optimism. Congratulations poured in from every
Labour organization in Great Britain and from Socialist parties
all over the world. The occasion was a great personal triumph
for Keir Hardie. This coming of age of the I.L.P. marked an era
in the progress of organized Labour and the propagation of
British Socialism.

The other main industrial area was in the western midlands.
Over the North Staffordshire coalfield were situated further
groups of collieries and ironworks. It was the coal from these
mines which fed the innumerable kilns of the Potteries, that

[1] J. R. Clynes, *Memoirs 1869-1924*, pp. 65-66.

produced about nine-tenths of all the porcelain and earthenware manufactured in Great Britain. A congeries of densely populated boroughs—among which Burslem, Stoke-on-Trent, and Hanley were the most important—together made up one great sprawling urban mass which was crossed and re-crossed by an intricate system of canals, railway lines, and electric tramways. The prospect was one of slated rooftops, slab-sided factories, squat and smoking pot-ovens, and tall chimney shafts stretching away to the smoky horizon. There were endless rows of small, dingy red-brick houses and drab, monotonous streets, interspersed with grimy gasometers, collieries with their winding gear outlined against the grey, wintry sky, little, low, gas-lighted shops, shabby public houses, desolate patches of waste ground, and works, works, works. . . . There were days when almost the entire region was submerged beneath impenetrable layers of slowly drifting smoke. The effect at night-time, when the fiery glow of furnace after furnace could be seen all round the horizon, has been vividly described by Arnold Bennett.

'It was a warm, cloudy evening. The last silver tinge of an August twilight lay on the shoulder of the hill to the left. There was no moon, but the splendid watch-fires of labour flamed from ore-heap and furnace across the whole expanse, performing their nightly miracle of beauty. Trains crept with noiseless mystery along the middle distance, under their canopies of yellow steam. Further off the far-extending streets of Hanbridge made a map of starry lines on the blackness. To the south-east stared the cold, blue electric lights of Knpye railway station. All was silent, save for a distant thunderous roar, the giant breathing of the forge at Cauldron Bar Ironworks.' [1]

The same writer, in his novels and short stories centred on the famous 'Five Towns', has immortalized the district and its inhabitants in the period under review — the great furnaces glowing red in the twilight, the long, unlovely streets, the smoky dusks and sooty dawns, the brightly-lit tramcars thundering down Trafalgar Road, the jollity and exhilaration of Christmas shopping in Hanley, the bustle and excitement of Wakes Week,

[1] Though the place-names in this excerpt are fictitious, they may be easily identified.

the few though luxurious motor-cars of that era speeding along the black and glutinous highways, the ever-present smoke clouds and 'the white window-curtains to change every week because of the smuts', and the gloomy little parlours 'crowded with mahogany and horsehair furniture, white antimacassars, wax flowers under glass, and ponderous gilt-clasped Bibles'; the friendships, jealousies, and enmities of the people of the Potteries, their all-consuming zest for life, their determination to get on in the world, their crudity and kindness, their total indifference to the squalid ugliness of their surroundings, their shrewdness and philistinism, the solid commercial prosperity of their root-less upper class, the sturdy independence of their work-people, their disconcerting directness of speech, and their dry humour.

Here was democracy, indeed, as it was understood in the American Republic. In the Potteries (as in many another indus-trial region) there were only the two classes, the employers and the employed; and a family who belonged to the former class in one generation might very well form part of the latter in the next — and *vice-versa*. The secure, stable, quietly permanent, hierarchical structure of society that existed in the countryside was almost unheard of in the 'Five Towns'.

Away beyond the Potteries, over the South Staffordshire coal-field, extended the grim industrial landscape of the Black Country. Again the close network of roads, canals, and railway tracks: it might almost be said that the entire area of the Black Country was one vast goods yard. Its manufactures included all kinds of hardware, as well as motor-cars, cycles, and electrical machinery. On the verge of this region was Birmingham, whose staple was metal-working in all its branches; its manufactories turning out a vast variety of goods ranging from steam-engines to sewing-machines. It had been claimed that the industries of Birmingham were more numerous and varied than those of any other provincial town on earth.

A smaller, though still highly important, mining and manu-facturing area was on the South Wales coast, centred around Swansea and Cardiff.

For good or for ill Great Britain had become an 'industry state', one that lived by commerce and manufacture and depended to an ever-increasing degree on the constant flow of shipping for most of the food consumed by her people and for much of the raw materials required for her works and factories. Owen Rutter thus vividly sums up the situation in the year 1913-14:

'Every day of the year Great Britain imported 3,000 tons of meat and 27,000 tons of grain, a million tons of butter, another million of tea, twelve million of sugar, seven of fresh fish, three of oranges and apples, 25,000 bunches of bananas, seven millions of eggs, besides great quantities of cotton, wool, ores, oil, rubber and timber and other commodities for the factories, much of which was redistributed about the world in manufactured form.'[1]

Sixty years earlier David Urquart had foretold, 'Our insular position leaves us only the choice between omnipotence and impotence. Britannia will either become mistress of the seas or will be swallowed up by them.' It was a simple statement of fact. For the inhabitants of these islands the maintenance of their cherished maritime superiority was a matter of life and death: there was no possible middle course. 'The stakes were very high', Winston Churchill has observed. 'If our naval defence were maintained, we were safe and sure beyond the lot of any other European nation; if it failed, our doom was certain and final.' What the severance of the vital sea-communications would mean to the teeming population of the United Kingdom was brought grimly home in Rudyard Kipling's well-known lines:

> For the bread that you eat and the biscuits you nibble,
>   The sweets that you suck and the joints that you carve,
> They are brought to you daily by all us Big Steamers—
>   And if any one hinders our coming you'll starve!

[1] Owen Rutter, *Red Ensign, A History of Convoy* (1947), p. 126.

CHAPTER 3

' *Welcome 1914* '

In London, the New Year was ushered in with the customary rejoicings. So dense were the crowds and so numerous the motor-cars and carriages in the streets of the West End that many extra police had to be called in to regulate the slowly moving stream of vehicles and pedestrians. The fashionable night-clubs of that era—the Four Hundred, Lotus, Murray's, and the rest—were thronged to capacity. There was a highly successful New Year's Eve ball at Covent Garden. But the most spectacular celebrations that night took place in the principal restaurants and hotels.

At the Carlton Restaurant, adorned with holly and mistletoe and hanging baskets of white and scarlet flowers, the New Year was impressively ushered in by means of a huge floral clock, on the dial of which the figures '1914' appeared on the stroke of midnight.

The central feature of the scheme of decorations at the Ritz Hotel was an avenue of festoons of foliage, scarlet blossoms, and chrysanthemums intertwined, while from the ceiling of the foyer was suspended an enormous illuminated cracker in red and green wrappings bearing the inscription '1914'. At midnight the chime of bells was accompanied by a stirring fanfare sounded by the trumpeters of the Royal Artillery.

At the Piccadilly Hotel, immediately after midnight, a blaze of many-coloured lights flashed out the seasonal greeting, '*Welcome, 1914*'. This was followed by a hilarious battle of crackers. At one o'clock in the morning the new ballroom was thrown open to the merrymakers, and the dancing began.

The ball at the Métropole included a performance of an old Provençal peasant-dance, the *farandole* — with its resounding drum and gay carnival trappings — perambulating from hall to hall, in place of the banned tango. When the multitude of guests sat down to rest, they were entertained by a troop of child dancers, who acquitted themselves so well that they were

rewarded with enthusiastic applause and bouquets of beautiful
flowers almost too large for them to carry.

At the New Year's Eve party at the Savoy Hotel there were
at least two thousand guests. The Savoy had always been famous
for its parties, and on this occasion it surpassed itself. At the
hour of midnight a fanfare of trumpets, sounded by the Cold-
stream Guards, heralded the New Year: as the last trumpet-blast
died away the great ballroom was plunged into darkness which
was suddenly pierced by a dazzling beam of light illuminating a
dais on which stood a pair of dancers to welcome in the New
Year. At the same instant a hundred large gold and silver bells
suspended under the ceiling suddenly dropped down cords: each
of these, on being grasped by the guests, released a shower of
crackers. After much cheering, hand-shaking, and many wishes
for a happy and prosperous New Year, the dancing was resumed.

Meanwhile, out of doors and indoors, there was 'a sound of
revelry by night'. Long before twelve o'clock a large and
exuberant throng, composed chiefly of Scotsmen, had assembled,
according to time-honoured custom, outside St Paul's Cathedral.
Surging to and fro under the street lamps, the crowd, larger than
in any previous year, beguiled the time of waiting with jests and
badinage. Parties of hilarious young men marched up and down
Ludgate Hill and Fleet Street blowing penny whistles and tin
trumpets. Presently, as the Old Year drew swiftly to its close, a
solemn silence fell upon them all; and then, as the great bell of
St Paul's struck midnight, a hurricane of cheers arose: hundreds
of handkerchiefs were waved, and hats and sticks brandished in
the air; from afar off came the hooting of ships' sirens down the
river and the ringing of church bells all over the City. The
uproar lasted for several minutes. Finally the crowd linked hands
and sang 'Auld lang syne'.

Welcome 1914!

It had been a glorious and exciting Christmas. The post had
reached the unexampled total of twenty-six million cards and
letters. The Christmas shopping had broken all records. The cold
and misty evenings had but enhanced the lure of the brightly
lit shop windows. Everyone seemed to be in cheerful spirits. The

trams and omnibuses bound for the outer suburbs were crowded with people laden with parcels. At Charing Cross and other termini parties of winter sports enthusiasts were entraining for the Continent. A considerably greater number were off to the country for Christmas.

The anxiety and foreboding which had overhung the political scene during the latter part of 1913—the growing labour unrest and alarming manifestations of class warfare, the increasing violence of Suffragette attacks upon persons and property, the intensification of party rancour resulting from the Government's fiscal and Irish policies, and the acute uneasiness of many Liberals and Radicals at the huge naval shipbuilding programme —were for the time being forgotten. Christmas brought a welcome respite from these cares. The current political gags in theatre and music hall only served to raise a laugh. In any case, savage as had been the party struggle during the last few years, it had done little to impede the flood-tide of British prosperity. Money was plentiful, and looked like being more so.

The 24th brought an abrupt fall in the temperature. That day it froze hard, while the air was crisp and dry. 'The tonic of a frost'—to quote the *Daily Telegraph*—was just what was needed to give the finishing touch to that Christmas of 1913. Several days later curling was in full swing on Wimbledon Common.

The crowds in the main shopping thoroughfares of the West End grew greater each day, reaching their maximum on Christmas Eve, when the streets were congested with a slowly moving mass of every kind of vehicle and vast throngs of shoppers threading their way past the huge plate-glass windows with their imposing display of goods. Here and there might be seen taxi-cabs and private motor-cars loaded with happy youngsters just home from boarding-school. For the younger children there was the rare delight of a visit to the Christmas bazaar in one of the great departmental stores, which usually included some such spectacular exhibit as 'Aladdin's Cave', 'Robinson Crusoe's Island', or 'The Palace of the Sleeping Beauty'. Everywhere were masses of shining, scarlet-berried holly and other evergreens, and forests of Christmas trees. (1913, incidentally, was memorable for the wholesale introduction of miniature electric-lamp sets on the children's Christmas trees in place of 'the twinkling but dangerous tapers of a former generation'.) The range of mechanical toys on display that year was remarkable—clockwork and electric train sets, motor cars, motor buses, traction engines, steamships, and aircraft (some of the latter actually driven by compressed air). Bassett-Lowke's new branch in High Holborn, with its superbly realistic scale models of the L.N.W.R. 'George V', the G.N. 'Atlantic', and other celebrated locomotives of the day, drew the males of all ages as a magnet.

It was a memorable Christmas in every way for the children of the metropolis. That year there were no less than thirty pantomimes running in London and its environs—though only two of them were in the West End. *The Babes in the Wood*, at the Lyceum, was a good old-fashioned pantomime which included a spirited combat between the two robbers. *The Sleeping Beauty Re-awakened*, at Drury Lane, was a much more spectacular affair. The advance booking reached record figures, and the great house was filled to its utmost capacity. The pantomime was a blend of the old fairy tale of *The Sleeping Beauty* and of *Beauty and the Beast*. One of the most beautiful scenes in it was where the Princess lay dreaming in her long sleep and the stage filled with all the toys and characters from the fairy stories she had known in her childhood — Dick Whittington, Aladdin, Cinerella, and the others could be seen emerging from the shadows. Another very effective scene was the one which showed the Prince and the Princess escaping from a blazing pine-forest. The harlequinade had lately been restored to something of its former importance at Drury Lane (oh, the memories of Dan Leno and Herbert Campbell!) and once again the delighted youngsters watched the antics of 'Whimsical Walker' the Clown, the business with the red-hot poker, the policeman, and pantaloon. The curtain fell on the final scene with the vast, joyful, madly excited crowd clamouring for Arthur Collins, and enthusiastically applauding that most flamboyant of conductors, Jimmy Glover, who, despite his recent severe illness, seemed quite in his usual form.

A favourite piece for the older children was *Charley's Aunt*, that hardy annual of the London stage, which was now entering on its twenty-first season. Youngsters of all ages were taken to see Max and Moritz, 'the almost human' chimpanzees at Olympia, and all the other exhibits there. There was *Maskelyne and Devant's Mysteries* at St George's Hall in Langham Place, the home of Magic and Illusion. There was Madame Tussaud's, a wonderland of waxen effigies of the famous and infamous—King George V and Queen Mary, Theodore Roosevelt and Woodrow Wilson, Lord Kitchener, Major-General Baden-Powell (founder of the Boy Scout movement), and Rudyard Kipling among the former, and a fair number of notorious murderers (lodged in the Chamber of Horrors) among the latter. There was the Anglo-American Exposition at the White City at Shepherd's Bush. Another popular resort for family parties was the current exhibition at Earl's Court (in 1914 it was 'Sunny Spain'), which had become a favourite rendezvous for all classes. The great attraction at Earl's Court, so far as the young were concerned, was the side-shows. Often, at night time, one could see young men and girls in evening dress sliding gleefully down the Helter-Skelter and shooting the Water Chute.

The last few years had witnessed the growing popularity of the children's play. Pauline Chase was making her final appearance in *Peter Pan*. At the Comedy Theatre there was *Alice in Wonderland*, and at the Globe *The Shepherdess without a Heart*. But the children's play which perhaps had aroused the keenest interest in recent years was *Where the Rainbow Ends*.

First produced three years earlier at the Savoy, *Where the Rainbow Ends* was not just another fairy phantasy; but, like *The Riddle of the Sands*, *The Man Who Stayed at Home*, and *When William Came*, was in fact a by-product of the Anglo-German naval armaments race. The two boys who, with their sisters, set out on a magic carpet with a genie on their perilous journey to 'the land where the rainbow ends' (which lay beyond an enchanted wood and the Dragons' Castle) wore the uniform of British naval cadets; and the underlying message of the play was—first, last, and all the time—the paramount need of a Big Navy!

After the passage of half a century, there are men and women that were children then who can still vividly recall the scene in the Garrick Theatre: the boys in their Eton suits and the girls in their party frocks and sashes—bright-eyed, eager, and breathless with expectation; the applause which heralded the arrival of the conductor, the young Roger Quilter, who had composed the music which so perfectly expresses the spirit of *Where the Rainbow Ends*; and the sheer rapture of that moment when the foot of the great curtain was suddenly aglow (like the magic carpet in Act I) 'with a lovely soft snap-dragon light'.

The four children in the play were accompanied by their pet lion cub and pursued by a wicked old uncle and aunt. St George of England was their protector and their enemy was the Dragon King, through whose domains the journey had to be made. After a series of breath-snatching adventures the children were ambushed by 'the lake at the end of the wood' by a force of flying Dragons and carried off to the enemy's stronghold in the Thundercloud Mountains, and there condemned to be cast at dawn from the battlements 'to perish on the jagged rocks below'. With her brother's white handkerchief and a red ribbon torn from their lion cub's collar the older girl deftly fashioned a St George's cross. The two cadets then scaled the castle turret and, after a hazardous climb, tore down the enemy's standard, hoisting the red-cross flag in its place. In a blinding flash of light St George of England appeared on the ramparts and challenged the Dragon King to mortal combat. After a thrilling fight the latter was vanquished and slain: the castle of the Dragons toppled down in ruins: the whole stage was bathed in the radiance of a glorious rainbow, and the two boys and their sisters arrived at last at their journey's end, in 'the land where the rainbow ends, where lost loved ones are found'.

This scene in the Dragons' Castle was, perhaps, the most exciting that had ever been staged in a children's play.

London in that last year of peace was recognizably the same London which is familiar to us from the essays of Max Beerbohm and G. R. Sims, and the black-and-white sketches of Phil May. Generation after generation it had gone on steadily growing, and swallowing up ever more meadows and fields, and woods and coppices, and villages and hamlets. By this time the huge amorphous mass of London reached almost as far south as the Caterham valley and nearly as far north as Epping Forest, and numbered more than five million inhabitants. Ealing, which was right out in the country down to the close of the nineteenth century, had been engulfed by what Cobbett in his day had called the 'great Wen'. What were once hedge-bordered lanes

were now trim suburban thoroughfares. Whole neighbourhoods
had been transformed out of recognition. Nevertheless, there
were still plenty of open spaces round such places at Mitcham,
Willesden, and Finchley. Elstree was as yet a peaceful village. So
was Greenford, and so was Perivale; and so were Banstead and
Woodmansterne.

Despite its vast extent and numerous foreign colonies, London
was still essentially an English city with a predominantly English
population where one might hear spoken the crisp, clear English
of the governing class at one end of the social scale and the
homely old Cockney dialect at the other. The various districts
making up London were more or less separate entities, each of
them differing in certain regards from its neighbour. Mayfair
was Mayfair, and Chelsea was Chelsea. Bayswater was not by
any means the same as Kensington. Belgravia was the abode
of the wealthy; artists lived in Chelsea, and prosperous business
and professional men out in the well-to-do suburbs like Purley
and Surbiton. Hoxton was the proper quarter for cabinet-makers,
and Bethnal Green for tailors.

Of all the picturesque figures who, in these bygone days, gave
life and colour to the London streets, the lamplighter was, perhaps, the most popular. He would come briskly along the pavement at dusk, with his pole over his shoulder. Lamp after lamp
would spring to life at his touch. The muffin-man would announce his presence by ringing a bell. The Punch and Judy show
man would beat a drum to attract an audience. Others, like the
cat's meat man ('*Mee-mee-eat!*') had their own particular cry.
Thus, there was the milkman ('*Milko-o!*'), the hokey-pokey man
('*Hokey-pokey, Penny a lump!*'), the coal man ('*Co-o-oals!*'), the
sweep ('*Swee-ee-eep!*'), the rag merchant ('*Any rags, bottles, or
bones?*'), and—best of all—the lavender-seller ('*Will you buy my
sweet blooming lavender?*').

Against the clopping of horses' hooves and the jingle of
harness and bells, usually it was not long before one heard, either
loud and close at hand, or else faint and far off, the strains of a
piano-organ playing some popular music-hall air. Thomas Burke
has vividly recalled the pathos of some of these tunes, heard in
such circumstances, in a passage which is well worth quoting:

'They were songs intended to rouse Homeric laughter, or to

prod you with memories of rude and raffish nights in the West End; and all they did was to play upon the nerves with a Verlaine tristesse. The airs of those songs, when I recall them, evoke for me the sadness of London streets in October twilights; crying children; the throb of London life coming muted over intervening roofs. Many a time, when wandering through rainy suburban byways, I have had my blood chilled almost to tears by a distant organ playing the latest comic song. . . . It isn't entirely due to Time that one hears the shyly-poignant note of grief. The note is there as clearly as it is in the airs of Tschaikowsky. It is the note of the London streets, and if you seek a true musical expression of London you are nearer to it in these rough comic songs than in such considered works as Elgar's Cockaigne overture or Vaughan Williams' London Symphony.'[1]

In the East End, as well as in other parts of the metropolis inhabited by the poorer classes, the streets at this time were full of quick-fire chaff and catch-phrases, which originated for the most part in the music halls. 'Git yer 'air cut!' 'Chase me, Charlie!' 'Here I come with my little lot.' 'Not in these trousers!' 'Keep yer 'air on.' 'Ginger, yer're barmy!' 'Any old iron!' 'What-ho, she bumps!' These catch-phrases, often highly amusing when used at the right moment and in the right context, made an irresistible appeal to the lively, quick-witted Cockney of both sexes.

For most of the poor life must have been a hard enough struggle. But their delighted response to these songs and jests serves to explain why, in spite of all the hardships, life in those days could also be cheery and gay. They could extract amusement from the most lugubrious topics, just as the small maidens on the pavement sang as they turned the skipping rope—

> I am a little beggar-girl
> My mother she is dead,
> My father is a drunkard
> And won't give me no bread . . .
> I look out of the window
> To hear the organ play—
> God bless my dear mother,
> She gone far away.[2]

[1] Thomas Burke, London in My Time (1934), pp. 135-6.
[2] Norman Douglas, London Street Games (1916), p. 71.

The town, like the country, abounded in characters. There were picturesque figures like Stewart Gray, 'the Apostle of Nature'; Old Humphreys, who kept a second-hand bookshop in Paternoster Row and on a Sunday, wet or fine, was to be found holding forth, on almost every subject under the sun, at his own particular pitch on Peckham Rye; Craig, 'the Surrey poet', who at every match at the Oval would peddle his doggerel verse and exchange witty badinage with a large and appreciative audience (Craig's poetry was terrible: but as a character he was an institution—impossible to imagine the Oval without 'the Surrey poet'!); the eccentric Captain Hunnable, of Ilford—champion of many a lost cause—a strange, wildly gesticulating figure in a white smock, with long dark hair tumbling over his shoulders (at the Croydon by-election in 1909 he had been likened to 'Peter the Hermit preaching the First Crusade'); and W. G. Waters, 'Spring Onions', the Stepney poet, who throughout most of his life had been a chronic drunkard — he was first gaoled for drunkenness at the tender age of thirteen, and had been 'inside' thirty-nine times — until, eventually persuaded to sign the pledge, he was employed as a messenger at Thames Police Court, in which capacity he was a favourite with all and still continued to woo the Muse ('I find that after fifteen years of teetotalism, I write better poetry. Every time I want a drink, I say to myself: "Spring—sit down and write a poem!"').[1]

There was the courtly old newsvendor who, in top hat, frock coat, and watered silk waistcoat, presented to him by club-men, used to sell the Pall Mall Gazette, 'with an air', at the bottom of Regent Street by Verrey's.

Another celebrated character was Herbert Anscombe. Possessed of a voice which could penetrate to the furthermost fringes of the crowd and a devastating method of disposing of hecklers, he was accustomed to harangue the multitude in one of the North London parks — 'weather permitting', records the late W. Pett Ridge, 'on Sunday mornings and, when public affairs became strenuous, on a week-day evening'. The following is a specimen of Anscombe's eloquence:

'Let me say at once that I am not, never have been, and possibly never shall be, in the private confidence of our leading

[1] Thomas Burke, Nights in Town (1915), p. 335.

politicians. I have no desire so to be. If any one of 'em came to me, and said, "Anscombe, can you keep a secret?" I sh'd turn on him, and I sh'd say, "My Lord," or whatever his name was, "go elsewhere". Go to the 'ired sycophants who surround and environ you. Go to the officials, bureaucrats, I venture to call 'em—who earn their princely salaries by pandering to you. But don't you dare approach, with your unworthy confidences and treacherous intrigues, 'Erbert Anscombe; for in doing so, my Lord," or whatever his name was, "I give you fair warning that you are coming——"

Here a deep indrawn breath. The right arm aloft, prepared to descend.

' "——coming to the wrong shop!" ' [1]

Characters like Old Humphreys, 'Spring Onions', and the others were, of course, outstanding cases; but a strong individualism distinguished, not only these humbler eccentrics of the streets, but also the great and famous. Politicians, painters, musicians, actors, comedians, lawyers, dons, divines, poets, bookmakers, journalists, and impresarios, by their demeanour, dress, and appearance, looked the part. The leading figures in the different walks of life stood out conspicuously from the common herd. Standardization was not as yet the rule of life.

It was an age, too, of intimate groups and coteries. In those days large numbers of men about town were regularly to be discovered, at certain understood times, in their customary restaurant, bar, or music hall.

The Café Royal in Regent Street, which in a remarkable degree reproduced something of the atmosphere of a Parisian café, had become the centre of some of the most interesting artistic, literary, and intellectual coteries in the kingdom. There were the painters from Chelsea, often accompanied by their models; the New Age set, presided over by A. R. Orage; Nina Hamnett and her circle; the coterie which revolved round T. E. Hulme, the mathematician and philosopher, and a number of other distinguished groups. T. H. W. Crosland, the brilliant satirist and poet, had haunted the Café for the last twenty years. Augustus John was a familiar visitor there. Winston Churchill came occasionally, and Horatio Bottomley was a 'regular'. The

[1] W. Pett Ridge, I Like to Remember, pp. 63-4.

urbane and soft-spoken Max Beerbohm wrote one of his happiest essays about the place. The two greatest singers of their day, Caruso and Chaliapine, patronized the Café. There, night after night, was discussed *ad infinitum* Ezra Pound's verse, Jacob Epstein's sculptures, August John's paintings, the rival schools of Futurism (it was in the Café Royal that the Futurist Manifesto had been solemnly signed by Marinetti and Nevinson, and hotly controverted by Wyndham-Lewis), and the imminence of a great European war. For decades the old Café had been a home from home for many of these Bohemians. Its polyglot clientèle would sink back in the comfortable red plush settees, beneath the smoke-begrimed, high, painted ceiling, and on occasion would break forth into their famous chant, to the air of 'Greensleeves'—

> Jove be with us while we sit
>   On the crimson, soft settees;
> Drinking beer and liking it
>   Most peculiarly at ease.
>
> That for life, and this for love,
>   'B' for bliss and 'P' for pain,
> Not till midnight will we move—
>   'Waiter ! Fill them up again.'

To the Café came 'rich man, poor man, beggarman, thief' . . . crooks, cadgers, pimps, bookies, trainers, owners, authors, publishers, poets, politicians, lion-hunters, and a growing army of sightseers attracted there by the legendary fame of this capital of Bohemia. It was worth seeing too. It had been said, and without exaggeration, that there was 'always something happening in the Café Royal'. It was within those hallowed walls that Marie Lloyd once chased the head waiter round the tables with a pair of long and dangerous-looking hat-pins; that G. K. Chesterton and Hilaire Belloc had gravely embarrassed their friend, E. V. Lucas, by singing cheerfully through the meal ('I was not brought up to sing in public places', observed 'E.V.' severely); and that Lord Alfred Douglas had the monumental row with Jacob Epstein over the Wilde memorial statuary.

Romano's in the Strand was renowned in story and song as the gayest, cheeriest little restaurant in town. Its clientèle was an extraordinary collection of people drawn from a great many different walks of life, ranging from country squires, Guardsmen, dons, and barristers to authors, playwrights, composers, journalists, and impresarios. Phil May in his day had been a frequent visitor. To Romano's came the 'Guv'nor' with a bevy of Gaiety Girls, and that very able band of writers who had made the fortunes of the *Sporting Times* (colloquially known as the '*Pink 'Un*'), and subsequently, under the editorship of 'Pitcher' Binstead, founded *Town Topics*.

One of the merriest of all these coteries whose aim was to enjoy life was the 'Junior Turf'. This was actually the cabmen's shelter in Piccadilly, which lay nearly opposite the Turf Club, where the 'three o'clock in the morning boys' were accustomed to foregather, to refresh themselves with eggs and bacon and fraternise with the cabbies. One of the 'regulars' at this alfresco night club was the distinguished explorer, Sir Ernest Shackleton, and among other callers were Beerbohm Tree, G. R. Sims, 'Costs' Booth, and 'Pitcher' Binstead.

The last two decades had witnessed one of the most glamorous eras in the annals of the London stage. This great theatrical renaissance had been ushered in by Henry Irving and Ellen Terry, and some years later there had appeared a brilliant galaxy of actors and actresses, including George Alexander, Lewis Waller, Herbert Beerbohm Tree, Cyril Maude, Marie Tempest, Irene Vanbrugh, and Lilian Braithwaite. The celebrated Shakespeare revivals by Irving at the Lyceum were followed by those of Tree at His Majesty's. At the Haymarket Theatre, the home of English comedy, there were revivals of Sheridan and Goldsmith. The productions of such modern dramatists as Pinero, Wilde, Bernard Shaw, Barrie, Galsworthy, and Somerset Maugham also appeared, as well as a series of Greek tragedies put on under the able Vedrenne-Barker management at the Royal Court Theatre. The era also saw the production of a large number of highly successful romantic plays like *The Prisoner of Zenda*, *The Three Musketeers*, *Under the Red Robe*, *If I were King*, *Monsieur Beaucaire*, and *Sweet Nell of Old Drury*. Nothing like this had been seen in England for centuries, nor has anything like it been seen since.

In the last years of peace, under the management of George

Edwardes ('the Guv'nor'), at his two famous theatres, the Gaiety and Daly's, with the entrancing music of Ivan Caryll, Lionel Monckton, Paul Rubens, and others, English musical comedy reached its highest peak. The beauty and brilliancy of some of these productions are among the most precious memories of the Old World whose doom and dissolution were now so swiftly approaching.

After its long record of triumphs in the late Victorian era the old Gaiety Theatre had closed in the summer of 1903, and the new Gaiety opened the following autumn with Gertie Millar as the leading lady and George Grossmith ('Gee-Gee') as the leading man in George Edwardes' production of *The Orchid*. The following decade was the most brilliant that the Gaiety Theatre had ever known. Dazzling show succeeded dazzling show. The long reign of Gertie Millar at the Gaiety reached its apogee, in 1909, with *Our Miss Gibbs*, with music by Ivan Caryll and Lionel Monckton. 'Gee-Gee', Teddie Payne, Robert Hale, and Gladys Cooper were also in the cast. *Our Miss Gibbs* ran for 636 performances, and broke all previous records.

The sparkle and glamour of the Gaiety Theatre were renowned throughout the English-speaking world. A Gaiety first-night was a social occasion of the first magnitude. All London would be there, pouring in through the lovely circular vestibule, with a rustle of silken gowns, gleam of jewels, and an elegance and an atmosphere which has vanished for ever, into the familiar brown and gold auditorium.

The Gaiety Girls were one of the sights of town. Sheaves of the most beautiful flowers would regularly arrive from their devoted admirers. A rustle of excitement would go round the tables whenever any of them entered a restaurant. At Romano's and elsewhere special tables were reserved for them. Several of the girls had married into the peerage. Young men of rank and fortune from all over the country flocked to see them. Night after night there would be the same eager throng of black-coated, silk-hatted young bloods assembled round the fabled stage door of the Gaiety. After the show the girls would be whisked off to supper at Romano's, Rule's, or the Cavour by their proud escorts.

At the 'Guv'nor's' other theatre, Daly's, in Leicester Square, the emphasis was on music rather than on comedy; indeed, the fare provided lay nearer light opera than musical comedy. Daly's long series of successes included such brilliant, sparkling productions as *The Geisha, A Greek Slave, San Toy, The Country Girl, The Cingalee, The Merry Widow, The Dollar Princess, The Count of Luxemburg,* and *Gipsy Love.* A first night at Daly's, as at the Gaiety, was a major social occasion. (It was nearly as difficult to get into the stalls or circle at Daly's as into the Royal Enclosure at Ascot.) The first night of *The Merry Widow* made theatrical history. George Edwardes had always believed that the crowning triumph of his career would come to him from the legendary city of Vienna; and come, at last, it had. London went wild over *The Widow*; picture postcards of Lily Elsie were in all the shop windows, and *Merry Widow* hats were seen in all the streets.

Marie Tempest singing 'O Mimosa San' in *The Geisha*; Gertie Millar, in her gray Quaker gown and white apron, singing 'Thee loves me, and I loves thee' and 'Tony from America' in *The Quaker Girl,* and dancing 'Moonstruck' in *Our Miss Gibbs*— perhaps her greatest triumph; the lovely ballroom scene in *The Country Girl*; Lily Elsie and Joseph Coyne dancing their immortal waltz in *The Merry Widow*; Dollis Brooke of Pelissier's Follies singing 'Moon, Moon, serenely shining'; the great Russian ballerina, Anna Pavlova, dancing 'The Swan' from Saint-Saen's *Carnaval des Animaux*—the very remembrance of these haunting melodies conjures up a rich and glowing picture of the London stage in those golden years. . . . Glorious nights, unforgettable memories!

The early years of the present century saw the Indian summer of that great national institution, the music hall, which had reached its zenith from twenty to thirty years before with the triumphs of George Leybourne, Bessie Bellwood, the Great Macdermott, Jennie Hill, and Dan Leno. Its origins may be traced back to the tavern sing-song of the mid-Victorian era, or perhaps somewhat earlier. It developed into a house of popular entertainment—half theatre, half beer-hall—presided over by a bibulous potentate known as the Chairman. (To sit at the Chairman's table was a much coveted honour.) Later on it became a theatre pure and simple, and, when the audience required liquid refreshment, they had to patronise one of the numerous bars on the premises.

'The music hall was a national product,' wrote J. B. Booth, 'it dealt with the national life, its mirth was the robust mirth of a masculine nation.' Gentle and refined characters like the poetess, Alice Meynell, tended to shudder at the crude and homely realism depicted on its boards. Max Beerbohm, on the other hand, frankly appreciated and admired the music hall.

From the music hall came the airs which set the whole kingdom singing and humming and whistling, as well as the jests and catch-phrases which went flying through the streets of England's cities and towns. For these were the songs and sayings of the people. One heard them whistled by errand boys and hymned on the piano-organ from Manchester to Margate, from Scarborough to Swansea. In the same way a catchword which appealed to the man in the street was taken to his bosom with enthusiasm and had a vogue which often lasted for many years.

The music hall reflected, fairly accurately, the character and temper of the common people, especially in times of stress. One of the most celebrated music-hall songs of all time, the Great Macdermott's 'We don't want to fight, But, by Jingo, if we do', played no small part in arousing public opinion during the Russo-Turkish War of 1877. Two decades later the South African War was responsible for 'Good-bye, Dolly Gray'.

The working-class Londoner of those days had none of the inhibitions of Kipling's 'Stalky' and his companions where The Flag was concerned. They loved it! They waved it! They swore by it! They had a robust and unshakeable confidence in both the fighting Services—though, faithful to our national tradition, the Navy, perhaps, held pride of place in their affections.

> Sons of the sea, all British born,
> Sailing every ocean, laughing foes to scorn,
> They may build their ships, my lads,
> And think they know the game;
> But they can't build the boys of the bulldog breed,
> Who made old England's name!

Their patrons loved the ornate display of golden and crimson upholstery, the bright lights, and the gleam of imitation marble which they saw around them. They loved the rousing overture

to *Zampa,* and similar pieces, which the maestro freely gave
them. They loved to sit there, in unbuttoned ease, in the richest
of fugs redolent of orange peel and peppermint drops, to listen
to men and women of much the same sort as themselves singing
and discoursing about life as they themselves knew it, and to
join in the cheery, raucous, rollicking choruses of the songs they
liked best — comic, vulgar, patriotic, or sentimental — to the
accompaniment of a loud and brassy orchestra.

The intimate relationship between stage and audience which
had been handed down from the earliest days of the music hall
still existed in full measure. The artists addressed the people in
the house as man to man, or woman to woman. They dealt with
types and topics with which everyone in the audience was inti-
mately familiar. Dan Leno and Bessie Bellwood had put on a
whole gallery of London types; and the tradition had been well
and worthily carried on by Marie Lloyd, Little Tich, Albert
Chevalier, and Gus Elen.

As one listens to the songs which have become part of the
warp and woof of English social life the London of long ago is
magically re-created before our eyes. The hen-pecked husband,
the coster and his Donah, the policeman, the railway porter, the
street arab, the sergeant-major, the *gamine* of the London streets,
all take the boards in turn. The rent, the lodger, 'Uncle' (the
pawnbroker), the mother-in-law, the naughty boy (and the
naughty girl!), poverty, drink, and goings-on in general are
among the favourite subjects for comment. Various articles of
diet (i.e. kippers, cheese, tripe) are agreed by all to be highly
amusing; so, too, are certain items of dress (i.e. garters, trousers,
'bloomers').

Certain artists were associated with certain songs; songs which
had made them famous, and with which their names will always
be linked. Thus, in this last year of peace there was Charles
Coburn with his 'Two Lovely Black Eyes' and 'The Man Who
Broke the Bank at Monte Carlo', Tom Costello with his 'At
Trinity Church' and 'The Ship I Love', R. G. Knowles with his
'Dear little Girly Girly', T. E. Dunville with his 'Little Boy—
Pair of Skates', Eugene Stratton with his 'Lily of Laguna' and
'Dolly Daydreams', Harry Champion with his 'Boiled Beef and
Carrots' and 'I'm 'Enery the Eighth I am', Marie Lloyd with her
'Oh, Mr Porter' and 'My Old Man said, Follow the Van', Florrie

Forde with her 'Down at The Old Bull and Bush', George Robey with his 'I stopped—I looked—I listened', Vesta Tilley with her 'Burlington Bertie' and 'The Army of To-day's All Right', and Clarice Mayne with her 'Joshua, Joshua' and 'I was a good little Girl'.

The year 1913 had seen the appearance of a number of new songs, most of which are still well known to us today. 'It's a long way to Tipperary', 'Get out and get under', 'Hitchy Koo', 'You made me love You', 'You're my Tango Girl', 'Who were You with last Night?', 'Hold your Hand out, Naughty Boy!', 'Joshua, Joshua, Nicer than Lemon Squash You are'.

London was then a city in which there was extreme wealth and extreme squalor. Often the two states existed in close juxtaposition. The spectacle of men, women, and children in miserable rags and abject, hopeless poverty was not so often encountered as in former days—at any rate, in the day-time. Rather, it was late at night, when most folk were in their homes, that human wretchedness and misery walked the streets of London. Degraded, drink-sodden women with infants in their arms would then steal silently through the shadows. 'There are a great many drunken people in London', observed Chaliapine, who later in the year was appearing at Drury Lane.

An hour or so after midnight the Thames Embankment presented a scene of mingled affluence and destitution that could scarcely be matched anywhere in the kingdom. The great hotels and luxurious chambers were still brightly illuminated. Within a stone's throw of the river there was all the comfort and elegance that riches could command. Yet outside these palatial buildings, hundreds of poor outcasts, both old and young, herded together in sheltered nooks and corners or snatched a few hours' uneasy rest huddled up on the seats along the Embankment. Some lay down, in utter exhaustion, on the pavement under the parapet. Hundreds more were to be found on the seats of the bridges over the Thames, or lying in long rows about Nelson's Column in Trafalgar Square. The rags they wore were of little avail to keep out the cold, and often they would wrap old newspapers around their bodies. Sometimes the police would discover one of these poor wretches frozen to death. Many others perished of hunger. There is a good deal of truth in an observation made about this time by W. B. Northrop:

'If the body of every pauper in London who starves to death were taken to Trafalgar Square, and there allowed to remain in State for a few days, instead of being quietly buried in a pauper's grave in some obscure cemetery, all classes would soon be brought to a realization of these terrible conditions.'[1]

The social and economic system, as it existed in the early years of this century, may be said to have exemplified the principle of the survival of the fittest. These poor outcasts from society, for one reason or another, represented the failures and unfit. Sometimes the more or less innocent victims of circumstances, but all too often, in fact, the authors of their own misfortunes, they had sunk lower and lower until they reached the bottom.

If there were not back-to-back houses in London like those in the North and Midlands, there were wide areas which contained greater aggregations of the very poor than could be found in any other part of the country. 'In Marylebone, Southwark, St Pancras, Holborn, Bethnal Green, Shoreditch, Stepney, and Finsbury upwards of 30 per cent of the inhabitants live in tenements of one or two rooms. In Finsbury the proportion reaches 45 per cent; in Shoreditch 37 per cent.' The appalling housing conditions were reflected in the vital statistics. While the infantile death-rate per thousand in districts such as Hampstead was under 94, in districts such as Shoreditch and Bethnal Green it ranged from 150 to 170.

Not even the schoolchildren of the poorest districts of Manchester or Newcastle-upon-Tyne exhibited the same degree of physical deterioration as those of Lambeth or Bethnal Green. It was stated that no less than one-third of the children attending elementary schools were inadequately or improperly fed. According to a report on conditions in the Lambeth district:

'There is bread and margarine for lunch, and the dinner is normally nothing but what a copper can purchase at the local fried fish shops, where the most inferior kinds of fish such as

[1] W. B. Northrop, Wealth and Want, p. 199.

skate are fried in unwholesome, reeking, cottonseed oil. They frequently supplement this with rotten fruit which they collect beneath barrows.'[1]

The following excerpt from a contemporary authority sheds further light on this evil:

'Those alone who have had to do with voluntary free breakfast schemes can have any idea of the terrible hunger of the children who attend them. The hugging of the mug of cocoa, the ravenous swallowing—it cannot be called eating—of the slices of bread, make one shudder to think that, but for such isolated voluntary effort, the poor children would in an hour or so be entering a school at which their attendance is compulsory—to study!'[2]

Not all these children, of course, went hungry through the poverty of their families. A fair proportion of them were the victims of parental heedlessness, ignorance, or neglect. The working-class Londoners of those days were a pleasure-loving race; and their young children might be left for hours to their own devices while the fathers and mothers were out enjoying themselves at the music-hall or public house. Again, many a baby would be taken out at night in all weathers and, on the parents' return home, undressed in the cold and put into chilly night-clothes in a cold bed—bronchitis, in consequence, levied a grievous toll on infant life.[3]

From time to time the public conscience had been stirred by the Revelations of Royal Commissions and Committees of the House of Commons regarding the evils of sweated labour. It appeared that large numbers of unfortunate men and women were engaged in toil under very unhealthy conditions, for anything up to sixteen hours a day, for a wretched pittance that was barely enough to keep body and soul together. Tailoring was one of the principal sweated trades. Box-making, chain-making, paper-bag-making, and the manufacture of artificial flowers were others. In London the sweating system existed chiefly in the

[1] *Ibid*, p. 46.
[2] L. G. Chiozza Money, *Riches and Poverty* (1913), p. 197.
[3] Helen Bosanquet, *The Standard of Life* (1906), pp. 238-9.

East End; newly arrived parties of immigrants from northern and eastern Europe provided a large proportion of its victims. The worst evils resulting from overwork and underpayment, however, had lately been ameliorated by the new Act; and much had been achieved by the resolute action of the trade unions.

'Forty years ago all chain-makers were sweated. The men were sweated as well as the women. The makers of the great chains that hold ships to their anchorage were sweated; so were the makers of the trivial chains that hold a gate to its post. The man who brought light into this darkness was Tom Switch, a Labour leader of the old school and the founder of the Amalgamated Society of Anchorsmiths and Shackle Makers. Tom Switch was not a Socialist. He had probably never heard of Karl Marx. He never talked of the Class War or understood the theory of "surplus value". His contempt for the young fire-eaters of today would be complete and undisguised. But he did a great work for his mates and raised them by his determined endeavours from a condition of being starved to a condition of being well paid and respected. Before he died he could boast that his union contained every worker in the country who was entitled to join it.'[1]

Margaret Bondfield was the moving spirit of a small but influential group of women in London who were engaged in vigorously promoting the industrial organization of women. Their mouthpiece, the Woman Worker, was founded and edited by Mary Macarthur, who, since 1906, had been Secretary of the National Federation of Women Workers. The activities of this group contributed materially to the progress of the Labour movement.

'Never were there more people with abundance of money to spend,' declared the Globe that Christmas, 'or more people without the commonest necessaries of life.'

The two statements are worth examining. The first is undoubtedly true. The second, however, is highly questionable. For though the rapidly expanding middle class had benefited greatly from the progressive increase in the national income, the mass of the working class had improved their position even more. Never had the workers been so continuously employed, or had

[1] Q. Mary Hamilton, Mary Macarthur, p. 81.

the level of wages been so high. Moreover, the cost of the expanding social services was borne by the upper and middle classes rather than by that part of the population which chiefly benefited from them. The existence of a limited area of extreme poverty must always be viewed against this background. When everything has been said that should be said about the unhappy outcasts on the Embankment and elsewhere, the evils of sweated labour, and the problem of unemployment, the fact remains that at this time the very poor represented a smaller proportion of the total population than ever before.

Still, if it be agreed that a well-known expression like 'the submerged tenth' is an exaggeration, it must be confessed that these unfortunates constituted a not inconsiderable minority; and their lot was growing even worse. Retail prices continued to rise. Coal was dearer; and the cheapest kinds of foods, notably bread, upon which the poor relied were certainly less nutritious than in former times. Moreover, urban rents were rising, overcrowding was on the increase, and, as has been said, housing conditions in the poorer quarters of the great cities were deplorable. 'What do I care for the Empire on which the sun never sets?' exclaimed a daughter of the slums. 'Down our court the sun never rises!'

CHAPTER 4

The opening of Parliament

There was a feeling of spring in the air and the sun shone brilliantly, when, in the early afternoon of February 10th, King George V and Queen Mary drove in state from Buckingham Palace to open Parliament.

The crowds which had gathered along the route were unusually large. It is doubtful whether so many thousands of people had ever assembled in the Mall—the principal processional way of the capital—on any previous occasion; and there was a great throng in Whitehall near the Horseguards. The whole route was lined with troops of the Brigade of Guards. Over the roofs of the great Government offices flags waved in the breeze, and the windows and balconies were filled with groups of spectators. On the crowded pavements below friendly London 'bobbies' directed visitors where to stand to get a good view of the ceremony. Though some of the people had been waiting for hours there was plenty to interest them. An almost continuous stream of vehicles—taxi-cabs, private motor-cars, and Ambassadors' coaches — swept southwards. The crowds in Parliament Square could see Lloyd George and other Cabinet ministers awaiting the Sovereigns' arrival at the foot of the Victoria Tower, where a military band played dance music. Behind the guard of honour, in their traditional place, stood the boys of Westminster School. M.P.s mingled freely with the other onlookers, and there was almost a holiday atmosphere about the occasion. Discussion turned on the weather, the present ceremony, and the prospects of the coming session. Finally all eyes were fixed on the cleared and sanded roadway between the double lines of motionless troops.

First, well in advance of the actual procession, came a Royal carriage containing the Crown and Sword of State with a jingling escort of Lifeguards. Presently the cheers of the huge crowds lining the Mall could be heard faintly in the distance—a

63

surge of applause which swelled and died away like the roar of
the sea; a momentary silence descended as the cavalcade
advanced through the Horse Guards; and then, as the opening
bars of the National Anthem crashed out, the Royal procession
in all its brilliancy and splendour appeared in Whitehall—six
Royal carriages, attended by postillions and wigged and
powdered footmen, and then the old State Coach, drawn by a
team of eight cream horses, bearing the King and Queen bowing
to left and to right, accompanied by a Sovereigns' escort of Life
Guards. The different shades of red and gold gleamed and
glistened in the bright sun. The clatter of horses' hooves mingled
with a blare of martial music, sudden hoarse shouts of command,
the jingle of accoutrements, and the loud, surging cheers of the
crowd. The glittering cavalcade wheeled to the right and
advanced slowly down Whitehall, evoking continual outbursts
of applause; and when at last the Sovereigns arrived outside the
Palace of Westminster the bells rang out in St Margaret's
Church, the Royal Standard was unfurled on the Victoria
Tower, and forty-one guns began to boom out in salute from
St James's Park.

The consummation of this ancient ceremony took place in the
House of Lords. On the entry of the King and Queen, heralded
by a fanfare of trumpets and preceded by the Earl Marshal and
the other great officers of State, shortly after two o'clock, the
great chamber, with its wealth of carved oak panelling and
stained-glass windows and red benches sloping from the floor,
which had hitherto been dimly lit, was suddenly flooded with
electric light: the scarlet and ermine of the peers, the snow-
white lawn of the bishops, the beautiful gowns and tiaras of
the peeresses, the full-bottomed wigs of the judges, the rich
uniforms of the Corps Diplomatique, and the knee-breeches and
gold chains of the Court officials, were seen in all their glory;
and when presently the whole assembly made their obeisance to
the Sovereigns, the general effect was likened to 'the waving of a
cornfield in the breeze'.

At the King's right hand stood Lord Haldane, the Lord Chancellor, the Duke of Norfolk, the Earl Marshal, and the Marquess
of Lincolnshire, the Lord Great Chamberlain. To the left of the
Queen stood the Duchess of Devonshire, the Mistress of the
Robes, and the other Ladies-in-Waiting. The lords and ladies

1. The country house (Wiston Park, Sussex)

2 A village smithy

resumed their seats, the 'Faithful Commons'—summoned by Black Rod—crowded in behind the Bar, and a solemn hush descended on the chamber. Then the Lord Chancellor, kneeling, presented the gracious Speech to the King, who, crowned and seated, began to read.

Parliament had assembled that day in a grave and anxious spirit. The feeling in both Houses was noticeably tense, and there was an unusually large attendance for what was regarded as the most critical session of modern times. In the course of the Speech from the Throne, the King referred briefly to his friendly relations with foreign powers and his forthcoming visit to the President of the French Republic, touched on the International Conference on Safety of Life at Sea, and expressed his concern at the recent severe drought in India which had resulted in widespread distress; and then spoke plainly of the issue that was uppermost in every mind.

'The measures in regard to which there were differences last session between the two Houses will be again submitted to your consideration. I regret that the efforts which have been made to arrive at a solution by agreement of the problems connected with the Government of Ireland have, so far, not succeeded. In a matter in which the hopes and fears of so many of my subjects are keenly concerned, and which, unless handled now with fore-sight, judgment, and in the spirit of mutual concession, threatens grave difficulties, it is my most earnest wish that the goodwill and co-operation of men of all parties and creeds may heal dissension and lay the foundations of a lasting settlement.'

The close attention with which this part of the Speech was received gave testimony of the growing apprehension through-out the whole country about the situation in Ireland. (The Christmas Day sermons had been full of gloomy references to recent happenings in Ulster.) Though the King's words did nothing to relieve this anxiety, they at least brought the matter out into the open. The Government had, in effect, admitted that the shadow of civil war overhung the land.

Shortly after, the King finished reading. Returning the Speech to the Lord Chancellor, he bowed to the assembled peers and peeresses, and quitted the chamber with his Queen.

C

Immediately after the Sovereigns' departure a hum of anxious discussion arose in all parts of the chamber, and was continued in the lobbies and corridors outside. Everyone was seeking to learn what really lay behind the careful phrasing of the King's Speech. It was surely significant that there had been a whole paragraph about such a non-controversial subject as the Safety of Life at Sea and not a word about the Government's bitterly assailed Welsh Disestablishment Bill. It was conjectured by some that the guarded reference to the Irish crisis betokened a new spirit of accommodation in the Cabinet; it might even be taken as a veiled hint of some last-minute reconciliation.

The pageantry of February 10th was a striking example of the abiding influence of the past over the present, and of the historical continuity of public life in this country. Once again the leaders of the Government and Opposition had given the customary banquet to their principal supporters on the night before Parliament reassembled. Once again the ancient custom of ceremonially searching the vaults below the Palace of Westminster which had been observed ever since Gunpowder Plot was duly honoured. The elaborately staged ceremony that had been enacted in the capital of the Empire was a tribute to the past as well as to the present glories of England. Here, as a contemporary journal truly observed, was symbolized 'the Might, the Majesty, the permanency of the Realm of England'—a fact of which every man, woman and child in the large crowds gathered outside to cheer the King and Queen on their homeward journey were, somehow or other, aware.

> Time, and the ocean, and some fostering star,
> In high cabal have made us what we are.

This was another of those memorable State spectacles to which Londoners of that generation had become accustomed. The thoughts of many in that great concourse must have gone back to the pomp and pageantry of the Golden Jubilee of 1887 and of the yet more magnificent display of the Diamond Jubilee ten years later. Many more would recall the scenes of stately mourning at Queen Victoria's funeral in 1901, and the impressive coronation processions of Edward VII and George V.

Great Britain was still the great World Power—to her, as in past centuries, belonged the Empire of the Ocean: an Empire upon which, according to our proud boast, the sun never set. It was a great and splendid era of our history which is conjured up for us by Benson's well-loved lines set to Elgar's stirring music.

> Land of hope and glory,
> Mother of the free.
> How shall we extol thee
> Who are born of thee?
> Wider still and wider
> Shall thy bounds be set.
> God, that made thee mighty,
> Make thee mightier yet!

Secure behind the shield of her Fleet, Great Britain had attained, in the mid-Victorian era, the apogee of her prosperity, power, and prestige. With an army insignificant in size compared with that of any of the other Great Powers she was able to extend and maintain her hold over an immense area of the earth's surface, and to impose the sway of the *Pax Britannica* upon countless millions of human beings of diverse races and creeds. If, in the words of a popular air of the 'eighties, 'A little British army goes a dam' long way', it was because that little British army would be carried to its destination by an overwhelmingly superior fleet. 'We alone of all nations', observed *Brassey's Naval Annual*, 'could place our armies at short notice in any part of the globe. This power of transport may be set in the scale against the superior numbers of foreign Powers.'

Our home population, in spite of evanescent war alarms, could scarcely imagine any serious threat to all this enduring peace and prosperity, to which, perhaps, no parallel had existed since the days of the Antonines. Wars and rumours of wars might periodically afflict the people's of the Continent. The frontiers of the Land Powers might be guarded by troops and fortresses. But war on the soil of England was something quite unthinkable —such a thing had not happened for centuries; the inviolable security of our island realm was indeed regarded by the inhabitants almost as part of nature's law. Mistress of the seas as we were, the trim white coastguard stations which drowsed in the sunshine around the long, indented coasts of Britain were all the defence we needed.

It was a phenomenon beyond the comprehension of Continental militarists like Clausewitz. But there was no belittling its significance. For all their superiority in territory and population, for all the immense conscript armies which they could command, the island State was beyond their reach, aloof and unassailable; its influence extended to the farthest corners of the globe—an ubiquitous and incalculable factor in the affairs of nations.

Seated that day on the Treasury Bench were the Prime Minister, H. H. Asquith, and the other Ministers, including David Lloyd George, Sir Edward Grey, and Winston Churchill, comprising one of the ablest and most distinguished Cabinets that ever ruled England. Across the gangway, on the Front Opposition Bench, sat Andrew Bonar Law, the Leader of the Conservative Party, with A. J. Balfour, Lord Hugh Cecil, F. E. Smith, and other of his principal supporters. Above them, sitting wigged and gowned in his high, canopied chair, was the Speaker, Mr James Lowther.

Asquith, now in his sixty-second year, had succeeded to the premiership on the death of Campbell-Bannerman in 1908. He belonged, like Grey, to the Imperialist wing of the Liberal Party, but worked in harmony with the Radical element in his Cabinet. With his massive brow, and flowing silvery hair, he looked—as, indeed, he had sometimes been called—'the last of the Romans'. A man of commanding ability, ripe judgment, detached judicial outlook, unshakable calm, and genial humour, he bore himself with dignity and firmness through the long and difficult term of his premiership. One of the greatest peace-time Ministers, perhaps, in our history, Asquith steered the ship of state through a period of epoch-making changes at home, and at the same time kept a watchful eye on dangers abroad. Above all, he showed himself a vigilant guardian of that maritime supremacy upon which, in the last resort, the safety and prosperity of Great Britain depended—never more so than during the long and acrimonious controversy in the Cabinet over the 1914 Naval Estimates.

The Chancellor of the Exchequer, David Lloyd George, was his junior by ten years. The poor village boy from Criccieth who, without money or influence, had become the second man in the Government, was now at the height of his formidable powers. He was a man of outstanding and diverse abilities; of ready wit, abounding energy, and indomitable courage: ambitious, shrewd, and frankly opportunist as to means. The hero and champion of British Radicalism, Lloyd George was the bugbear of the conservatively minded and of the comfortable classes generally. What they thought about him in the country houses, in the West End clubs, in cathedral closes, and in the more prosperous suburbs, can well be gauged from the cartoons in *Punch*. His budgets, revolutionary in their range and scope, marked a turning-point in our social and political history. He was the architect of the Liberal victory over the Parliament Bill in 1911 which abolished the ancient prerogative of the peers. With his lively Celtic imagery and gift of withering invective he was among the best half-dozen debaters in the lower house. His mordant phrases scorched and seared. In a famous passage he declared that the House of Lords had 'ceased to be the watch-dog of the Constitution, and had become Mr Balfour's poodle'. When the Duke of Devonshire, somewhat imprudently, characterized the Welsh Disestablishment Bill as 'robbery of God', Lloyd George fiercely denounced the part played by this nobleman's ancestors in the spoliation of the monasteries and spoke of 'hands dripping with the fat of sacrilege'. But it was on the platform that Lloyd George really excelled, swaying the emotions of a vast multitude; and it was there that his greatest triumphs had been won. His speech before a crowded audience at Limehouse, on July 30, 1909, was a masterpiece of cogent and sustained invective. A few months later he discoursed upon the 'rare and refreshing fruit' to be hoped for from his Budget land taxes; and, in reference to the Old Age Pension Act, conjured up a pathetic picture of the aged toilers who stood at the workhouse gates 'wistfully awaiting the turn of the key with nothing between them now and their redemption but the greed of the Lords'. Lloyd George possessed an unsurpassed gift of histrionic appeal. He was, as his biographer, T. E. Raymond, once wrote, 'a master in the art of leading up to "loud cheers" '. In 1913 Lloyd George had been on the rampage once more, as a sequel to his other triumphs, with his newly launched Land Campaign. Once again he was tilting furiously at his old opponents, the landowners. He said he looked forward to a contented, prosperous population in a new and better Britain, and to a countryside 'where the valleys stand so thick with corn that they shall laugh and sing'.

From December 1905 Sir Edward Grey, as Foreign Secretary, had represented England to Europe and the world at large. Throughout these years his reputation had been steadily rising, owing partly to the moderate and conciliatory policy he pursued, and partly to his own fine qualities. Grey had handsome, aquiline features and a slender, well-knit frame; almost to the end of his career there was about him an air of youth, an almost boyish appearance. He spoke in a steady, even, passionless voice. 'A moderate, patient, wise man', commented the American Ambassador, 'the biggest Englishman I have met'. Possessed of an almost passionate love of nature and the open air, and a master of the complex art of fly-fishing (a book he wrote on that subject is justly accounted a classic), he passed most of his leisure hours during the session at his fishing lodge on the banks of the Itchen. A cardinal point of Grey's policy was the maintenance of our historic maritime supremacy—for the preservation of which it was necessary at all costs to prevent a German hegemony in Europe. Hence the understanding with France. Convinced in his innermost soul that war was inevitable, though hating the idea of it, Grey took no active steps to prevent its onset. It is at least within the bounds of possibility that had he done so he might have acted as intermediary between France and Germany and thus have turned the course of history.

'But the idea of bringing the two estranged nations together, and so assuring the peace of Europe, was too odd for Sir Edward Grey to entertain; every weekday he industriously attended to business, with no plan and little imagination, and he did not observe the current of the times with the same loving comprehension as he did his trout stream on Sunday.'[1]

It must be confessed that Grey, the man, was continually

[1] Theodor Wolff, *The Eve of 1914*, p. 92.

troubled in conscience on account of the shifts and contrivances of Grey, the statesman; as, year by year, he found himself drawn deeper and deeper into the meshes so skilfully woven for his entanglement by the French Ambassador, M. Paul Cambon. The military conversations which he allowed to be carried on between the General Staffs of Great Britain and France had not unnaturally come to be regarded on the other side of the Channel as tantamount to a definite commitment to stand by the latter in the event of a hostile attack.

Winston Churchill, the son of a brilliant but wayward Conservative leader of the late Victorian era, was at this time in his fortieth year—younger by more than ten years than the Chancellor of the Exchequer and by more than twenty than the Prime Minister. A direct descendant of the first Duke of Marlborough, he had been in turn soldier, war correspondent, and politician. While still quite a young man he had seen a good deal of active service in the frontier wars of the day, and had written a number of distinguished books on these campaigns. Entering the House of Commons in 1901 as a Conservative, he had later gone over to the Liberals on the Protection issue. Lloyd George was the first of his new colleagues to welcome him to their ranks; and the two men had worked in close accord throughout the constitutional crisis which ended in the passage of the Parliament Act. Churchill had early attained to Cabinet rank, and was Home Secretary from January 1910 to the autumn of 1911, when he succeeded Reginald McKenna at the Admiralty. It was then that four of the most memorable years of his life began. At a week-end party in the country a young man just down from Oxford, coming down to dinner before the other guests, discovered the ebullient Winston Churchill leap-frogging over the chairs in the drawing-room and chanting:

> Yip-i-addy, i-ay-i-ay,
>   Yip-i-addy-i-ay,
> I don't care what becomes of me;
> I'm the First Lord of the Admiraltee,
> Yip-i-addy, i-ay, i-ay.[1]

On October 8, 1911, Churchill took his place at the head of the long mahogany table in the Board Room of the Admiralty

[1] L. E. Jones, *An Edwardian Youth*, p. 213.

where so much of England's history had been made. From the
first his thoughts and energies, like those of his friend and
mentor before him, Admiral Lord Fisher,[1] were centred on 'the
efficiency of the Navy and its instant readiness for war'. The
Navy became his overriding passion, and the Admiralty yacht,
Enchantress, his other home. 'He visited practically every dockyard, shipyard, naval establishment and important ship in the
British Isles and the Mediterranean', says Marder. 'No First Lord
in modern times has displayed equal zeal in this direction.'
During the first eighteen months of his term of office, Churchill
spent no less than one-third of his time at sea.

A few other members of the Government have also to be mentioned. John Morley, now in his seventy-sixth year, was by far
the oldest member of the Cabinet. He had held a distinguished
place in English letters before ever he entered the House of Commons. A pupil of John Stuart Mill and the friend of Gladstone,
he was a veteran of the great age of British Liberalism. Despite
his friendly relations with Grey, Morley showed a growing
uneasiness at the *ententes* with France and Russia. Formerly
Secretary of State for India, he now held the office of Lord President of the Council. Richard Burdon Haldane, the learned
lawyer-philosopher who had become one of the ablest War
Ministers in modern times, had recently revolutionized the
organisation of the British Army. Among his principal measures
were the creation of a General Staff; the establishment of a
Territorial Army, primarily for home defence, as an integral part
of the national forces; the development of the Officers' Training
Corps, and plans for the speedy mobilization of 160,000 men in
the event of war. To the same end plans had been prepared in
concert with the French G.H.Q. for dispatching an expeditionary
force across the Channel to a position on the left of the French
line. John Burns, now President of the Board of Trade, was the
first working-class man to attain to Cabinet rank.

John Redmond was the leader of the Irish Nationalists who
sat below the gangway; a Party in alliance with the Liberals,
whose goal was the liberation of their homeland from English
rule, and Ireland 'a nation once again'. Redmond, like Asquith,

[1] John Arbothnot Fisher, who was First Sea Lord from 1904 to 1910, was the
most distinguished officer which the Navy had produced since the age of
Nelson and the creator of the dreadnought battle fleet.

was essentially a Parliamentarian, and he thought only in terms of constitutional methods and processes. He was perilously out of touch with the realities of the situation in Ireland.

Bonar Law had succeeded Balfour in the leadership of the Conservative Party after that Party's defeat in the constitution struggle of 1911. Canadian by birth, of Ulster Protestant stock, the son of a Presbyterian minister, the new leader was without Cabinet experience and practically unknown to the general public. Law's first steps were cautious and hesitant; but as he gradually gained experience and confidence he became increasingly associated with the die-hard policy of his Carsonite allies. In the Austro-Serbian crisis which arose in the summer of 1914 this was of more than national importance: for, almost to the last, Law was blind to the realities of the European situation. In the words of his biographer, 'The Irish problem filled the horizon to the exclusion of everything else'.

Arthur James Balfour, the late Conservative leader and an ex-Prime Minister, was by far the most distinguished member of his Party and one of the most accomplished debaters that the House had ever known. In recent years, however, to all outward appearances his star was waning, and he seemed to have had his day. There were few at this time who would have predicted that some of the most important years of Balfour's life still lay ahead. He had been a regular member of the Committee of Imperial Defence since 1912 and took a close and intelligent interest in Naval affairs. In the main he supported Bonar Law's Irish policy but remained unaffected by the fierce fanaticism which inspired Law and the Carsonites.

Lord Hugh Cecil, who was the youngest son of the Marquess of Salisbury, had made his reputation in the Church Schools controversy at the beginning of the century. The band of young Conservative bloods who followed him became known as the 'Hughligans'. During the ferocious Party war which preceded the passage of the Parliament Act these 'Hughligans', in the most violent scene which had occurred within the House in living memory, had effectively prevented Asquith from being heard.

Another of the rising young men of the Conservative Party was F. E. Smith, who, after a triumphant career at the bar, had entered Parliament in 1906 and had made one of the greatest maiden speeches in the annals of the House of Commons. He was closely associated with Carson in the anti-Home Rule campaign on both sides of the Irish Sea.

Sir Edward Carson, the 'uncrowned King of Ulster', sat with the other Unionist leaders on the Front Opposition Bench. He had taken the measure of the Liberal Cabinet and had made his plans; he had nailed his colours to the mast, and now awaited the outcome of the struggle with composure. A few weeks earlier he had flatly refused any compromise on the Home Rule issue short of the total exclusion of Ulster.

In the turmoils that lay ahead the House of Commons was fortunate indeed in having such a man as its Speaker as James William Lowther. His ripe experience, imperturbable temper, genial, unforced humour, and unfailing tact saved many a scene. 'The hon. member', Lowther had once gravely informed a garrulous Irish Nationalist, 'must put his interruption in the form of an interrogation.' 'This', he had observed drily, on another such occasion, 'is a debate, not a *conversazione*.' After a succession of clean-shaven Speakers, Lowther was bearded, and an impressive figure in his full-bottomed wig and flowing robes.

At the outset of the session the Opposition advanced purposefully to the attack by moving an amendment to the Address, humbly representing 'that it would be disastrous to proceed further with the Government of Ireland Bill until it has been submitted to the judgment of the people'.

Asquith in reply was conciliatory, but evasive. He hinted at much, but gave away nothing to a crowded and deeply attentive House. 'Is it unjust to call all this the skilful manoeuvring of the old Parliamentary hand?' asked the *Daily Telegraph*. 'We must wait and see, but it was evidently the speech of a Minister who desires smooth Parliamentary waters for as long as he possibly can get them.'

Be that as it may, the sobriety and restraint which marked the opening of the debates in both Houses came as a welcome relief after the bitter and intransigent temper which had prevailed in the previous session. During the last few days there had been talk of coming disorder in the Commons: but in the event nothing of the kind had occurred. The debates for the most part covered the usual well-trodden ground; the same arguments and counter-arguments were used, but there was a noticeable lowering of the temperature.

CHAPTER 5

Action and reaction

The present administration had to its credit a record of social legislation unprecedented in any comparable period, before or since, reflecting the spirit of the new Liberalism which inspired such men as Asquith, Lloyd George, Grey, and Masterman. Old Age Pensions; Labour Exchanges; the Eight Hours Act for the mines; free dinners for necessitous schoolchildren; the more complete protection of merchant seamen; the Small Holdings Act; the Sweated Industries Act; the payment of M.P.s; a revolutionary and comprehensive system of national insurance, and the reorganization of the fiscal system—all these formed part of the immense programme of reforms secured by the last Liberal Government to rule Great Britain. Early in 1913 Asquith had been able to declare:

'We are now in the eighth year of our Administration, and how do matters stand? By universal admission our trade, at home and over the seas, was never so prosperous, or the percentage of unemployment in this kingdom so small. We have placed on the Statute Book the two greatest social reforms, measured by the extent of the relief which they give against the vicissitudes of life, which Parliament has ever enacted—the Act for Old Age Pensions and the National Insurance Act. We have made provision, in the face of great difficulties and exigencies, for maintaining unchallenged the Command of the Sea which is essential to our national and Imperial life. In carrying out these costly purposes we have not only not added a penny to the debt of the nation, but we have diminished its aggregate capital liabilities at a faster rate, and by a larger sum, than have any of our predecessors.'[1]

Much, therefore, had been done to alleviate the sufferings of

[1] H. H. Asquith, *Fifty Years of Parliament*, II, p. 130.

the very poor, and to secure the general run of manual workers against the common vicissitudes of life. But all these benefits had been achieved, partly at the expense of the more successful and more prosperous among the working-class population, and, to a much greater degree, at the expense of the middle and upper classes. To many of the latter, indeed, it seemed almost as if the country were on the verge of a social and political revolution. The general situation has been well summed up by Williamson:

'The old *laissez-faire* governments of mid-Victorian times had aimed chiefly at preserving order and giving fair play to all by the removal of injustices. The new reformers acted on the principle of "doing something" for some part of the community at the expense of some other part. The process did not produce contentment, even among the gainers.'[1]

The older generation of working-class people, especially the farm labourers, were by no means unanimous in their approval of these measures brought in by the Liberal Government. There was much food for reflection in the criticism of one old stager:

' . . . Hear 'em talk at election time, you'd think they'd got us into Heaven, pretty nearly; but if we could get the old times back again, when there was work for any one as liked it, and any one could keep a pig, and farming paid a man to do it proper, not like what they do now, all weeds as they call a vallow, and sellin' their hay off by September, why, we'd do without this outdoor relief, for that's what it is, and it won't alter it to call it a Pension—no, not if it was four hundred a year.'[2]

Against the Ministry were ranged all the most formidable Conservative forces in the kingdom. Already they had witnessed, in impotent wrath, the onset of something like a political and social cataclysm. 'The landslide in England towards a Social Democracy proceeds steadily', recorded Beatrice Webb, 'but it is the whole nation that is sliding, not the one class of manual workers.'[3] To vary the metaphor somewhat, the 'wind of change'

[1] J. A. Williamson, *The Evolution of England*, p. 455.
[2] John Halsham, *Old Standards* (1913), p. 197.
[3] M. Cole, *Beatrice Webb's Diaries* (1952), p. 18.

had become a mighty rushing wind. It seemed to the Conservatives that there would be no stopping the triumphant advance of the Radical Juggernaut. They had been out-manoeuvred in the country and out-voted in the Commons and were thirsting for revenge. Suddenly they saw and seized their opportunity. The Liberal solution of the perennial Irish problem was open to grave objection, and involved the Government in a predicament far more serious than that in which the Opposition had lately been placed by the Protection issue. The year 1914 saw the climax of the bitter party warfare which had been raging for nearly a decade.

The English are not normally political extremists: as a rule they have played the party game with instinctive moderation and restraint; but, at this particular time, they were becoming adept in the perilous pastime nowadays known as 'brinkmanship'.

There was a strange tendency to play with fire. Party leaders outvied one another in extravagance of language and sentiment; the exchanges became increasingly violent; and continually the warring factions edged and shoved each other nearer and nearer towards the verge of catastrophe. In the Mother of Parliaments such unseemly interjections as 'Traitor!', 'Swine!', 'Dirty cad!', 'Liberal scum!' and 'Pothouse crowd!' were becoming all too familiar. Nor was this rancour and fury confined to the males. One of the great ladies of London society had recently stood at the top of the stairs leading down from the Ladies' Gallery to the Lobby shrieking insults at the editor of the *Westminster Gazette* as he made his way below. The cleavage was wider and deeper than any which had existed in English society. As the newly appointed United States Ambassador, Walter Page, observed in the summer of 1913:

'You can't imagine the intensity of the party feeling here. They had just had a 'division' an hour or two before in the House of Lords on the Home Rule Bill. . . . The Great Lady, who was our hostess, told me, with tears in her voice, that she had suspended all social relations with the Liberal leaders.

At lunch—just five or six hours before—we were at the Prime Minister's, where the talk was precisely on the other side. Gladstone's grand-daughter was there and several members of the

Cabinet. Somehow it reminds me of the tense days of the slavery controversy just before the Civil War.'

Pledging his Party to the unconditional support of the Ulster Unionists, Bonar Law had begun to make speeches almost as violent as Carson's. At a great Unionist rally at Blenheim in July 1912 he declared: 'I can imagine no length of resistance to which Ulstermen will go in which I shall not be ready to support them, and in which they will not be supported by the overwhelming majority of the British people'. Later, in the autumn, there was a memorable scene in the House of Commons in which Ministers were angrily denounced as 'traitors' by certain Opposition extremists. An hour's adjournment by the Speaker failed to restore peace; and, on a cry of 'No more business in this House!' from Sir Edward Carson, a well-sustained chorus of 'No more business!' and 'Adjourn! Adjourn!' arose. Once again the Speaker adjourned the House—this time until the following day. Then, as the First Lord, accompanied by Colonel Seely, the Minister for War, was making his way along the Treasury Bench, he and his colleague were assailed with wrathful shouts of 'Rats!'[1] Finally one of the infuriated War Hawks across the gangway, completely losing his temper, snatched up the Speaker's copy of the Standing Orders and flung it at Winston Churchill, striking him on the side of the head.

During 1912-13 the Home Rule Bill, providing for the government of Ireland (with certain restrictions) by an Irish Parliament and Cabinet, passed through the Commons and was rejected, early in 1913, by the Lords. Again it was passed with a large majority in the House of Commons and again thrown out by the Lords. It would automatically become law under the terms of the Parliament Act in the course of 1914. The opportunity afforded by the Bill was eagerly seized upon by their opponents as ground of attack upon the Government generally.

In 1913 civil war was quite openly being threatened both by Ulstermen and Unionist leaders throughout this country. The veteran Field-Marshal Lord Roberts of Kandahar, affectionately known as 'Bobs', flung himself enthusiastically into the fray on the side of the Ulster Unionists; large numbers of whom, both

[1] Both Churchill and Seely had changed their political allegiance some years earlier.

men and women, had signed a covenant to resist Home Rule by force of arms. Early in 1914 a British Covenant in support of the Ulster Covenanters was signed by a number of leading men

AN ULSTER "CONVERSATION."

(Sir Edward Carson, in his speech in the House on Wednesday last, said the Government had failed to find a solution of the Irish question, and shirked the issue at the hands of the people.)

CARSON: "None of those solutions will do—this is what we want!"
ASQUITH: "I see. It's not a solution you want—it's a DIS-solution!"

(From *Reynolds's Newspaper*, February 15th, 1914)

including the Duke of Portland, Lords Milner and Roberts, the Dean of Canterbury, Rudyard Kipling, and Professor Dicey.

Among the ministerialists there was no such enthusiasm for the Irish cause as had inspired the followers of Gladstone; the Liberal support of Irish nationalism was essentially a matter of expediency. The Liberals were actually outnumbered in the House by the Conservatives. The ministerialists' majority rested on an uneasy coalition; had Redmond and the Irish Nationalists refused to vote with the Government, Asquith's ministry must have fallen.

Throughout the first half of 1914 the Irish question overshadowed all else. It was apparent that the Opposition extremists were prepared to support the most desperate measures of their

Ulster allies to avenge the defeat of their Party in the Parliament Act. The Conservative defiance to law and precedent might be morally indefensible: there was no question, however, that it was succeeding. Whatever happened in the other provinces, Home Rule could never be imposed upon the stubborn Ulster Protestants by force. But the ferocious racial hatreds of the Irish parties were not properly understood by the Government; and Asquith, for all his great qualities, was reluctant to face these vital issues promptly and squarely — the fatal habit of procrastination and delay had been growing on him in recent years. Intent on holding together his majority in the House of Commons, he seemed blind to the realities of the situation outside the walls of Westminster. Forces had been unleashed in the sister islands which were beyond the sway of argument or reason. In the first few weeks of the session the debates in the Commons reached a degree of passion and fury such as had not been known since the days of the great Reform Bill.

'My task in trying to preserve some semblance of decency and order in these successive scenes of tumult and invective was not easy', observed the Speaker, 'but I was greatly assisted by the calm and dignified way in which Mr Asquith presented the Government case from time to time, though some of his colleagues did not see fit to follow his example.'[1]

The position of the King at this stage was one of great embarrassment. Whether he acted or whether he refrained from acting, he was always in danger of antagonizing some important section of his subjects. If he should make an imprudent move, it was almost inevitable, as Asquith had remarked, that 'the Crown would become the football of contending factions'.

The Princess of Pless related in her memoirs how, early in the New Year, she dined at Crewe House and sat between the Duke of Devonshire and the King, with whom she discussed the ominous darkening of the nation's prospects. 'During our conversation I said, "1913 has not been a very lucky year for you, Sir"."I am afraid", was the reply, "1914 does not promise to be much better." '[2]

A minor but potent cause of exacerbation in public life was provided by the Marconi case. Recent years had witnessed the

[1] Lord Ullswater, A *Speaker's Commentaries*, II, p. 156.
[2] Daisy of Pless, *My Diary*, p. 266.

remarkable expansion of the new system of wireless telegraphy
developed by the brilliant young Italian inventor of that name.
During 1913 vague rumours that certain members of the
Cabinet had been speculating in Marconi shares gave rise to
angry exchanges in the House of Commons and finally to the
setting up of a Select Committee to inquire into the whole
affair.

Among those implicated, according to the City rumours, was
the Chancellor of the Exchequer. 'The rich man's hatred of a
great "People's Minister",' exclaimed the *Daily News* indig-
nantly, 'winged the lies and double-distilled the poison.' Be that
as it may, these rumours became increasingly circumstantial; and
though Lloyd George spoke angrily of allegations which had
been 'passed from one foul lip to another behind the backs of
the House', it had not escaped the notice of cynics, both inside
and outside Parliament, that, while denouncing these rumours,
he had wholly omitted to deny them.

The Opposition fastened eagerly on what was termed 'the
Marconi scandal'. The papers were full of it. Trains, buses, trams,
clubs, restaurants, and public houses rang with the name
Marconi. For weeks it was the one topic which dominated practically everything else. The proceedings of the Select Committee
were followed with rapt attention by the general public. The
true facts — or, at any rate, some of the true facts — were
extracted with difficulty from embarrassed witnesses. After a
debate the Ministers concerned expressed their regrets, which
were accepted by the House. Well on into 1914, while the Select
Committee was pursuing its inquiries, the affair continued to
embarrass the Government.

The imminent disestablishment of the Anglican Church in
Wales at the insistent demand of Welsh nonconformity and
Welsh national sentiment added further fuel to the flames of
party rancour. It was a measure long called for; and it might be
said that the issue was quite as much political as ecclesiastical.
The principle of establishment had become intolerable to the
non-anglican majority, and was not infrequently associated with
the penalization of dissenters. (Lloyd George in his youth had
actually been promised advancement by the local curate on condition that he gave up his religion and turned Anglican.) The
churchmen rather rashly secured the aid of such unlikely cham-

pions as F. E. Smith[1] and other Conservative leaders. Like the
Irish Home Rule Bill, the Welsh Disestablishment Bill would
shortly become law under the operation of the Parliament Act.

Two other factors contributed to the increasing violence of
public affairs.

It had been strongly contended by the supporters of female
suffrage that the Liberal Party was morally committed to a
policy of votes for women. Asquith's Government, however, disagreed. During this time the suffragists kept up an unceasing
agitation all over the country.

There was a good—though by no means unanswerable—case
for female suffrage; and it was commanding increasing support.
But the pace of advance was not rapid enough to satisfy the
extremists. Accordingly, under the ruthless and determined
leadership of Christabel Pankhurst from her refuge in Paris and
of her mother Emmeline in London,[2] the militant suffragists of
the Women's Social and Political Union resorted to organized
outrage on persons and property. 'The argument of the broken
pane', Mrs Pankhurst declared, 'is the most valuable argument
in modern politics.' Some of the women and girls concerned in
these demonstrations showed great powers of ingenuity,
resource, and courage. Though they were repeatedly arrested
and imprisoned the stir that they created resulted in more converts and more subscriptions to the cause. The imprisoned

[1] The Welsh Disestablishment Bill, stated 'F.E.' unctuously, had 'shocked the
conscience of every Christian community in Europe'. The Liberal wit, G. K.
Chesterton, then in his prime, promptly replied with the famous broadside
beginning:

> 'Are they clinging to their crosses,
> F. E. Smith,
> Where the Breton boat-fleet tosses,
> Are they, Smith?
> Do they, trembling, fasting, bleeding,
> Wait the news from this our city?
> If the voice of Cecil falters,
> If McKenna's point has pith,
> Do they tremble for their altars?
> Do they, Smith?'

[2] Mrs. Pankhurst and her daughter, together with two other leading
suffragettes, had lately attained the high honour of a place at Madame
Tussaud's.

women went on hunger-strike and had to be forcibly fed. Public uneasiness about the inevitable brutality of forcible feeding increased to such an extent that presently an expedient was devised, a measure which was popularly known as the 'Cat and Mouse Act', under which the hunger-strikers could be released and afterwards re-arrested at the will of the authorities. In 1913 the Suffragettes resorted to the firing of unoccupied houses, many of which were burned to the ground. During that year the damage committed by the militants was estimated by the *Daily Mail* at no less than £½ million. One of the bravest and most fanatical of these women, Emily Davison, flung herself in front of the King's horse at the Derby that year, bringing down horse and jockey and herself sustaining such serious injuries that she died a few hours later. Political meetings were liable to be interrupted at any moment with shrill cries of 'Votes for Women!' In 1913 militancy was at its height. Letter-boxes were deliberately set on fire, plate-glass windows ruthlessly shattered, pictures in public galleries defaced, and Cabinet Ministers assaulted. This campaign of organized violence greatly increased the tension of political life.

'They interrupted public meetings and even the debates of Parliament, fought the police in the streets, and destroyed a great amount of property. To slash a priceless picture, to pour corrosive chemicals into a letter-box, or to break an unoffending tradesman's windows was to demonstrate the qualities of citizenship. The whole age was a little mad, with the madness of those whom the gods mean to destroy.'[1]

The hostility of the militant suffragettes to the stubborn and scornful males who continued to resist what they considered to be their legitimate demands was returned, with interest, by the males. Some of these women made a practice of chaining themselves up to railings and swearing to stay there till they received the vote. Asquith was unimpressed by this argument. 'A man might as well chain himself to the railings of St Thomas's Hospital', he remarked one night at a dinner-party, 'and say he wouldn't move until he has had a baby.'

Another sign of the times was the growing labour unrest in

[1] J. A. Williamson, *The Evolution of England*, p. 455.

THE DISTRIBUTION OF WEALTH

(From the *Labour Leader*, January 8, 1914)

many parts of the British Isles. During the years 1911-13 there had been an epidemic of great strikes, more serious than any hitherto experienced: the railwaymen, seamen, miners, and London dockers had all, one after another, 'come out'. In the torrid summer of 1911 savage rioting had occurred at Liverpool and Llanelly and troops were called in; they were forced to fire, and several of the strikers were killed. In 1912 the struggle between the dockers and the Port of London Authority, then dominated by Lord Devonport, was accompanied by the intimidation of non-strikers and fights with the police. At a huge assembly of strikers held on Tower Hill, Ben Tillett, the founder and General Secretary of the Dockers' Union, had got the whole meeting to repeat solemnly after him, 'Oh, God, strike Lord Devonport dead!' These strikes had left behind a legacy of bitter feeling; and, in the case of the Seamen's Union and certain others, both sides in the quarrel were preparing to renew the struggle at the first favourable opportunity. During the winter of 1913-14 there were strikes and lock-outs in the coal and building trades. There was a threat of sympathetic action on the part of the transport workers and the likelihood of the numbers out of work rising to 150,000. 'The great industrial crisis which has arisen in London', declared the *Observer* on January 25th, 'shows no sign of settlement'.

During the year 1914 the unrest spread to other parts of the country. The trade unions were increasing rapidly in membership and activity. By 1914 more than four million of their members were affiliated to the T.U.C. 'They no longer speak for a minority,' the *Labour Leader* declared, 'and sometimes a small minority at that, but for practically the entire occupation for which they stand. This of itself is quite a revolutionary change.' The action of the militant trade unions of Dublin greatly strengthened the more extreme element among the British trade unionists; and during the period in question the triple alliance of three great basic services — the miners, railwaymen, and transport workers—was successfully brought into being.

Even the Church of England, apparently, was affected by the prevailing spirit of militancy. Since the previous winter the Kikuyu controversy had been greatly agitating ecclesiastical circles. It was taken very seriously by some; but it is doubtful whether the majority of lay folk ever really understood what the

quarrel was all about. The Welsh Disestablishment Bill which
was then going through Parliament was a major political issue
and had excited much the same feelings on either side as the
Irish Disestablishment Bill of 1870—there was, after all, a considerable amount of property involved. But the Kikuyu issue was
purely doctrinal. 'To account for the heat of the Kikuyu controversy by the contrast between the fiery African sun and the
temperate climate of the English Church', observed the *Nation*,
'is a theory which would have commended itself to Mr Buckle.'
In July 1913 a joint Communion service had formed part of a
conference of Protestant missionaries at Kikuyu in Uganda; in
consequence of which the Bishop of Zanzibar, who was distinctly
'High', had charged the Bishops of Uganda and Mombasa, who
belonged to a different school, with heresy. The controversy
filled many columns in the *Times* and engendered a good deal of
warmth in the Athenaeum and other haunts of the higher
clergy. 'I pray God', remarked Lord Halifax, 'that controversy
may not be the occasion of a schism which will rend the Church
of England in two.' 'I doubt if the Church of England was ever
more seriously threatened than it is now', the Bishop of Durham
declared at the end of the year, and went on to speak of these
developments as 'totally subversive of Catholic order and doctrine'. The opposing faction promptly accepted the challenge.
'The religion of the nation of England, as a whole', pronounced
the Dean of Canterbury, 'is irrevocably Protestant.' When the
combatant prelates appealed to the Archbishop of Canterbury,
the Primate (like the House of Peers in the famous lines from
Iolanthe) 'did nothing in particular, and did it very well'. And
there, for the time being, the matter rested.

CHAPTER 6

The Irish crisis

The temperature of the debates on Irish affairs rose ominously in the ensuing weeks. Discussion centred on the position of the large Protestant Unionist majority in north-eastern Ireland. 'Ulster', declared Carson, 'will be the field on which the privileges of the whole nation will be lost or won.' The Anglo-Irish ruling class—the 'Ascendancy'—now prepared for a last desperate stand. Since the Unionist policy was to use the uncompromising resistance of the Ulster Protestants as the means to block Home Rule throughout Ireland, it is understandable that no real progress was made in the direction of reconciling these differences. Meanwhile, the Ulster Volunteers controlled the situation. By March something like 110,000 Ulstermen had enrolled and the railways, post offices, and other Government premises in north-eastern Ireland were all more or less under their control.

In the last resort the only possible solution to the problem appeared to be to exclude the loyalist areas from the scope of the Home Rule Bill altogether. To this Irish Nationalist sentiment was, needless to say, strongly opposed. Nevertheless, early in March, Asquith announced his intention to bring in an Amending Bill, granting to each of the Ulster counties the right of opting out of Home Rule for six years, during which period there must be at least two general elections in the United Kingdom offering the electorate two chances of confirming this exclusion—otherwise, at the termination of the period, the counties in question would automatically come under Home Rule like the rest of the island. This proposal was at once rejected by Sir Edward Carson, who insisted, 'be exclusion good or bad, Ulster wants this question settled now and for ever' and went on to declare, 'We do not want a sentence of death with a stay of execution for six years'; he made it very clear that he and his followers would accept nothing short of final exclusion. There appeared to be no way out of the *impasse* that had been reached. Moreover, though by no stretch of the imagination could Ulster be considered either united or homogeneous, 'King Carson' invariably spoke as if he had the entire province at his back. 'Whatever Ulster's rights may be,' Churchill had earlier declared, 'they cannot stand in the way of the rest of Ireland. Half a province cannot impose a veto on the rest of the nation. The utmost they can claim is for themselves.' But Carson would not have it.

By this time the quarrel raging daily on the floor of the House had spread to the galleries, and presently there was whispered talk in bars and smoking-rooms of a regular set-to, on March 19th, up in the Speaker's Gallery. It appeared that, while the Prime Minister was speaking, Lady Londonderry had been carrying on a continuous and disparaging commentary, which Asquith's daughter, sitting nearby, not unnaturally resented. High words passed between the two; and at the height of the row, it was reported, the fair ladies had actually slapped each other in the face. The indignant Mrs Asquith then addressed a hurried appeal to the Speaker, who had drily replied that he had as much as he could manage 'in keeping order amongst the devils below, without having to control the angels above'. Next day, however, the Speaker thought it well to direct his Marshal to police the gallery.

Before proper consideration could be given to Asquith's proposal there were disturbing reports of growing disaffection to the Government among Army officers. In encouraging these officers to join in the political fray the Unionists had, of course, gone far beyond the limits of constitutional opposition. Certain of their extremists, like Lords Halsbury and Willoughby de Broke, had even been considering using the Army Act as a pawn in the party game. The Leader of the Opposition was negotiating in secret with Lord Roberts (who had lately recommended a commander-in-chief for the Ulster Volunteers) and with that incorrigible intriguer, General Henry Wilson (then Director of Military Operations at the War Office). But any such manoeuvre was rendered unnecessary by what presently occurred in Ireland.

The full facts about the grave crisis which developed during the third week in March 1914 are never likely to be known. It was the subject of passionate and prolonged controversy—the flames of which are even now scarcely extinguished. The truth would however appear to be that each side in the quarrel was increasingly apprehensive of a coup on the part of the other. This was really the context of the Curragh incident. The Government suspected the Opposition of planning an immediate rebellion in Ulster. The Opposition suspected the Government of plotting to overthrow the dissidents in that province by overwhelming naval and military force. The Irish Nationalists for their part suspected—and not without reason—both Government and Opposition.

In Unionist circles the First Lord of the Admiralty was widely regarded as the villain of the piece; with Colonel John Seely, the Secretary for War, as his accomplice. Lord Morley had once told Winston Churchill that he would end his days on St Helena; and according to Sir Almeric Fitzroy the First Lord appeared to be 'more flattered by the comparison than dismayed by the prospect'. Be that as it may, the latter's somewhat Napoleonic proceedings in the next few days were responsible for the exacerbation of an already alarming and explosive situation.

The opening move in what might be described as the Government's belated counter-offensive was made by Churchill in a bellicose speech at Bradford on the 14th. In his concluding passage the First Lord responded to the challenge of the Carsonites in these ominous terms:

'If Ulstermen extend the hand of friendship it will be clasped by Liberals and by their Nationalist countrymen in all good faith and in all good will, but, if there is no wish for peace, if every concession that is made is spurned and exploited, if every effort to meet their views is only to be used as a means of breaking down Home Rule, and of barring the way to the rest of Ireland, if Ulster is to become a tool in Party calculations, if the Civil and Parliamentary systems under which we have dwelt, and our fathers before us for so many years, are to be brought to the crude challenge of force, if the Government and the Parliament of this great country and greater Empire is to be exposed to menace and brutality, if all the loose, wanton and reckless chatter we have been forced to listen to all these many months, is in the end to disclose a sinister and revolutionary purpose, then I can only say to you, "Let us go forward together and put these grave matters to the proof".'

A week later, at Huddersfield, the Chancellor of the Exchequer, in his most provocative 'Peers v. People' style, similarly, responded to the Tory challenge. 'We are confronted', he declared, 'with the greatest issue raised in this country since the days of the Stuarts. Representative government in this land is at stake.' With his usual wit and humour, Lloyd George proceeded to 'play down' the more melodramatic aspect of the Ulster crisis. The religious apprehensions of the Ulstermen, however keenly felt, and their idealism, however genuine, were, he believed, much exaggerated.

'Is their faith menaced by oppression? They talk as if the fires of Smithfield were to be lit up in North-East Ulster. You have as much chance of doing it as you have to restore the altar of the Druids in this country! . . . I don't say that Ulstermen are not prosperous, industrious, thrifty, brave, gallant, but they are not the only gallant people in the British Isles. You might imagine, reading the Tory newspapers, that they were. Look at these frothy descriptions of the Ulster Volunteers in the Tory Press. There has been nothing like it since Milton's description of the Heavenly Host. (Laughter, and a voice: "Go on, David!")'

In his peroration, Lloyd George recaptured something of the crusading ardour of his great Budget speeches of 1909-10. He declared that the Irish question must now be settled once and for all; after which the Liberal Party would be free to return to its proper task of social reform.

'Let us settle it in order to get rid of it. Has another generation to pass away in wretchedness? . . . Is England so poor that she cannot afford to feed, to shelter, and to clothe, her own sons and daughters? Is Britain so mean that she will not share her wealth to do so? Is Britain so callous and hard-hearted that she is indifferent to the wretchedness of her own household? These are the questions which, above the din and clang of partisan and sectarian fury, I mean to continue to ask until the proud flag of

Britain shall no longer be ashamed by waving over squalid homes and hungry children.'

The 'Welsh magician' was at the top of his form. There was a merry twinkle in his eye as with matchless art he played deftly upon the emotions of his crowded audience. The northerners were held spellbound by Lloyd George's magnetic personality; they listened entranced, and a roar of delight greeted each witty sally. After speaking for well over an hour, he sat down amid tremendous and sustained applause. This speech at Huddersfield was one of Lloyd George's outstanding performances and may be reckoned as one of the contributory factors in the impending crisis.

Events now moved rapidly to a climax. On the same day that Churchill spoke at Bradford, as a result of reports to the effect that mischief was brewing in Ulster, Seely had instructed the Commander-in-Chief in Ireland, General Sir Arthur Paget, to take certain precautions with regard to various depots and magazines in the northern counties. After a long consultation between Seely, Churchill, and Sir John French, it was determined to dispatch reinforcements to the depots in warships as well as by rail. 'It was also decided to move a battle squadron and a flotilla from Arosa Bay, where they were cruising, to Lamlash, whence they could rapidly reach Belfast. It was thought that the popularity and influence of the Royal Navy', observed Churchill hopefully, 'might produce a peaceable solution, even if the army had failed.' On the 19th the 3rd Battle Squadron was ordered by wireless to proceed immediately to the Firth of Clyde. Two cruisers from Bantry Bay were also dispatched to the vicinity of Belfast.

Aware that discussions were going on at the War Office, but ignorant of the details, Carson and Bonar Law concluded that the Government were about to take strong action in Northern Ireland, and prepared to resist. The drama was carried a stage further when Carson's threatening words and demeanour, as he stalked wrathfully out of the House on the 19th, after a fierce altercation with Joseph Devlin (the leader of the Ulster Nationalists), conveyed the impression that some decisive action —perhaps the proclamation of the Provisional Government in Ulster—was imminent. 'I feel I ought not to be here', exclaimed the Ulster leader, 'but in Belfast.' (There was a mocking cry, 'With your sword drawn?') Carson banged the dispatch box in front of him, with the retort, 'If this is the last word of the Government, what more have we to do here? Let the Government come and try conclusions with them in Ulster.' Pointing a menacing finger at the Treasury Bench, he cried, 'You will be sheltering yourselves behind the Army. Under your directions they will become assassins.'

Amid the enthusiastic plaudits of the Conservatives, the Ulster leader hurried off to Euston and the boat-train for Belfast.

Next day there were rumours of the impending arrest of Carson and his colleagues. But in the evening the news reached London that General Hubert Gough and most of the officers of the Cavalry Brigade at the Curragh had resigned their commissions rather than be ordered against Ulster. On Saturday the papers were full of it. In clubs and drawing-rooms the greatest excitement prevailed during the week-end, and there was endless rumour and conjecture. How the Commander-in-Chief in Ireland, General Sir Arthur Paget, had attempted to browbeat and coerce these officers. How General Gough had stood firm. How there had been a head-on collision between the Army and the Government. How powerful support would certainly be forthcoming for these officers at home. How one regiment had actually mutinied. For a while the wildest reports found credence.

In the purlieus of Whitehall the newspaper posters carried such startling intelligence as 'Grave National Crisis' and 'Soldiers Throw Down their Arms!' 'The biggest story since the Boer War', was the comment passed in the *Daily Mail* office, which promptly rushed an army of special correspondents across to Ireland to cover the crisis. On Friday, the 20th, the Cabinet sat till after midnight; and over the week-end the War Office stood open, day and night, to receive an apparently endless stream of distinguished callers, beginning with the Prime Minister, Lord Roberts, General Gough, Winston Churchill, and the King's Secretary, Lord Stamfordham, as well as a host of excited journalists.

The immediate occasion of the Curragh crisis was a piece of arrant bungling on the part of General Sir Arthur Paget, which had simply played into the hands of the Unionist military caucus. Paget delivered a muddled and irascible address to the cavalry officers stationed at the Curragh, concluding with a characteristic outburst against 'those dirty swine of politicians'. Gough remained unimpressed and stood to his guns. On the following day, the 21st, he and a number of his colonels were summoned to the War Office.

It need hardly be said that, in the ensuing negotiations, these officers were assiduously supported and encouraged by the Director of Military Operations, who, having by now thrown decency, discipline, and the King's Regulations to the winds, was busily putting the finishing touches to the nearest thing to a *pronunciamento* ever compassed by British generals. 'I was at Bonar Law's at 9.30 a.m.', wrote Wilson in his diary that Saturday, 'and told him how serious everything was, and how on my present information I thought it would be imperative to back Hubert. . . . I told Sir John there was still time to stop the breakaway of the officers if he made Asquith take instant action, but it must be done at once or the General Staff would break away next.' Whitehall that morning was in a ferment of activity. The Prime Minister, having heard of Churchill's orders to the 3rd Battle Squadron, immediately had the orders countermanded. In the evening Sir John French, the Chief of the Imperial General Staff, was summoned to Buckingham Palace. 'I had an interview with Sir John French,' wrote the King (who had learned of the troop movements and the drama at the Curragh for the first time from the newspapers), 'and impressed upon him the gravity of the situation and that if great tact were not shown there would be no Army left.'

On the 22nd there were further conferences and consultations at Buckingham Palace, 10 Downing Street, and the War Office. The Archbishop of Canterbury spent an hour and a half with the Prime Minister, before the latter left for an audience with the King. Wilson was having the time of his life. 'Great coming and going here all day of a number of fellows all wanting to know what they are to do. . . . I gave Bonar Law my copy of Hubert's report of what A.P. said, and told him he might use it.'

'Is this the eve of Civil War?' the *Daily Mirror* exclaimed on the 23rd. 'The menacing shadow of strife hangs over the country, and the record of the past few hours is a record of alarums and excursions, of troops hastily rushed into Ireland's Unionist province, of warships hovering around Belfast harbour, and of great generals and statesmen holding private audiences with the Sovereign.'

The comings and goings of Ministers that day were followed with quite exceptional interest by a large crowd gathered outside 10 Downing Street. The Prime Minister's earliest caller was General Paget, who had travelled overnight from Ireland; after him came General Gough; and finally the Cabinet began to appear—John Burns strolled up in his blue reefer suit, looking calm and unconcerned; Lord Haldane arrived in some haste; Churchill and Seely, modestly avoiding the public gaze, hurried in by the back entrance.

The crucial discussion of the Army crisis was held that morning at the War Office. Seely, Sir John French, Gough, and the other *dramatis personae* strode in past a curious crowd of spectators and a number of Press photographers. Tension in high military circles was at its height; Lord Roberts had cut Sir John French dead in the street; the future Field Marshal Sir Douglas Haig had conveyed a warning to French that, if Gough were penalized, the resignation of every officer in the Aldershot Command was to be expected. It was evident that the King had not exaggerated the gravity of the situation. Trying desperately to find some way out of the *impasse*, Seely was outmanoeuvred at every stage. He was induced to part with a written pledge which was subsequently repudiated by the Government. Having gained their point, the officers withdrew their resignations. Gough proceeded to execute a public 'gloat', first in London, and presently at the Curragh, where he was fervently cheered by the whole brigade. Wilson had likewise been 'gloating' at the War Office, claiming that 'The Army have done what the Opposition have failed to do', and adding hopefully that it 'will probably cause the fall of the present Government'.

In a thronged and feverishly excited House of Commons the

Prime Minister rose in the afternoon to make his anxiously awaited statement.

Asquith was visibly shaken by these events. He had already sent in the Government's version of the army crisis to the *Times*, which, if it was not open to criticism on the grounds of *suggestio falsi*, could scarcely be acquitted of *suppressio veri*.

He categorically denied any intention of launching a military campaign against the recalcitrant Ulstermen. He was not believed by the Opposition, any more than the Opposition were believed by the ministerialists when they declared that the officers at the Curragh had only been acting within their rights. Throughout the sitting speakers were heard with difficulty through a running stream of heated interjections, assertions, and denials. It was the first of what was fated to be a long series of turbulent debates revolving around the alleged 'mutiny' and the alleged 'plot'.

It was soon apparent that the Prime Minister's statement had done nothing to relieve the anxiety of his followers, many of whom suspected that the Cabinet had, in effect, capitulated to the dissident generals. British Liberalism was shocked to its core. The prevailing mood of angry suspicion was reflected in a strong article which appeared in the *Manchester Guardian*.

'There is profound indignation in the Liberal Party at the outrageous attempts of an aristocratic faction to tamper with the Army. Hitherto the Army has been kept aloof from all our party struggles. Now some of the more reckless elements in the Tory Party are endeavouring to use it as a counter in the party game. . . . Some Conservative journals have published poisonous comment on the subject of the Army. Mr Tom Mann was sent to prison for less dangerous doctrine.'[1]

The House of Commons was profoundly moved. Not even at the height of the Parliament Act crisis was there such tension as that which prevailed next day in the Lobby. On all sides was heard unsparing criticism and condemnation of the Cabinet's attitude. For the first time in the history of the coalition the

[1] Tom Mann had been gaoled in 1912 for advising the troops not to shoot down their fellow workers during industrial disturbances.

3
Sussex shepherds

4. Upper Baker Street

The muffin man

The knife grinder

Government was threatened with a formidable revolt of the rank and file.

On the mere suspicion that their leaders had come to terms as General Gough and his officers, the Radical and Labour members (as the *Westminster Gazette* declared), 'swept the debate out of the hands of the Front Bench and spoke their minds in a series of impromptu speeches, the like of which have not been heard in the House of Commons in this generation'. It is significant that the outburst of rage and fury embraced not only the Conservatives and Carsonites—it was directed also against their own Government and the King.

Early in the debate Ramsay MacDonald referred to a written pledge having been extorted by General Gough from the War Office, and to its having been taken away by the latter 'as something in the nature of a trophy'. Soon afterwards another of the Labour members, the ex-navvy, John Ward, speaking openly of 'the recent mutiny among officers at the Curragh', asked if 'it was proposed that Brigadier-General Gough should form a Government?' The inquiry was followed by a hurricane of applause which reverberated to and fro between the crowded ministerialist and Nationalist benches.

The temperature of the House rose ominously in the course of a speech by a young Conservative, L. S. Amery, which appeared to imply close political contacts between the Opposition and certain high-ranking officers. It was shortly after this that a group of Labour members took the lead and raised the level of the whole debate.

The speech of the evening was undoubtedly made by John Ward. From his place on the Front Bench below the gangway, with his eyes blazing with indignation and fierce sweeping gestures which matched his angry rhetoric, Ward — a huge, hulking giant of a man — dominated the House. The subject of his diatribe was what he described as 'the aristocratic conspiracy against the State'.

'The question for decision', he concluded, 'was whether the discipline of the Army was to be maintained, whether it was to continue to be a neutral force to assist the civil power, or whether in future the House of Commons, representing the people, was to submit its decisions for approval to a committee of officers, a military junta.' Ward wheeled round from the

D

Tories to face the Speaker, and, raising his clenched fist in the air, uttered the pregnant words: 'We have now to decide whether the people, through their representatives in Parliament, are to make the law of the country absolutely without interference from King or Army'.

At this stage some 300 Liberal, Labour, and Irish members rose as one man and vociferously applauded John Ward for three or four minutes on end. Within the memory of the oldest member there had never been anything like the spontaneous outburst of emotion which followed Ward's protest. For once the Opposition had nothing to say, and sat in stricken silence. Later in the evening, at the National Liberal Club, where he had been taken by a friend, Ward received a thunderous ovation—*'for saying what we all think'*.

In the course of the debate the Conservative leaders endeavoured, not very convincingly, to draw a distinction between soldiers ordered to put down a rebellion in Ulster and soldiers sent to quell disorder during a strike. The Labour members would have none of it. They saw very clearly that, if on account of officers' consciences the Army could not be used in Irish troubles, it could not logically be used in industrial troubles either.

'There is no institution', J. H. Thomas observed, 'however great or sacred, in this country that I will not take my stand in smashing if it attempts to interfere with the constitutional liberties of the people.' Thomas, who was the secretary of the railwaymen's union, intimated that he would have to advise his men to use their funds to purchase rifles in readiness for the next strike. 'General Gough', he declared, 'may feel keenly the Ulster situation. Tommy Atkins will feel not less keenly the industrial situation.'

On the following day, the 25th, the diminutive but truculent Tory member, L. S. Amery, successfully 'drew' his former schoolfellow, the First Lord of the Admiralty, while the latter was endeavouring to defend his rather dramatic orders to the 3rd Battle Squadron (according to Lord Stamfordham, who was looking down from the gallery above, Churchill was 'livid with rage').

L. S. AMERY: Will the right hon. gentleman state whether he expected and hoped that the purely precautionary measures to look after stores would lead to fighting and bloodshed? (Opposition cheers.)

THE SPEAKER: The hon. member can form his own judgment from what has transpired. (Government cheers.)

THE FIRST LORD: As the question has been asked, perhaps with your permission, Mr Speaker, and that of the House, I may repudiate that hellish insinuation. (Uproar, and loud Opposition cries of 'Withdraw'.)

THE SPEAKER: The First Lord will see that I could not permit an expression of that sort to be used, whatever indignation the First Lord may feel at the suggestions made.

Later in the evening, when Churchill rose to continue the discussion, there were angry cries of 'Resign!' When the tumult momentarily subsided, he declared:

'Every effort has been made with the greatest dialectical skill by the right hon. gentleman the Senior Member for the City of London (A. J. Balfour) and by the Leader of the Opposition who emulated his dialectical force without his dialectical subtlety to show that it is always right for soldiers to shoot down a Radical or a Labour man, and always wrong——'

There were furious shouts of 'Liar!' . . . 'Withdraw!' . . . 'Rub it in!' . . . 'Withdraw!'

'As I say, great efforts have been made to show that when it is a Tory quarrel then the Army ought to act. But in any matter where Liberals are concerned, then, of course, no gentleman would demean himself by doing his duty to the Crown and Parliament.'

Outside the Houses of Parliament an angry murmuring arose against the Army in politics, particularly from the Radical strongholds of the North. The truth was that the Labour members' protests had made a deep impression in the country at large and awoke indignant echoes in the Liberal press. 'Is the United Kingdom to be a democracy or an oligarchy?' demanded the *Manchester Guardian*. 'Is the nation to govern itself, or is it to be governed by a caste?' 'It is not Ulster or Home Rule that is the real issue', the *Star* declared. 'It is whether representative institutions are to be upheld.' 'A soldier has defied the Parliament from which he and his comrades draw their military existence and pay', observed the *Nation*, 'and has gone back to his quarters in triumph, the most popular figure in the Army.' 'The Government', the *Daily Chronicle* said, 'must not flinch in dealing with the situation thus created.'

Following the Curragh incident, the Secretary for War resigned. Later Seely withdrew his resignation; then finally resigned a second time. Asquith thereupon took over the War Office himself. 'The Army', he declared, 'will hear nothing of politics from me, and in return I expect to hear nothing of politics from the Army.' Asquith's prompt and decisive action averted what might easily have been a great national calamity. His calm, steadying influence effectively prevented the mischief from spreading, and a potentially dangerous rift in the Service (for not all officers shared Gough's and Roberts's views) was gradually healed. Had he played the party game as recklessly as certain of the leading spirits on both sides of the House, our Army would assuredly have been paralyzed in what was to be the hour of our greatest need only a few months later—even if the country had not already been plunged into civil war.

'Asquith's device', one of the Irish leaders, the veteran Tim Healy, told his brother, 'saved them from what appeared to be a hopeless position. . . . The Government have emerged with the loss of a few tail feathers.' But Asquith was unable to restore the situation in Ireland, where affairs continued to go from bad to worse, and the prospect of settlement by constitutional process became increasingly remote. 'Ulster controls the situation', remarked Sir Almeric Fitzroy,[1] 'and, it would seem, the fate of the Ministry.'

A fierce cry of triumph had gone up from the Unionist press. 'The Army has killed the Home Rule Bill', boasted the *Morning Post*, 'and the sooner the Government recognizes the fact the better for the country.' That the 'military junta' had effectively disarmed the Government could scarcely be disputed by the ministerialist newspapers. Among them Roberts, Wilson, Gough, and their following had successfully flouted the will of Parliament.

[1] Clerk of the Privy Council.

'The Conservatives', wrote the United States Ambassador, a few weeks later, to President Wilson, 'have used Ulster and its army as a club to drive the Liberals out of power; and they have gone to the very brink of civil war.'

CHAPTER 7

'The sure shield'

The decade preceding the First World War was distinguished by rising tension between the Powers, ominously recurring international crises, and warlike preparations on a scale unprecedented in history. It was the last phase of the era which has become known as the 'armed peace'. With each successive crisis the Powers accelerated and intensified their preparations.

The ubiquitous fear and suspicion which now overshadowed Europe like a thundercloud had originated in three main causes: the irreconcilable Franco-German antagonism which was the legacy of 1870-1, the rivalry of Russia and Austria for the hegemony of the Balkans, and — a crucial factor from 1908 onward — the naval shipbuilding race between Germany and Great Britain. It was this last which really determined our relations with the neighbouring Powers; for the whole of the European foreign policy of Great Britain centred, in the last resort, upon the command of the sea.

The German Navy Law of 1900, providing for a vast shipbuilding programme extending over twenty years, marked a turning-point in the history of European relations; slowly but surely the rift between Germany and Great Britain widened. Such a programme, if carried out in its entirety, would make Germany at least the second naval Power in the world. Other developments, like economic jealousy, played the part in producing this estrangement. But the crucial factor was the growth of the German fleet. The work was pressed forward with unresting energy. Not since the days of Colbert and Seignelay had a European government set to work steadily, systematically, and effectively to develop a great sea power. At the same time the rapid expansion of the coastal fortifications, harbours, docks, canals, arsenals, factories, plant and machinery of the Reich kept pace with the intense activity of the shipyards. The great German steel industry, centred mainly on Essen and Düsseldorf, advanced from strength to strength. Within a very few years Anglo-German naval rivalry had become one of the major issues in international politics. No longer was our greatest political danger the combination of the French and Russian navies, but, as Winston Churchill was later to declare, 'a very powerful homogeneous navy, manned and trained by the greatest organizing people of the world, obeying the authority of a single Government and concentrated within easy striking distance of our shores'.

If the truth had only been known, it was not so much the numbers as the quality of the new fleet which rendered it so formidable a rival to our own. The keen, high technical efficiency of the German Navy was not sufficiently appreciated on this side of the North Sea. In the course of the naval armaments race which ensued the Germans constructed a battle-cruiser that was very nearly unsinkable; on the eve of the First World War they had evolved an efficient, reliable, and revolutionary type of fighting-ship in the shape of the sea-going submarine; the German mine was far ahead of ours; and in other classes of material also their technique was markedly superior. Year by year the German crews advanced in knowledge and experience of seamanship and gunnery. As Scheer has justly said of this fleet created by Tirpitz, 'it reached an extraordinary state of maturity in a very short time'.

At this crisis of our fortunes the immemorial prestige and majesty of the Royal Navy, based upon its age-old mastery of the oceans, was by no means an unmixed blessing. It was in large measure responsible indeed for the formidable *vis inertiae* that too frequently obstructed the path to progress. The strenuous endeavours of Admiral Sir John Fisher—First Sea Lord during the years 1904-10—had done much to bring the Service up to date. Fisher was a man of volcanic driving force and apocalyptic vision, whose thoughts and energies were centred on one aim and purpose only—the maritime supremacy of Great Britain. 'The efficiency of the Navy and its instant readiness for war' was his slogan, and 'Ruthless, relentless, remorseless' his declared policy. Step by step, in the face of strong, occasionally violent, opposition, he had sheared away the encrustments of nearly a century of peace and had the decks cleared for action. But the time still left was all too short, and the 'living tradition' of naval warfare inherited by the officers of Nelson's day had been broken, with disastrous consequences, in the long Victorian peace.

Henceforth the naval strategic front shifted from the south to the east. The potential enemy was no longer France but Germany; and, if ever it came to war, the battleground would not be the Channel, but the North Sea. Though at the outset no great alarm was felt in this country, the Admiralty, in the next few years, took steps to meet the new situation which was arising. 'It is a fact', David Hannay declared at this time, 'that the mere existence of the German Navy subjects Great Britain to the risk that in conceivable circumstances she might be attacked in a formidable way. The Channel is unfavourable to an enemy acting against Great Britain. That is not equally the case with the North Sea when the enemy is a northern power not confined to the Baltic.'[1] With the rapid growth of German naval power Great Britain was confronted by a danger she had not experienced since the Dutch wars in the seventeenth century. It would be manifestly much harder for our Navy to guard against raids or invasion from Germany than it had been from France. On the southern front, it was possible for our torpedo craft, effectually supported by our battle squadrons, to keep the enemy's ports of embarkation under close and continual observation: every point of strategic consequence from Chatham to Berehaven was strongly guarded; and in close proximity to the line of ports were stationed the principal military garrisons of the kingdom — Aldershot, Salisbury, and the Curragh. The North Sea front was relatively weak. Our torpedo craft watching the Heligoland Bight would have no base nearer than Harwich, 240 miles away: to which every few days they must return for rest and replenishment, necessitating three reliefs, for which their numbers were by no means sufficient. With the exception of Chatham, there was not a single base on the whole east coast where the Fleet could lie secure. From the Thames estuary to the Shetland Islands, there were numerous and extensive landing places where the enemy might disembark his forces; nor did there exist in this region any large military establishments like those covering the Channel front. Last but not least, Germany's own North Sea coast was one of immense natural strength. Three

[1] David Hannay, *The Navy and Sea Power* (1913), pp. 245-6.

great rivers—the Elbe, Weser, and Jade—discharged themselves into the North Sea through a vast congeries of sands; behind this labyrinth of channels, banks, and shoals, swept by swirling tides and often enveloped in impenetrable mists, lay Germany's principal naval and commercial ports and her richest trade. It was apparent that the traditional British strategy of close blockade could only be carried into effect against Germany in the face of the most formidable difficulties.

The Moroccan crisis of 1911 had revealed certain grave deficiencies in the British High Command. In the autumn of this year Winston Churchill went to the Admiralty to provide for closer co-operation between the Navy and the Army and generally to take over the work of naval preparedness. All endeavours to come to terms with Germany on the shipbuilding question had ended in complete deadlock; Germany refused point-blank to slow down her rate of construction unless she were first assured of British neutrality in a European war: a proposal which the British Cabinet refused to entertain. Great Britain and France, now 'allies in all but name', drew closer together; and this inevitably increased the dependence of Germany upon her ally, Austria.

One of the principal results of this hardening of the *Entente* was the redistribution of British naval strength. In consequence of the Anglo-French Naval Conversations, France in 1912 moved all her capital ships into the Mediterranean, while ours were brought home. The whole of the British battle fleet, together with its cruiser squadrons, flotillas, and ancillary vessels, was now concentrated in the North Sea.

Churchill's immediate task as First Lord was the creation of a Naval War Staff to deal with the major problems of naval strategy. But a strong prejudice existed in the Service against the whole principle of a general staff; and the scheme was first postponed, and later introduced on but a limited scale: with the result that at the outbreak of war, as Churchill has observed, 'we had more captains of ships than captains of war'. The functions of the Naval War Staff were purely advisory; it possessed no executive authority. And it was through the lack of such an organization at the head of affairs that the Navy was in certain respects inferior to the German in technical preparedness.

Churchill's term of office was also marked by important changes in naval strategy. Down to the year 1911 the war plans of the Admiralty had been based on the traditional policy of the close blockade of the enemy's ports; but, owing to the development of the torpedo-boat, submarine, and mine, such an operation was now deemed impracticable; and it was abandoned in favour of the strategy of 'distant blockade'. The new dispositions entailed the blocking of the outlets from the North Sea by basing the battle fleet on Scapa Flow in the Orkney Islands and holding the Straits of Dover with flotillas supported by the older battleships. In this way the Germans would be effectively cut off from the outer seas. The policy of distant blockade was embodied in the Admiralty War Orders of 1912.

At the same time special precautionary measures were taken by the First Lord and his advisers to guard against a 'Bolt from the Blue', or surprise attack before the main concentration of the Fleet could be effected. The danger of such an attack was materially increased by the new developments in naval warfare; particularly by the advent of the submarine. 'I was accustomed', Churchill recalls, 'to check our dispositions by asking the Staff from time to time, unexpectedly, "What happens if war with Germany begins today?" I never found them without an answer which showed that we had the power to effect our main concentration before any portion of the Fleet could be brought to battle. Our Fleet did not go for its cruises to the coast of Spain until we knew that the German High Seas Fleet was having its winter refits. When we held Grand Manoeuvres we were very careful to arrange the coaling and leave which followed in such a way as to secure us the power of meeting any blow which could possibly reach us in a given time.'[1]

Saturday, October 12, 1912, had witnessed the launching at Portsmouth of the new super-dreadnought, the *Iron Duke*, which, less than two years later, was to be the flagship of the

[1] W. S. Churchill, *The World Crisis, 1911-1914* (1923), pp. 150-1.

battle fleet. That was a name that would be mentioned in history.

It was a fine autumn day; and there was a record attendance of more than 60,000 people packed in the gaily decorated stands which had been erected round the stern of the great ship. The ships in harbour and at Spithead were dressed overall in flags from early morning to noon. In a stand near the starboard bow of the *Iron Duke* the Royal Marine Artillery band was stationed. Mingling with the strains of martial music, the blows of the hammers knocking away the last remaining block proclaimed the fact that the new vessel was almost ready to take the water.

The guard of honour drawn up at the foot of the principal staircase presented arms as a motor car drew up containing the Duke and Duchess of Wellington and Admiral Sir Hedworth Meux, the Commander-in-Chief at Portsmouth. The First Lord, who had walked over from Admiralty House to the ship, ascended by another staircase; he was recognised and enthusiastically cheered by several hundred workmen gathered about the ship.

After a short religious service, concluding with the customary hymn, 'Eternal Father, strong to save', the Duchess of Wellington prepared to name the ship in the traditional manner. Shattering the bottle of wine which was suspended beneath a bouquet of beautiful flowers over the bows, she pronounced the words: 'I wish good luck to the *Iron Duke* and all who sail in her!'

There was a mighty outburst of applause while the dockyard mateys were busy with the final preparations. Shortly after noon, a bugle sounded the call for everybody to stand clear for the launch. Then, with a few deft blows with the mallet on the chisel, the Duchess quickly severed the cord which held the weights suspended over the dogshores. A storm of cheering arose, and, above the uproar, in which the sirens of almost every ship in the harbour took part, could be heard the inspiriting strains of 'Rule, Britannia', played by the Royal Marines in the adjoining stand. Slowly at first, then with steadily increasing momentum, the great ship glided down the ways and finally took the water with a tremendous splash.

Such was the dramatic scene which had been enacted over and over again in the last few years before Armageddon as on both

sides of the North Sea dreadnought after dreadnought swept
down the slips and in due course took its place among the rival
battle fleets.

In these years of tension and crisis the whole nation had, in
fact, become Navy-conscious as never before or since in time of
peace. There had been nothing like the patriotic fervour excited
by these launchings since the Napoleonic Wars. It is difficult, if
not impossible, for the present generation really to understand
what the Navy meant to the England of their parents and grand-
parents. Jane's *Fighting Ships* had become a best-seller. The word
'dreadnought' was on everybody's lips. The Royal Navy was
very much the Senior Service; it was their strength and their
pride; it was the guarantee of the safety and prosperity of their
island home and their world-wide Empire; it was 'the sure shield'
to which their King was later to allude in a much-applauded
passage.

The space devoted to naval affairs in the national press, the
crowded and enthusiastic meetings of the Navy League, the
anxious care with which people studied the statistics of the rival
armaments preparing on either side of the North Sea — even the
ubiquitous sailor suits of the small boys — all gave eloquent
testimony of this perpetual preoccupation with the Command of
the Sea.

On the parade grounds of Osborne and Dartmouth successive
terms of naval cadets swung past their Captain to the stirring
strains of Boyce's immortal 'Heart of Oak'. As they marched,
the young faces grew set and stern; for the old ballad, which had
originally appeared in the Year of Victories, 1759, went back,
far beyond the easy-going peace-time routine and leisurely
'hurrah cruises' of the pre-Fisher Navy, to the great days of
Hawke and Nelson; once again, to the fiercely exhilarating
double-double beat of 'Heart of Oak', with all its proud traditions, the drums were beating to quarters. Not a few of these
youngsters came of families with historic Service associations.
The Navy was in their blood.

During the last year of peace the whole business of preparation for war was speeded up and the North Sea was the scene of strenuous battle practices approximating nearer and nearer to the real thing. 'Your battle-ground should be your drill ground', Fisher had declared in years past. 'What was the good of the old system of drill and manoeuvres in the Mediterranean under blue skies and smooth waters when if war ever comes you'll have to fight among the fogs and shallows of the North Sea'. A growing sense of urgency permeated the Service. Impelled by the keen spurs of competition and promotion, our officers scorned delights and lived laborious days in the dedicated pursuit of efficiency. Their men, particularly the guns' crews, were trained within an inch of their lives. As one of the most perspicacious of the younger school of officers has testified: 'This sea service in the years prior to the outbreak of hostilities was one long preparation for war. We expected war, we were ready for it, and almost wished for it.'[1]

The summer manoeuvres of 1913 were on the largest scale, the area of operations extending into the Atlantic off the west coast of Ireland, and the Intelligence Department working day and night. In this exercise the 'Blue' fleet, under Vice-Admiral Sir John Jellicoe, attempted to break through the 'Red' fleet, under Admiral Sir George Callaghan, in order to attack the east coast. Two merchantmen, chartered as troopships, carried a large force of Marines. Jellicoe succeeded only too well: troops were landed in the Humber and higher up the coast and a number of successful raids were made in other directions. The manoeuvres in fact had to be hurriedly curtailed for fear of teaching the Germans as well as ourselves. As it was, a great outcry arose in the press about the vulnerability of our coasts. Meanwhile, from the direction of the Norwegian coast, where the German High Seas Fleet, under the command of Admiral von Ingenohl, was engaged in similar exercises, came the sound of heavy firing; and Rear-Admiral Beatty noted with interest that the Germans appeared to be regularly 'jamming' our wire-less signals (a stratagem which they were to repeat with success at Jutland).

The ever-increasing expenditure entailed by the recent Programmes culminated in the 1914 Naval Estimates for £52½ millions, which gave rise to an acute and prolonged controversy

[1] J. M. Kenworthy, *Sailors, Statesmen—and Others* (1933), p. 47.

in the Cabinet and a memorandum from the First Lord re-stating the Admiralty case, containing the pregnant words:

'We must begin by recognizing how different the part played by our Navy is from that of the Navies of every other country. Alone among the great modern States we can neither defend the soil upon which we live nor subsist upon its produce. Our whole regular Army is liable to be ordered abroad for the defence of India. The food of our people, the raw material of their industries, the commerce which constitutes our wealth, has to be protected as it traverses thousands of miles of sea and ocean from every quarter of the globe.'

Towards the close of this memorandum Churchill laid stress on certain harsh realities of the international situation in a striking passage which, when years later he was writing his memoirs, he toned down considerably.

'We are not a young people with an innocent record and a scanty inheritance. We have engrossed to ourselves, in time when other powerful nations were paralysed by barbarism or internal war, an altogether disproportionate share of the wealth and traffic of the world. We have got all we want in territory, and our claim to be left in the unmolested enjoyment of vast and splendid possessions, mainly acquired by violence, largely maintained by force, often seems less reasonable to others than to us. . . . There has not been the slightest abatement of naval and military preparations. On the contrary, we are witnessing this year increases of expenditure by the Continental Powers beyond all previous experience. The world is arming as it has never armed before.'[1]

The struggle which had continued for years between the navalists and their opponents in the ministerialist ranks now came to a head. The rapidly growing expense of the Navy was a standing embarrassment to a Liberal Government anxious to implement its plans of social reform. It was the subject of unsparing criticism on the part of the Radical and Labour members.

[1] Compare the document in its original form, as quoted in A. J. Marder's *From the Dreadnought to Scapa Flow*, I, p. 322, with the revised version in Churchill's *The World Crisis*, I, pp. 175-6.

For nearly five months — from the autumn of 1913 to the following spring — the controversy and tension mounted. The Chancellor of the Exchequer, in a much talked-of interview with the *Daily Chronicle*, had strongly criticised all this heavy expenditure on armaments and had recalled how Lord Randolph Churchill (Winston Churchill's father) had resigned on this very issue. At the height of the conflict a former First Lord, Reginald McKenna, together with other critics of the Estimates, had protested to Asquith that 'the total is unprecedented; the increase is unexampled at a time of international calm'; in January the resignation of Prince Louis of Battenberg (the First Sea Lord) and the entire Board of Admiralty was a strong probability; and Asquith began to think of dissolving Parliament.

In the Cabinet, the Admiralty case was powerfully upheld by Winston Churchill; and in the end, with the silent but unswerving support of the Prime Minister, he won—the Estimates being accepted virtually in their entirety. A similar controversy meanwhile raged in the press, which as usual was divided on party lines, the Liberal newspapers in the main supporting the champion of economy, David Lloyd George, and the Opposition journals fiercely attacking him.

'Mr. Lloyd George', observed the *Daily Chronicle*, 'can do no better service to his country or his party than by lifting high the old banner of retrenchment. . . . There is not a banker or a merchant in the City, whatever his political opinions, who does not view with grave misgiving this tremendous expenditure on armaments.' 'The present action of the Chancellor of the Exchequer', the *Daily Telegraph* declared, 'is a wilful trespass upon the province of the Admiralty and of the Foreign Office.'

With the opening of the new session, as we have seen, the Irish question began to dominate the Parliamentary scene and greatly strengthened Churchill's hand. 'The prospect of a formidable naval agitation', he relates, 'was recognised as uninviting. In order to strengthen myself with my party, I mingled actively in the Irish controversy'. In the acrimonious debates of March and April the First Lord was in the forefront of the fray; and his critics were increasingly distracted from the Naval Estimates by the rising fury of the fight over Home Rule.

CHAPTER 8

The coming of spring

The weather during the third month of 1914 was abnormal. Instead of the dry, cold winds for which March had always been noted, there came day after day of steady, relentless downpour. The oldest people in the southern counties could scarcely recall such a wet March.

It was followed, however, by one of the finest Aprils on record. Before Easter most of the ghylls and coppices were bespangled with primroses and wild anemones; already the oakbuds were turning reddish, the hedgerows were bursting into foliage, and, with the return of the warblers to our shores, the Dawn Chorus was, daybreak by daybreak, growing louder and fuller.

Down at Wiston, as in many other places throughout England, all the people as a matter of course went to church on Good Friday morning. For the men working on the land it was a holiday—provided, of course, that they went to church. Friday was a day of heavy cloud alternating with periods of bright blue sky and warm sunshine. In the afternoon a good many of the children picked primroses and took them up to the rectory. In 'Peggy' Copse and the spinneys at the foot of the Downs, in among the hollows and dells behind the schoolhouse, and on the verges of the neighbouring lanes and footpaths, parties of small girls and boys industriously filled paper bags and baskets with innumerable bunches of primroses, which were used next day in the decoration of the church.

Easter Sunday was, like Christmas, a day quite different from every other in the year. Seldom had there been such perfect weather for the Easter feast. The sun shone down upon a smiling countryside where the woods and coppices and ghylls and hedgerows were already putting on their mantle of young green. From all parts of the estate the families who had lived and laboured there from time immemorial — Dalmons, Goatchers, Carters,

Dales, Golds, Charmans, Maples, Timberleys, Meetens, Merritts, and Standings—were slowly wending their way to church along lane and field-path. Singly, in couples, or in groups, they came from Hole Street and Weppons Farm, Mouse Lane, Rokers, Roundrobin, Buncton, and Buddington. The old grey church beside the great Tudor manor-house was thronged from wall to wall. Daffodils and fresh green foliage adorned the pulpit, font, and altar rail; ivy was twined round the pillars, and primroses in mossy beds filled all the window ledges. The happy country sounds—the call of the chiff-chaff, the rustle of the breeze in the churchyard elms, the lowing of cattle, a magpie's busy chatter, the distant bark of a dog, and the song of the skylark—floated in from the woods and meadows. The air was full of the fragrance of flowers, and there was a general feeling of serenity and contentment abroad—a quiet confidence that some day, at last, everything would come right. The strains of the joyful Easter hymns resounded to the rafters.

> Christ the Lord is risen today;
> Christians, haste your vows to pay . . .

The traditional date of Heathfield Fair fell three days later. It was formerly believed that, on this day, the first cuckoo of spring would be let out of a basket by an old woman at 'Hefful Fair'; and on April 14th south country folk usually reckoned to hear the cuckoo for the first time.

Thursday, April 23rd, was St George's Day and Shakespeare's birthday. It was a typical April day of sunshine and shower, blue and white skies, young green foliage and flower-decked meadows, cuckoos calling from glade to glade, gorse and geans in full bloom, and immense drifts of bluebells. Over countless church towers that day there flew the red cross of St George, the patron saint of England. The traditional procession from Shakespeare's birthplace to his tomb in the parish church of Stratford-on-Avon was headed by the American Ambassador, Walter Page, who later delivered the address. Shakespeare, when all is said and done, was as much an American as an English inheritance; and this address, given by a former editor of the *Atlantic Monthly*, made a deep impression on his audience and the country at large.

The freshness and beauty of an English April had been celebrated in literature from the days of Chaucer and Shakespeare. Much of the landscape on which their seeing eyes had rested had not greatly changed over the intervening centuries. Long stretches of the Pilgrims' Way were much the same, in 1914, as they had been on that morning long ago when Chaucer's immortal band of pilgrims had set out from the sign of the Tabard, at Southwark, for the far-famed shrine at Canterbury, 'the holy blisful martir for to seke'. The Forest of Arden was still the same lovely woodland in which Rosalind and Celia had wandered in disguise. The national character, too, was but little changed. England was still truly English through and through. Particularly in the countryside, the large majority of the people bore English names and had recognizably English features. The characters which Shakespeare knew and loved still flourished in our midst. You might encounter Nick Bottom and his mates waxing garrulous over their pint-pots in many a village alehouse. The Merry Wives of Windsor had their counterparts in most English country towns. Gloucestershire (and other counties) still produced Justice Shallows in abundance. Juliet's nurse was to be found nightly up in the gallery of almost every music-hall in the land.

The spring advanced with rapid strides that year. The flowers of May were already in bloom while it was still April. By St George's Day almost every wood in certain parts of the country had become a sea of bluebells; there were bluebells, too, in the ghylls, roughs, coppices, combes, shaws, holts, and hedgerows—everywhere around was to be seen a shimmering haze of cobalt. The high, windswept headlands of Devon and Cornwall were carpeted with squills and sea-pinks. On the chalk downs of the southern counties the furze flamed into flower.

Wave after wave of delicate, fragrant fruit-blossom spread across the length and breadth of England. Among the earliest orchards in bloom were those of pear, plum, and damson round about Malvern, and the masses of pure white cherry blossom encircling Canterbury and elsewhere in Kent. Later in the spring the whole Vale of Evesham became a sea of glowing blossom; and all over the western midlands, and down in the west country, innumerable cider orchards put on their pink and white mantles.

The plumage of birds, too, was unusually bright and gay. An

immense number of swifts had arrived in southern England, and the nightingales were already nesting in early May.

In winter time the children of Wiston had trudged, on many a dull and dreary day, through wet, miry lanes; sometimes the great beech-clump high up on Chanctonbury Hill was blotted out by mist; often they had to wend their homeward way in the deepening dusk—but now, 'i' the sweet of the year', the walk to and from school was a daily delight.

Weppons Lane had become a tunnel of green. The tall Lombardy poplars, planted by the old squire, that were such a feature of the estate, had begun to break into leaf. The copses and meadows were gay with flowers. They would see the ever-changing play of sunlight and shade on the bare slopes of the Downs. They would listen to the yaffle's loud laugh ringing through the spring woods. They would smell the strong scent of sweet brier after rain. The shrill *peewee* of the plovers, the dry, staccato call of the chiff-chaff, the cooing of the wood-pigeons, the drumming of the spotted woodpecker, the high, needle-like note of the goldcrests, and the tap-tap of the nuthatch began to be heard. The girls would linger in the sunlit meadows to pick cowslips, while their brothers ranged the hedgesides for birds' nests. Like their fathers and mothers before them, the children would shelter from some passing shower under the friendly Umbrella Tree which grew beside the Steyning - Washington road.

Every day brought something new. There was the warm, sunny day in early spring when the first brimstone butterfly appeared. There was the day when they heard the first cuckoo. There was the day when the swallows returned to Malthouse (there were always swallows under the eaves at Malthouse, and the air was full of their soft twitterings). There was the day when the strong, vibrant note of the nightingale was heard. There was the day when a cloud of orange-tip butterflies fluttered over the ladysmock by the roadside in the bright April weather.

The spring sometimes brought a glimpse of a couple of mad March hares boxing away with their fore-paws in some new-ploughed field; of a vixen playing with her cubs in an outlying rough or unfrequented meadow; of solemn young owlets who could be drawn up from the nest below by an old stocking cautiously lowered within a hollow tree; of a brood of small, downy moorchicks setting out with their mother on their very first swim in a corner of the sedge-girt lake below Buddington, and of an old prowling badger high up in the hanging woods on the chalky slopes of Chanctonbury Hill.

Every day the dusk fell just a little later, and the nightingale sang in the fresh, clear April nights under the glittering stars.

The surrounding countryside was rich in wild flowers. There were acres and acres of waving daffodils in the glades of Ashington. First violets, and then cowslips, grew luxuriantly under Owlscroft. Primroses and bluebells flourished everywhere, and the rarer oxlip, as well as certain species of orchis, could be found by those who knew the right places. Later the woodland glades were full of purple foxgloves, and clumps of creamy meadow-sweet appeared under the hedgerows.

There was fine, sunny weather for May 1st, though a rather cold breeze was blowing. The traditional May Day ceremonies were observed in various parts of the country. In Berkshire, in the Vale of the White Horse, the girls arose in the early morning to wash their faces in the May dew. In Rutland the school-children went from house to house displaying their May garlands and chorusing their May Day song:

> Good morning, lords and ladies, it is the first of May,
> We hope you'll view our garland, it is so very gay.
> The cuckoo sings in April; the cuckoo sings in May,
> The cuckoo sings in June; in July she flies away.

At daybreak the choristers of Magdalen College, Oxford, climbed to the top of their tower and sang the Latin hymn, *Te Deum Patrem colimus*, while the crowd in the High Street and in the boats on the river listened below; the ceremony ending with the ringing of bells. At Southampton, according to ancient custom, the May Day songs were chanted from the battlements of the historic Bargate. At Bampton in Oxfordshire and in many other places throughout the country the Morris dancers held their annual frolic, and the children danced around the village maypole.

On the morning of May 1st, too, the Padstow Hobby Horse gambolled out of the low parlour of the Golden Lion into the midst of an excited and deeply interested crowd of onlookers. As, some ten hours earlier, the clock in St Petroc's church at Padstow struck midnight, a party of singers had assembled in the darkened street and, to the accompaniment of an accordion, burst into the 'Night Song':

> Unite and unite and let us all unite,
> For summer is acome unto day.
> And whither we are going we will all unite
> In the merry morning of May.
> The young men of Padstow they might if they would,
> For summer is acome unto day.
> They might have built a ship and gilded it with gold,
> In the merry morning of May.
> The maidens of Padstow they might if they would,
> For summer is acome unto day.
> They might have made a garland of the white rose and the red,
> In the merry morning of May.

The ceremony of the 'Oss at Padstow had been enacted year after year from time immemorial. The fronts of the houses were adorned with branches of sycamore, and men and boys wore primroses and cowslips in their hats and caps. The ancient ritual never varied. The rider of the 'Oss was covered with a black tarpaulin stretched over a hoop-shaped frame. Above the fantastic mask, tapering to a tuft of horsehair, which was the 'Oss's head was a big black and white dunce's cap, inscribed with the mystic letters 'O.B.' The 'Oss was accompanied by the clubman or 'teazer',[1] armed with a painted and cardboard club, also by a man dressed up as a woman called 'All Sorts', a seaman, and a couple of musicians. With his head cocked on one side, the 'Oss proceeded to perform a ritual dance with the clubman; and then, together with his train, he first set out for the neighbouring hamlet of Treator, and afterwards, on his return, perambulated

---

[1] The part of the 'teazer' is virtually hereditary. It was played in 1914 by John Henry McOwen; and it is played today by his grandson.

the old town to bring the 'Summer and the May' into every house and cottage in Padstow, while the narrow streets resounded with the tuneful strains of the 'Night Song'.

> Unite and unite and let us all unite,
> For summer is acome unto day.

From time to time the crowd would encourage the 'Oss with the time-honoured cry of ' 'Oss, 'Oss, we 'Oss'; upon which the 'Oss would suddenly plunge forward and corner some maiden against the wall, where, despite her squeals, he would proceed to 'cape' her—i.e. he would turn his back, lift his hood, and then bring it down over her head. Occasionally, too, the tune would change from the 'Night Song' to the slower but no less melodious 'Day Song':

> O where is St George, O where is he, O?
> He's out in the long boat all on the salt sea . . .
> Up flies the kite and down falls the Lark O,
> Aunt Ursula Birdhood had an old ewe [yow],
> And she died in her own Park O.
>   And for to fetch the summer home, the summer and the May O,
>   For summer is acome O, and winter is ago.

At the words 'O where is St George' the 'Oss would crouch on the ground with the 'teazer' before him, and then the children would crowd around to pat and stroke him. Then, at the end of the verse, with a sudden bound, the 'Oss was on his feet again and dancing gaily with the 'teazer' as the 'Night Song' broke out once more; and the crowd moved on with them, singing lustily, through the narrow streets.

> Up Merry Spring, and up the merry ring,
> For summer is acome unto day.
> How happy are those little birds that merrily do sing
> In the merry morning of May.

The arduous role of the Hobby Horse taxed the physical endurance of the man who carried the 'Oss to the limit. Hour after hour he would be gambolling up and down the steep and stony ascents leading up from the harbour-side. On occasion he had been known to clear the churchyard wall at a single leap. (In former times, the 'Oss was accustomed to chase the girls through the churchyard; but the parson had put a stop to this.) Once he had jumped from the quay on to the deck of a foreign merchantman — to the consternation of the crew, who had promptly taken to the rigging. The May Day revels were kept up till the early afternoon.

Next week the weather was again fine, though there was a rather keen high wind, for Furry Day at Helston. The festival of May 8th was the outstanding event of the year for this little, grey, hilly Cornish town. It had been the custom for centuries, on that day, for the leading citizens of Helston to dance through the principal houses and gardens of the town; and for weeks past the inhabitants had been busy with their annual indoor and outdoor cleaning in readiness for the great day.

From an early hour the people had been crowding into Helston, on foot and in every kind of conveyance, from all parts of the west country. The principal streets were gaily decked with flags; and arches of green boughs had been set up before the doors of many of the houses and shops. The pavements were thronged with spectators, and every window and balcony over-looking the route of the dance was crowded.

Sharp on the stroke of noon, the dancers—twenty-five couples, the gentlemen in morning dress and the ladies in garden-party frocks, adorned with buttonholes and sprays of lilies of the valley —issued from the Corn Exchange. Headed by a brass band play-ing the ancient Furry tune, these couples tripped, hand in hand, straight across the road and down Meneage Street, then back again on the other side of the street, down the old Market house steps into Church Street, through two shops and the doctor's house, entering by the back door in Church Street and emerging from the front door in Cross Street; then across the road and around the gardens of Lismore, through Lismore House back into Cross Street, up the drive to Penhellis, into the house and around the gardens, and out into Tanyard Lane; and through Lady Street into Coinagehall Street, around the old bowling green, and back up Coinagehall Street to the Corn Exchange.

The gardens of Helston that day were gay with blossom; the lilacs and chestnuts, as well as most of the apple-trees, were at their best. The people, too, were gay at the coming of spring and at all the bustle and jollity around them. The long line of couples stretched away down the street, vanishing into a house at one door—dancing all the time—and coming out again by another, tripping between the branches of lime and lilac that had been set up before the portals. The quaint old tune went on and on as though it would never stop; women stood in doorways tapping out the measure with restless feet; many from among the crowd bustled along in the wake of the dancers.

Long, long would all those who were present remember this Furry Day of 1914. For, though in the years to come the crowds would flock to the town as of old to watch the ladies and gentlemen of Helston go through the motions of the historic ceremony, this was fated to be the last Furry Day in which such complete and carefree confidence in the future prevailed; nor would things ever be the same again.

CHAPTER 9

Melodrama in Ulster

Spring had come early to town that year. On the last day of March the rows of little green chairs were out in Hyde Park, the squares and gardens of Belgravia rang with birdsong, and in the neighbouring streets there was a smell of tarred blocks under the hot sun.

Three days later, on the afternoon of Saturday, April 4th, twenty-two great processions, representative of all classes of people, from M.P.s and clubmen to businessmen and artisans, converged on an area of Hyde Park beside the Serpentine where a monster demonstration was to be held to protest against the use of the Army and Navy to impose Home Rule upon Ireland and to demand that this grave issue should at once be submitted to the electorate. From time to time brass bands played patriotic tunes. One contingent marched along to the strains of 'Tommy Atkins'. The banner of the citizens of Dulwich proclaimed proudly that 'Dulwich defies Devlin'. The biggest procession of all represented the City of London ('City of London supports Loyal Ulster'). Though there had been larger gatherings in the Park in the past, it is doubtful if there had ever been so many well-dressed persons among them—on the 4th silk hats were everywhere.

The proceedings opened at four o'clock with the singing of the war hymn of the Ulster Unionists, 'O God, our Help in Ages past', and 'God Save the King'. Among the many speakers that afternoon were Sir Edward Carson, Austen Chamberlain, Lord Charles Beresford, F. E. Smith, Walter Long, Lord Robert Cecil, and (the first time on record of an ex-Prime Minister declaiming in Hyde Park) A. J. Balfour.

Sir Edward Carson, figuratively speaking, proceeded to hoist his colours to the mast-head and stood back to admire the effect.

'Whatever happens we will keep the old flag flying, and it will

be a brave man who will come to Ulster and pull it down. The
Army won't pull it down. The Navy won't pull it down. The
people of England won't pull it down. It will fly, as it has always
done for hundreds of years, as the symbol of civil and religious
liberty, which we have inherited in Ireland, and which we will
never allow, with God's help, to be taken away from us.'

The Ulster Volunteers were encamped during Easter in almost
every park in the province (the larger landowners hereabouts
were Unionists to a man). There were all the auxiliaries of a
regular army—engineers, commissariat, transport, medical, and
signalling corps. There were camps of instruction with rifle
practice, signalling, and ambulance drill. On all sides were to be
seen columns of stalwart, soldierly men equipped with bando-
liers, haversacks, and water-bottles, marching and counter-
marching. The Ulster Volunteer Force appeared to have everything, indeed, but arms. And this deficiency, as we shall see, was
shortly to be remedied.

On Easter Monday Carson reviewed the South Antrim contingent on their parade ground near the banks of Lough Neagh.
With him at the saluting base were the Commander-in-Chief of
the Ulster Volunteers, Sir George Richardson, Lord and Lady
Londonderry, Lord Charles Beresford, and Captain James Craig.
After the march past Carson delivered a short address, in which
reference was made to Ulster's hour of peril and to memories of
the great siege of Londonderry in 1689.

A few weeks later, speaking at Lewes, one of the Unionist
back-benchers, Sir William Bull, denounced the whole Home
Rule project root and branch. He submitted Ireland was a contented spot and there was no need for this Home Rule Bill. He
did not believe the rank and file of Ireland wanted to be separated
from the Union. God had planted Ireland on the flank of the
United Kingdom and they could never allow her, whatever her
wrongs might have been in the past and with whatever unfair-
ness they might have treated Ireland, to become a separate
nation. For geographical reasons they must not allow it.

For their part, the ministerialists were no less obdurate and
determined. 'For months', declared the *Nation*, 'these Carsonite
levies have been treated as if they were a lawful army. The
Imperial Government has affected not to see them. Not a magis-

trate has been struck off the Commission of the Peace; not an officer who has been planning the defeat of Parliament has been removed from the Army List.'

When the Commons reassembled after the Easter recess, the Prime Minister was subjected to an almost nightly barrage of questions from the Unionists about the 'Pogrom Plot', based on material readily supplied to them by their allies in the Army. Every question and answer was received with taunts, jeers, and interjections shouted from some quarter of the House. The young Conservative member, L. S. Amery, played a leading part in these exchanges. Feeling ran high. On one occasion a Conservative shouted something more than usually provocative across the floor of the House, which brought down the stern rebuke of the Chair.

'If', said the Speaker severely, 'the hon. member wants to say offensive things, he had better go out into the Lobby.'

One of the angriest scenes in the session occurred on April 21st, when Asquith curtly refused to agree to Bonar Law's request for a 'judicial inquiry' into the recent military and naval movements in Ulster.

Bonar Law insisted that Ministers had made statements which had been 'proved to be false'. Now, the epithet 'false', though not unparliamentary, is strong language for the House of Commons; and a storm of protests from the ministerial benches mingled with the applause of the Opposition.

Asquith's face flushed with anger at the allegation; but Bonar Law persisted.

'Only statements on oath', he said scornfully, 'would be any good.'

There followed thrust and counter-thrust and the tumult around the antagonists reached a crescendo.

'Allegations', cried Asquith at last in thunderous tones, 'have been made against the honour of Ministers. The place to meet them is here—in the Grand Inquest of the nation.'

By now the whole House was in an uproar, and shouts of 'Marconi Committee' were heard.

'Why are you afraid', Bonar Law demanded, 'to take the sworn testimony of all who took part in the recent occurrences?'

'We are not in the least afraid', rejoined the Prime Minister.

'If the Leader of the Opposition makes a charge against the honour of Ministers he must make it here!'

And with that he brought his hand down on the dispatch box in front of him with such emphasis that the sound of the blow rang from end to end of the chamber.

'I have already accused the Prime Minister of making statements which are false', exclaimed Bonar Law defiantly; 'and he has refused to take an opportunity of either explaining or withdrawing them.'

In the end Asquith was induced to agree that the Opposition's motion of inquiry into the developments that led up to the Curragh crisis should be debated on April 28th and 29th.

Early that morning, in radiant spring weather, King George and Queen Mary, accompanied by the Foreign Secretary, had left for Paris.

Seldom had the Bois de Boulogne looked fairer than it did when, in the afternoon sunshine, the Royal train drew up at the little, white-painted station set in the midst of groves of trees where the President and Madame Poincaré were waiting to receive their guests. At the start of the drive the King appeared tired and a little anxious. This was the first State visit of his reign to a foreign capital, and, not unnaturally, he was inclined to be nervous. However, he need not have been; the entry of the Sovereigns into the French capital was greeted with a joyous enthusiasm that eclipsed even the warmth of the reception accorded to his father, Edward VII. It was estimated that something like two million people turned out that day to view the procession.

For several hours enormous crowds had been gathering outside the little station and all along the Avenue du Bois de Boulogne. Windows, balconies, roofs, and tree-tops, even, overlooking the route were packed with spectators. Expectancy mounted as the great moment approached. Away in the Bois the boom of a gun announced the Sovereigns' arrival. There was a sudden stirring in the crowd. The lighthearted chatter and laughter ceased, and all eyes were turned towards the cleared and speckless roadway between the double lines of troops. Then, as the procession of carriages, with its gleaming escort of Cuirassiers mounted on beautiful dark bays, rolled slowly down the Avenue du Bois de Boulogne towards the misty grey shape of the Arc de Triomphe, a tremendous cheer arose—'*Vive la Reine!*' '*Vive le Roi!*' In the first carriage were the King and the President; in the second, the Queen and Madame Poincaré; Sir Edward Grey sat with the French premier. The air was full of sunshine and the flash of steel. Band after band struck up the National Anthems of the two countries. Along the route the long lines of troops— Zouaves, Lancers, Dragoons—successively saluted at the word of command. A solid roar of acclamation accompanied the procession all the way along the Avenue. From time to time a few unmistakable British *hurrahs* could be heard amid the swelling chorus of Gallic *vivats*.

The cortège swept round the Place de l'Etoile, where were stationed the artillerymen in their sombre dark blue uniforms beside their beloved '75s'; on down the broad avenue of the Champs Elysées, thronged with thousands upon thousands of cheering spectators, where the long rows of chestnuts were bursting into leaf and flower, and the red and blue of the French infantrymen, with the scarlet plumes of the mounted officers, and the drawn swords and gleaming breastplates of the Cuirassiers, made a brave show against all the fresh green foliage in the background; and on to the Place de la Concorde.

Here were assembled the largest crowds of all, and here the roar of applause was deafening. The carriages rolled slowly over the Pont de la Concorde and into the courtyards of the Ministry of Foreign Affairs at the Quai d'Orsay, where the Sovereigns were to reside during their stay in Paris; thereupon the long lines of troops came to the present, the band struck up 'God Save the King' and the 'Marseillaise', and all heads were bared. As the President escorted the Queen up the crimson carpeted steps, followed by the King and Madame Poincaré, the Royal Standard rose slowly to the masthead between the two tricolours on the roof of the Quai d'Orsay.

In the evening Paris was ablaze with illuminations and the King and Queen drove through cheering crowds to a State banquet at the Elysée Palace. During these days Paris had become, indeed, a City of Light. Around the Elysée, where myriads of fairy lamps were twinkling, immense crowds were assembled. In the surging chorus of cheers three different cries could be distinguished — 'Vive l'Angleterre! 'Vive le Roi!' 'Vive la reine Mary!' The last, according to *Le Temps*, was the loudest and most insistent of all; for in the space of a few brief hours Queen Mary had captured the hearts of the Parisians. At the banquet, the President and the King proposed the official toasts, and graceful allusions were made to the *entente cordiale*—the tenth anniversary of which they were then celebrating. On the morrow the Sovereigns drove out to a great military review at Vincennes, and in the evening attended a gala performance at the Opera.

On the last morning of the visit Grey went to the Quai d'Orsay at the request of the French Foreign Minister. In the course of the discussion, the suggestion was made to him that there should be some consultation between Great Britain and Russia as to the parts to be played by their respective navies in the event of Great Britain taking part in a war. To this proposal Grey, after some hesitation, agreed.

In view of the space he devotes to this matter in his memoirs it would appear that Grey was not altogether easy in his mind: even though he ends by convincing himself, as he usually did, that the course he followed was the right and proper one. Nevertheless, the fact remains that this country had been drawn deeper into the meshes of Paul Cambon's guileful diplomacy, restricting still further her freedom of decision. And, not for the first time, the British public was lulled into a false sense of security, deluding itself that in the *Entente* policy we enjoyed all the advantages of an alliance without its obligations; whereas the position was actually the reverse of this, since, when it came to the point, it would be found that we had assumed all the obligations of an alliance without its advantages.

It was at this stage that the Ulster insurgents succeeded in bringing off another daring stroke.

Among the signatories of the Ulster Covenant was a dour and fanatical Presbyterian of Scottish lineage named Frederick Crawford, who, following the example of one of his ancestors that signed the Solemn League and Covenant in 1683, had insisted on inscribing his name in his own blood. For several years past

Crawford had been engaged in smuggling small quantities of arms into Ulster and by this time possessed an unrivalled experience of the international gun market. With the full support and co-operation of Sir Edward Carson, he now embarked on the most audacious exploit of his career.

Long afterwards Crawford recalled how in a dramatic interview with Carson he insisted that his backers must run the risk of imprisonment equally with himself. Were they willing to back him to the finish in this dangerous enterprise? If they were not, he would not go; but if they were, he would go even if he knew he would not return. It was for Ulster and her freedom that he was working, and that alone.

'I so well remember that scene. We were alone; Sir Edward was sitting opposite to me. When I had finished, his face was stern and grim, and there was a glint in his eye. He rose to his full height, looking me in the eye; he advanced to where I was sitting and stared down at me, and shook his clenched fist in my face, and said in a steady, determined voice, which thrilled me and which I shall never forget: "Crawford, I'll see you through this business, if I should have to go to prison for it". I rose from my chair; I held out my hand and said, "Sir Edward, that is all I want. I leave tonight; goodbye." '[1]

With a cargo of 35,000 Mauser rifles and three million rounds of ammunition, purchased by Crawford in Hamburg, he at last arrived in the *Fanny*, after a series of amazing adventures and hairsbreadth escapes, safely in Irish waters, where the contraband cargo was quickly transhipped to another vessel, appropriately named the *Mountjoy II*.[2] During the night of April 24-25th the guns and the ammunition were disembarked at Larne, Donaghadee, and Bangor.

'We arrived in Larne at about 10.30 p.m. The harbour was brilliantly lighted, but we had difficulty in getting alongside, and did not succeed for almost an hour. The boat for Belfast was on the other side. Willing, though amateur, hands started to tran-

[1] Fred Crawford, *Guns for Ulster* (1947), p. 29.
[2] *The Mountjoy* was the supply ship which in 1689 had brought provisions in the nick of time to the starving garrison of Derry.

ship the cargo of the forehold into her. Number 2 hold was opened and the arms were landed on the wharf. As each crane-load was landed, a motor-car came along quietly, gathered as many bundles as it would hold, and then drove off rapidly in the darkness to its destination.'[1]

Subsequently the *Mountjoy II* unloaded part of her cargo into a motor-boat which carried the arms to Donaghadee. When the motor-boat arrived in the little harbour she found the berth alongside the single crane occupied by another vessel, whose skipper at first refused to move at that time of night.

' "There's something special on," James Craig, who was in charge at Donaghadee, shouted into the companion-way, "if you move up you can charge your own demurrages." "That's spoken like a gentleman", said the skipper, and then as he came on deck, and saw the aspect of affairs: "Can I gi'e ye a hand?" '[2]

This operation, in which about 12,000 persons were involved, and the Signalling Corps of the Ulster Volunteers played an essential part, was remarkably well organized. Early that night the local Volunteers had been mobilized, and a procession of motor-cars and motor-lorries nearly three miles long had started out from Belfast. Telegraph and telephone communications had been systematically disrupted, highways blocked, and coast-guards imprisoned in their quarters. The police put up no resistance at all, and, in fact, made no attempt to restrain the gun-runners. The unloading was speedily completed, and the arms dispatched to all parts of Ulster. The night sky was illuminated by headlights. It was a masterpiece of planning and transport.

'The "Coup" was really successful in every detail', Sir George Richardson wrote to Carson. 'Nothing went wrong. Not a rifle or one round of ammunition astray. The "Mausers" are little beauties, being fascinating weapons—and very popular.'

It was not until noon on the 25th that the news of the gun-running reached Dublin Castle. Great were the rejoicings in the Protestant North, and great was the wrath in the Catholic South.

[1] Fred Crawford, *Guns for Ulster* (1947), p. 56.
[2] Ian Colvin, *Life of Lord Carson*, II, p. 374.

Nanny and little girls watching the riders in the Row

ere the Rainbow Ends'

| MISS T TEMPLE S "BETTY" | MISS ESME WYNNE AS "ROSAMUND" | MASTER GUIDO CHIARLETTI AS "CUBS" | MR. REGINALD OWEN AS "ST. GEORGE" "WHERE THE RAINBOW ENDS." | MASTER PHILIP TONGE AS "CRISPIAN" | MASTER SYDNEY SHERWOOD AS "JIM BLUNDERS" |

6. H. H. Asquith, the Prime
Minister

David Lloyd George, the Chancellor
of the Exchequer

A SEA-CHANGE.

Tory Chorus (to Winston). "YOU'VE MADE ME LOVE YOU, I DIDN'T WANT TO DO IT."

Winston Churchill and the 1914
Navy Estimates

Sir Edward Grey addressing
the House

The London newspapers came out with special editions. They were eagerly purchased by the hordes of cloth-capped, rosetted Lancastrians who were up that day for the Cup Final at the Crystal Palace (the first Cup Final ever attended by the King), on their way to the northern termini. The news spread swiftly throughout the capital. Until a late hour that night groups of people could be seen studying the papers by the light of the street lamps. Among the first to congratulate the 'King of Ulster' was Lord Roberts, who hurried round to Carson's house in Eaton Place full of triumph and satisfaction.

'I could not have done it better myself!' the old soldier declared, on his departure.

The two days' debate in the Commons which followed that night's work was one of the most acrimonious and crucial of the session. When Carson entered the chamber on the 27th, the ministerialists welcomed him with ferocious applause. 'Your King! Your King!' they adjured the Unionists. 'Hats off to your King!' The Opposition renewed the charge of a plot against Ulster, and Austen Chamberlain rose to move that there ought to be 'a full and impartial inquiry into the naval and military movements recently contemplated by the Government against Ulster'. The Lobby that evening was full of rumours and conjectures as to the Government's next move. Next day the Unionist attack centred on Winston Churchill, who, in reply, made one of the most powerful and most provocative speeches that had ever been heard within the walls of Parliament.

Not without justification, Churchill characterized Chamberlain's proposal as 'the most audacious vote and the most impudent demand for a judicial inquiry in our records'; and he went on to remind the House that 'the first maxim of English jurisprudence is that complainers should come into Court with clean hands. Here we have the right hon. gentleman the member for Dublin University [Sir Edward Carson] and the hon. member who sits behind him [Captain James Craig] fresh from their gun-running exploits.'

A loud cheer went up from the ministerialist benches. In the midst of the uproar Carson rose and attempted to speak, but

E

Churchill refused to give way. Amid all the noise and confusion some members on the ministerialist side were heard to shout mockingly to Carson, 'Behave like a King'.

'You behave like a cad!' responded the Ulster leader.

Then, as the cheering and the counter-cheering gradually subsided:

'So, what we are now witnessing in the House', went on the First Lord at last, 'is uncommonly like a vote of censure by the criminal classes on the police.'

Once more pandemonium! The Radical members shouted their approbation. The Welsh nonconformists yelled themselves hoarse. Whatever rifts may have been threatening in the coalition ranks, the Liberals, Radicals, Labour members, and Irish Nationalists were as one in their fervent approval of these sentiments.

'The Conservative party, the party of the comfortable, the wealthy, the party of those who have most to gain by the continuance of the existing social order, are here committed to naked revolution, committed to a policy of armed violence, and utter defiance of lawfully constituted authorities, committed to tampering with the discipline of the Army and Navy, committed to obstructing highways and telegraphs, to overpowering police, coastguards and Customs officials, committed to smuggling in arms by moonlight, committed to the piratical seizure of ships and to the unlawful imprisonment of the King's servants—the Conservative party as a whole is committed to that.'

'All this talk of civil war has not come from us', he declared, 'it has come from you. For the last two years, we have been forced to listen to a drone of threats of civil war with the most blood-curdling accompaniments and consequences.

'What did they mean by civil war?' he added. 'Did they really think that if a civil war came, it was to be a war in which only one side was to take action? . . . I wish to make it perfectly clear that if a rebellion comes, we shall put it down, and if it comes to civil war, we shall do our best to conquer in the civil war. But there will be neither rebellion nor civil war unless it is of your making.'

The First Lord, however, concluded his discourse that night on a very different note. Having so far spoken as a party politician, he now appealed to the House as a statesman; and told of the incalculable harm that was being done to our country's influence and standing in the world through all this internecine conflict.[1]

'Anxiety is caused in every friendly country by the belief that for the time being Great Britain cannot act. The high mission of this country is thought to be in abeyance, and the balance of Europe appears in many quarters for the time to be deranged. Of course, foreign countries never really understand us in these Islands. They do not know what we know, that at a touch of external difficulties or menace, all these fierce internal controversies would disappear for the time being, and we should be brought into line and into tune.

'I am now going to run some little risk on my own account for what I will now say. Why cannot the right hon. and learned gentleman [Sir Edward Carson] say boldly, Give me the amendments to this Home Rule Bill which I ask for to safeguard the dignity and the interests of Protestant Ulster, and I in return will use all my influence and goodwill to make Ireland an integral unit in a federal system.'

Though public opinion in the country at large was inflamed to nothing like the same degree as that in Parliament, the press took up the quarrel with enthusiasm. In the Liberal newspapers the exploits of April 24-25th were denounced as acts of gross and glaring illegality. 'The Real Ulster Plot', proclaimed the headlines in the *Birmingham Gazette*. 'Brazen Act of Warfare.' 'While the Prime Minister keeps an open door for peace proposals', observed the *Edinburgh Evening News* scornfully, 'the Orangemen keep an open door for rifles and ammunition.' 'Friday night's scheme', the *Newcastle Daily Chronicle* remarked, 'was only successful because the plotters have succeeded in reducing the armed forces of the Crown to impotence.' 'We are face to face with open and flagrant rebellion', the *Daily News* declared, 'fomented and encouraged by the leaders of the Conservative Party and officered by men in the pay of the State.' On the opposite side, the leading Conservative journals warmly espoused the cause of the insurgent Ulstermen. 'Apart from the very remarkable skill and astuteness shown in the arming of

[1] Only a few days before General Wilson had crossed the Channel to reassure his French allies about the situation in Ireland, which was attracting a good deal of attention in France and other Continental countries.

Ulster,' declared the *Globe*, 'the English public will not fail to be impressed by the extraordinary self-restraint with which the operation was carried out.' 'Ulster', said the *Observer*, 'has replied to the plot with a vengeance.' 'They are arming openly in defence of their liberty and religion,' the *Times* announced, 'and will put no trust in a Government who move by stealth against them.'

The pretence that Carson all this time had merely been bluffing was wearing very thin. The Ulster Volunteers—determined, disciplined, drilled, and now properly armed — represented an insurmountable barrier to Home Rule. The Liberal press was held up to ridicule by its opponents. 'Their gibes and sneers at Ulster Volunteers with their wooden guns are heard no more in the land', the *Morning Post* declared, 'and the rulers of the country are faced with a problem the solution of which is fraught with the gravest consequences.'

The coercion of Ulster was outside the bounds of practical politics. It clearly could not be done. In the last resort Ulster would fight; and, in the eyes of their many sympathizers in this country, Ulster would be right. The Government had manifestly lost control. Though the Prime Minister had declared on the 27th that in view of 'this grave and unprecedented outrage' the Government would immediately 'take appropriate steps to vindicate the authority of the law', in the event nothing was done; the Ulster insurgents were left in possession of the field, and Asquith continued to vacillate and wait upon events.

'What happens?' *Town Topics* demanded in derision. 'Nothing. He doesn't get as far as spitting on his hands, much less fighting. The Cabinet turns the thing upside down and looks at it from all sides, but it can't alter its nature. Ulster stands there immovable and resolute, with 100,000 men and something like that number of modern rifles.'

Sir Almeric Fitzroy with a good deal of justice censured Government and Opposition alike for the respective share of each in bringing the country to the very verge of catastrophe.

'The Government', he declared, 'are open to the charge of slackness and want of forethought in dealing with the elements of Ulster discontent, of not having measured its force or prepared themselves for the solution of an inevitable problem—charges grave enough in all truth; and the Prime Minister, though his lethargy has been redeemed by moments of resolution, is answerable for the violence and intrigue of colleagues he has either feared or not cared to restrain; but neither he nor they have used the resources of order to foment anarchy, nor tampered with the foundations of executive authority.'[1]

[1] Fitzroy, *Memoirs of Sir Almeric Fitzroy*, II, p. 548.

CHAPTER 10

'England, home, and beauty'

The House of Commons at this time no longer sat on Friday night; and whenever he could manage to do so the Foreign Secretary caught the evening train for Winchester. Otherwise he would rise at five o'clock the following morning and catch the earliest train from Waterloo. Three hours later he would be standing in the dorway of his little cottage beside the Itchen, drinking in the pure Hampshire air and gazing at the swiftly flowing stream, with the prospect of a full day's fishing ahead. This was the cherished haven to which Grey, for a brief week-end and 'for a few precious days late in May or early in June', would escape from Parliament and politics.

An avenue of gnarled and ancient lime-trees extended from the lane above to the left of the cottage; and, beyond the last of these lime-trees, was an old chalk-pit—a tangle of oak, ash, and thorn, hung about with masses of ivy and traveller's joy—a sheltered, sunny place where the owner loved to watch and listen to the birds. Though to Grey's lasting regret the nightingales which had formerly haunted the hollow no longer bred there, a pair of blackcaps and many other species nested unfailingly, every spring, in this sanctuary.

The village of Itchen Abbas, then consisting of a few thatched cottages grouped around the church, which Cobbett had long ago described as 'one of the prettiest spots in the whole world', lay out of sight among the trees a short distance along the lane. Grey's cottage was encircled by a sweet-briar hedge, with rose-beds at the back and a small lawn in front; and, across the fair green valley of the Itchen—at this point scarcely more than two hundred yards wide—rose thick woods which in spring-time rang with ceaseless bird-song. A more perfect refuge for a dry-fly fisherman and a lover of birds it would hardly be possible to imagine.

Grey's delight was not merely in the terrain of his sport—the pools and bays of which he had such intimate knowledge, the crystalline waters of the 'Aquarium' where every trout was plainly visible, the stream swirling down to Winchester beneath the low wooden bridge opposite his cottage, the sedge-grown banks and tangling weed-beds which so often defeated the fisher-man—but in all the sights and sounds and scents of spring. His eyes noted the flash of gleaming blue as a kingfisher flew low over the water-meadows as keenly as they measured the morning rise. While he fished he was aware of the song of the blackbirds in a neighbouring spinney and the scent of honeysuckle and sweet briar after rain. These were the moments, above all others, for which Grey lived. This was the prospect to which, as he has related, he looked forward with longing from Monday to Satur-day when in town, and bore about with him 'like a happy secret'.

During the early half of June that year the water-meadows were bright with ragged robin and cow parsley; along the verge of the Itchen and of its tributary brooks the yellow iris and forgetmenot flourished. Grey's fishing extended for some three miles upstream on either bank. For some years past he had been ruefully conscious of the fact that his baskets of trout compared poorly with those of his younger days, before he had attained high office and henceforward 'dragged the weary clog of office work to the Itchen'. Nevertheless, he passed some happy hours in the bright June weather strolling beside the brimming chalk-stream, viewing the swirl below each patch of weed where a trout might sometimes be seen to lurk, matching his skill and his fine gut against the largest and strongest fish, and returning home in the warm dusk over the rough, tussocky ground just as the grasshopper-warblers were beginning to sing.

The sense of release which Grey experienced on these occa-sions was a very real thing. The country was still the country fifty years ago. Urban civilization and urban institutions had not then put out their tentacles so far or so comprehensively throughout the length and breadth of the island. The line of demarcation between town and country was far more pronounced. Grey vividly recalls the contrast, on leaving London for his Hampshire retreat, between the hot adamantine pavements of the city and the fresh spring grass and the soft country dust about his feet in the quiet lanes round Itchen Abbas.

In that beautiful and, as yet, virtually unspoiled landscape there was an almost complete absence of harsh mechanical din. Motors were still mercifully sparse; road-rollers and traction-engines were also comparatively few; the occasional puff-puff of a passing train scarcely jarred on the ear. Though it was never absolutely still and silent in the country, at any rate in day-time, the general effect was indescribably soothing and restful. The common sounds of rural England were the ring of the scythe against the whetstone, the clang of sheep-bells on the southern hills, the dry rattle of a reaping-machine, the lowing of cattle, the tinkle of the hammer on the anvil in the village smithy, the ring of a woodcutter's axe, and, at the close of the day, the drowsy chur of a nightjar in the warm summer dusk.

The narrow, winding country lanes—dusty in summer, desperately muddy in winter—were still much the same as they had been a generation before in the time of Richard Jefferies; or even earlier, indeed, in the days of William Cobbett or Parson Woodforde. In these peaceful byways children might safely play and dogs lie basking in the sun. The traffic, such as it was (and it varied greatly, according to time and circumstances) was usually slow and for the most part horse-drawn and pedestrian. Periodically a lane would be blocked by the passage of a herd of cattle or a flock of sheep. In the late spring wagons loaded high with hay would ply between the meadows and the rickyard. At regular intervals a carrier's cart would rumble past on its way to the local market town or railway station. There were occasional governess-carts, floats, traps, vans, and cyclists, and of recent years, in gradually increasing numbers, motor-cars and motor-bicycles.[1] But often, for hours on end, a lane would be absolutely empty. In spring and summer the roadside verges were gardens of wild flowers, grasses, and herbs. The hedges were gay with blackthorn blossom, pink and white may, wild roses, and honeysuckle. Mile after mile, twisting and turning, rising and falling,

---

[1] The impact of the automobile on that peaceful countryside is amusingly described in a contemporary children's classic, Kenneth Grahame's *The Wind in the Willows*.

the white road led on through the trim and ordered English land-scape.

Gradually but surely, alas! all this was passing: only for another decade or so would the old sleepy charm of many of our country lanes remain. A lament for the passing of the old order, as exemplified in the children's pony-cart, was voiced this summer by the *Times*:

'Seldom does one see now about the country lanes that low, roomy, solid box on wheels, or the smarter, but equally safe, little governess cart, with the wise, lazy, tubby old friend of the family tucked into the shafts. He was a useful old fellow, in moderate country homes, that tubby fellow. His keep was inex-pensive and his services many. He would oblige by mowing the lawn, or fetching and carrying the washing or the luggage. Greatest service of all, he was the *corpus* upon which the children learned how to hold the reins and to get the feel of a horse. His proudest and most beneficent office was to take the children out driving. . . . He dawdled his way kindly and com-fortably along at his own pace. But he could go when he liked, and there was always something—a heap of stones, a traction-engine, or a piece of waste paper—of which he pretended to be afraid. . . .

'And then the cart! What a lot it could find room for in the way of children and rugs and coats and campstools and picnic things, or baskets of blackberries in September or sprays of wild roses—never to be saved alive—in June. It sturdily declined to upset, even when one wheel climbed the bank, in taking a corner; and in a collision with a gate-post it was not the cart which suffered. It went on from year to year, never looking any shabbier, never seeming to have less room for the legs that year by year were growing longer.

'What with harnessing and unharnessing, with taking it in turns to drive, or open the gates, or stand at the pony's head, or even (when very young) to hold, not use the whip, there was something for everybody to do. And of course it was much jollier when the party could be trusted out without nurse or governess—people always affected with a desire to get to some particular place and to get back at some particular time. Potter-ing about the quiet roads, with the pony now going, now crop-

ping grass by the roadside, children learned their way about the
country, with plenty of time to inquire into its wonderful details
of human, animal, and vegetable life. . . . Old clothes, an old
pony, and an old cart—they meant much to the education and
to the happiness of children.'

Despite the ravages of the Industrial Revolution, despite the
inexorable spread of towns and suburbs into what had quite
recently been open country, England was still a lovely land.
Farms, barns, bridges, churches, cottages, hamlets, villages,
entire towns, even, melted harmoniously into the surrounding
landscape. So many of the dwelling-places of men and beasts
alike had been built of local stone or brick, and in accordance
with the well-tried tradition of local craftsmen; nor was there
ever any lack of skilful hedgers, thatchers, woodmen, carpenters,
and others who took intense pride in their work, and whose
patient toil had added incalculably to the neat and ordered
appearance of the English countryside.

Grey's friend, the naturalist W. H. Hudson, who knew that
countryside so well, had written of the 'old thatched cottages,
unlike, yet harmonizing, irregularly placed along the roadside;
each with its lowly walls set among gaily-coloured flowers; the
farm with its rural sounds and smells, its big horses and milch
cows led and driven along the quiet streets; the small ancient
church with its low, square tower, or grey shingled spire; and
great trees standing singly or in groups or rows'.

It was a mellow, mature, balanced civilization. In spite of the
ominous acceleration of modern urban trends and tendencies,
there were hundreds of homely little towns all over the country
wherein was preserved much that was old and cherished. There
were quiet and dignified High Streets whose comely Tudor or
Georgian fronts were still unspoiled by ruthless commercial
development. There were comfortable old country inns which
ministered to the wants of the modern motoring public as
formerly they had ministered to those of travellers on horseback
or by stagecoach. There were spacious lawns and bowling greens
whose velvet sward had been lovingly tended for centuries. In
almost every shire in the land there were grey old cities which
had grown up around some ancient minster or abbey. The two
historic universities, Oxford and Cambridge, had never appeared

so entrancingly fair as in this last summer of the long general peace.

For the past twenty years British agriculture had been slowly recovering from the great depression which had reached its nadir about 1894. Since the heyday of the industry in the 'sixties and early 'seventies the acreage under the plough had shrunk by more than one-quarter. Seen from the height of the Downs, much of the fertile farmlands which, during the month of August, had formerly been golden with corn, was now green meadowland. A large part of the working population had already left, and were continuing to leave, the land. The high farming of the mid-Victorian era was a thing of the past: it had gone, never to return. However, slowly and painfully the industry had finally managed to adapt itself to the new conditions; and by 1914 English agriculture was, by and large, in a more flourishing condition than it had been for many a long year. 'That large tenant farmers were doing pretty well then', declares A. G. Street, 'there is no question. As I have said, they did their duty by the soil, and, in the words of the Scripture, it repaid them, some twenty, some sixty, and some a hundredfold.'

On market days they would foregather in the neighbouring country town, where, after attending to their business, they would sit down with their cronies to a substantial repast, known as the 'market ordinary', which cost them, perhaps, about three shillings. The farmer's recreations, as well as his work, were centred on the land.

'In those times, the farmer's sole interest was his farm. What went on in the world outside of farming he didn't know, and didn't care. The farm supplied all his amusements also: shooting, hunting, fishing, local tennis—one didn't go to Wimbledon in those days to watch tennis, one concentrated on the best method of dealing with one's neighbour's devastating first service, a very real and urgent problem—an occasional point-to-point meeting, a puppy show, and countless other festivities pertaining to one's calling. One never got away for a moment from the atmosphere of farming. Both farmers and labourers might have been justly called narrow-minded clods by townsmen in those days, but as guardians of the soil in their particular district they were unbeatable.'[1]

Notwithstanding the long depression, the wages of the farm workers had continued to rise. So far as money wages were concerned, indeed, the men were a good deal better off, in 1914, than ever their predecessors had been. The average wage of a man in the South Country was between thirteen shillings and fifteen shillings, and for a boy between five shillings and seven shillings. The wage of a shepherd, cowman, oxherd, or carter was between eighteen shillings and twenty shillings. These wages were supplemented by substantial sums earned during the hay and corn harvest. Cottage and garden were often rent free, or let at a very low rent. Privileges were no longer so numerous or so substantial as in days gone by, but they were still an important item in the farm worker's budget. They usually included the right of gleaning, or 'leasing', which provided plenty of flour for the winter; a certain quantity of firewood, and a supply of skim milk. On many estates the men were allowed to rent an allotment, which furnished them with vegetables and fruit both for their own use and for sale, and sometimes the feed for one pig was also allowed (not infrequently the owner of the animal helped himself *sub rosa*—so much so that it used to be said significantly, ' 'Twas maäster kept the pig!').

The diet of the cottagers was richer and more varied than in the past. Good home-baked bread and either cheese or bacon was the favourite luncheon fare of the men working in the fields, and the traditional Sussex pudding and flead cakes were still popular. Boiled cabbage figured largely in the cottage menu, but there were also other vegetables grown in the garden or allotment. Considerable quantities of tea were drunk at home both by men and women; and home-made wines, often of surprising potency, were brewed every year with loving care. Butcher's meat appeared on the cottager's table far more frequently than of yore. The recent improvements in the lot of the farm workers were sometimes the subject of sharp criticism on the part of the older generation, as the late Arthur Beckett has testified:

[1] A. G. Street, *Farmer's Glory* (1932), p. 46.

'Work,' once said an old labourer to me with fine irony, 'why, they doän't know what work be! When I were a young marn it were work from fower in the marnin' till sunset, an' naun to eat but a bit o' fat pork fur brakfust, an' bren-cheese fur dinner, 'cept t'were harvest-time. Now they ain't satisfied onless they has their beef an' mutton dinners as well as pudden'; an' onless they 'as their 'ollerdays, same as if they were gents, they make a hem of a row. I doän't know what they be comin' to, nohows.'[1]

Along the whole range of the South Downs, from Butser Hill to Beachy Head, was to be heard the deep, mellow clangour of the sheep-bells as the flock moved slowly over the close, wiry turf, streaming fanwise up the shoulder of a hill and down into the next hollow. It was the characteristic music of the downland, mingling with the song of the skylarks and the sough of the breeze in the bents, and, further off, in the vicinity of the Channel, with the swash of the waves at the foot of the white chalk cliffs. The deep-toned cluckets could be heard at a great distance over the hills. On hearing them the shepherds would say, 'Here come the old cluckers'.

Sheep-breeding was the mainstay of the downland farms, particularly in Sussex. The big hill farms of the South Downs were at present enjoying a more than average share of the general prosperity; and their owners were men of substance, farming from 500 to as many as 3,000 acres of downland.

On the South Downs between Eastbourne and Seaford, around Lewes and Brighton, and between Steyning and Midhurst, a large number of the flocks were of considerable size, totalling many hundreds of ewes and tegs. The shepherd and his mate would be in charge of the ewe flock, while the tegs would be entrusted to the 'teg boy'. These great flocks moving along the bare hillsides had been a familiar sight to travellers since the days of Arthur Young.

On a hill farm nearly everything depended upon the shepherd. On his accumulated store of knowledge and experience hung the welfare of the flock. Shepherding was essentially a family calling; it was handed on from father to son: not a few of the

[1] Arthur Beckett, *The Spirit of the Downs* (1909), pp. 17-18.

shepherds had as long a pedigree behind them as that of the sheep which they tended. Those who followed this calling frequently passed long years of service on one farm—sometimes an entire lifetime.

The older generation of shepherds were apt to look down on the younger ones, and called them 'hurdle-pitchers'. When past work, old Shepherd Aylward of Lavant, in West Sussex, used to remark in bad weather, 'Now I wonder how my sheep are faring; that young one won't be looking after them. I wish I could go and see to them.'[1]

Many of these shepherds, with their weather-beaten complexions and flowing beards—a few of them still attired in the old slate-coloured roundfrock and carrying a huge old umbrella—were sufficiently picturesque figures as they stood, motionless, up on the hillside, or trudged in the wake of their flock to a sheep-pond. Close at hand, ever ready and watchful, was the shepherd's other self—his dog. (The Old English or Sussex sheepdog was generally preferred to the collie.) The smithy at Pyecombe, near Brighton, which had once fashioned crooks that had a great vogue throughout the county, now turned out 'Pyecombe hooks' no longer; but some of the village blacksmiths in Sussex still made crooks to order.

Here and there in the South Down country an ox-team might still be seen at work, ploughing, harrowing, and carting the hay and corn. The use of oxen as draught animals was quite common in the county down to the middle of the last century; but nowadays they were used on less than half a dozen farms.

At Exceat Farm, on the highway between Seaford and Eastbourne, there were eight 'yoke' or pairs of oxen. They were worked in pairs under such names as Lamb and Leader, Duke and Diamond, Gallant and Golding, Turk and Tiger, May and Magog. (Lamb was the master bullock and yoked on the off-side.) One, two, or three 'yoke' of oxen were used according to the work in hand. The control of an ox-team was a highly skilled job, and was often handed on from father to son, or from uncle to nephew. An ox-herd's wages were between eighteen shillings and twenty shillings, and those of his boy between five shillings and seven shillings.

An ox would be broken in at the age of two and worked for

[1] Gosset, *Shepherds of Britain* (1911), p. 26.

five or six years, when it would be fattened and sold to the butcher. It was shod with flat iron plates, nailed on each side of its cloven hoof. The oxen were quiet, gentle, patient animals, which moved forward or stopped, and went to left or right, in obedience to the guttural sounds of the ox-herd's voice. The latter was armed with a goad, but it was seldom used. A good team would plough as much as an acre in one day. When an even, steady draught was needed oxen were far superior to horses. Often an ox-team would shift some heavily laden wagon which had stuck fast in the mud when a horse-team had tried and failed.

Half a century ago these great, slow, black oxen could be seen at work on the slopes of the Downs between Exceat and Crowlink bottom. It was here that W. H. Hudson had watched them, one summer's day, from the hill above the ancient village of West Dean, which lay in a hollow of the Downs to the east of the winding Cuckmere. This was one of the loneliest spots in Sussex. The rough coast road between Seaford and Eastbourne was little used. A mile or two to the south were the white chalk cliffs of the Seven Sisters and Beachy Head, and the spacious saltings beside Cuckmere Haven. Fringing the cliffs were thousands of acres of bare, windswept turf interspersed with thickets of thorn and furze. Occasionally a motor-car would pass within view of one of the oldest things in England—an ox-team slowly drawing the plough on a manor mentioned in Domesday Book, where oxen had been used since Saxon times.

The atmosphere of peace and serenity which permeated the English countryside in summer also hung about the sunlit cliffs and beaches. For close on a century no enemy had appeared in the seas around our island. The memory of the great war against the French Revolution and Empire receded further and further into the background of the national consciousness. In the aftermath of the long Victorian peace, there was difficulty even in envisaging the possibility of a threat to these peaceful shores.

The yarns of our longshoremen no longer dealt with Napoleon's threatened invasion of England, the depredations of enemy privateers, or the enormities of the press gang: but with

wrecks and gales and epic passages. Along the Devon and
Cornish shores children on holiday would hear from friendly
fishermen as they worked about the boats tales of Cruel
Coppinger, Nick Carter 'the King of Prussia', the loss of the
Good Samaritan, and other sagas of the West Country. On other
parts of the coast there would be stories of Grace Darling, daring
rescues on the Goodwin Sands, famous smuggling affrays, 'Bully'
Forbes, the finish of the great China tea race of 1866, the mystery
of the Flannan Light, and historic blizzards and 'breezes'.

The coast, like the countryside, was for the most part still
unspoiled. There were important mining and industrial centres
on the north-east and north-west littorals and also on the coast
of South Wales. There were continuous stretches of the Essex,
Kent, Sussex, Hampshire, and Devonshire coasts which had
become major seaside towns. Even so, by far the greater part of
our shores remained inviolate, and the visitor could usually be
as solitary as he or she chose.

Some of the finest walks in the kingdom were by way of the
well-trodden coastguard path which, for many hundreds of
miles, followed the line of the shore from headland to headland,
and around each bay and cove. Sometimes the path would come
down near the water's edge, and sometimes climb high above it :
but always it commanded an extensive view of the sea. Along
the limestone cliffs of Filey and Bridlington running out to Flam-
borough Head; along the low flat shore of East Anglia past the
once busy ports of Southwold, Dunwich, and Aldeburgh; round
Dungeness and along the edge of Romney Marsh to Rye, past
the old 'Ship' (the sole place of refreshment in thirteen thirsty
miles) to Hastings; over the high chalk *massif* of Beachy Head
to Birling Gap and the Seven Sisters; along the tangled undercliff with its wealth of flowers and wild life between Lulworth
Cove and Ringstead; along the rugged cliffs and moorland
between Prawle Point and the Bolt Head; past the pinnacled
headlands of West Penwith—Carn Du, Tol Pedn, and Pardeneck
Point—to Land's End; and 'round the land' up the south shore
of the Bristol Channel, westward down the coast of South Wales,
and so on up the long western shore to the border and beyond.

Many a marsh and estuary was then a sanctuary for birds and
other wild life. Buzzards, ravens, and peregrine falcons nested
on the more inaccessible headlands. Seals bred in the depths of

dark sea-caves on the wilder parts of the coast. Certain of the scarcer species of butterflies haunted the high ground above the cliffs. On St Boniface Down in the Isle of Wight there was the glanville fritillary, and along the undercliff near Ringstead in Dorset there was the lulworth skipper. Parts of the coast were still a happy hunting ground for botanists in search of the rare white poppy, broad-leafed centaury, golden sapphire, matted sea lavender, and certain species of orchids.

For days on end scarcely a soul would be seen on such lonely coastal tracks as those which led around the Lizard peninsula or about St David's Head. Only the herring-gulls floated, wailing, along the cliff-edge; and far below a few sooty-necked cormorants flew low over the surges which fretted on the rocks at the foot of the cliffs.

There was, however, one figure which was, sooner or later, certain to appear—that of the coastguard. Usually a bearded, middle-aged reservist, in his trim bluejacket's uniform, with his telescope tucked firmly under one arm, he would tramp steadily on along the path by the edge of the cliffs. On and on he would march, to a point about mid-way between his own and the neighbouring coastguard station. There he would meet the coastguard from the latter, and, after exchanging local news, set out on the return journey by the way he had come.

Fifty years ago the seas around the British Isles swarmed with a multitude of small craft, both sail and steam, engaged either in the fisheries or in the coasting trade. An arresting and impressive spectacle on the coast in those days was the departure of the fishing fleets, often in the level rays of the setting sun, for the night's fishing, and their return to port from the fishing grounds the following morning, often in the silver mists of sunrise.

The four leading fishing ports were Grimsby, Hull, Aberdeen, and Lowestoft. Since the 'seventies and 'eighties the North Sea fishery had been worked on a hitherto unprecedented scale. Each year in early summer a huge fleet of fishing vessels would fish for several weeks on the grounds situated some fifty miles to the northward of the Shetlands; and then, as the herring slowly moved down the coast in immense shoals covering an area of many square miles, they would be accompanied by a vast fleet of drifters from many ports, arriving eventually off Yarmouth in the early autumn. The Yarmouth fishery was the greatest in the world. Extending for more than forty miles to seaward off the Norfolk coast was a series of long, narrow, more or less parallel banks, where in places the water shoaled to two or three fathoms. In the deeps between these banks the boats would shoot their nets and drift up and down with the tide. Large-scale trawling similarly dates back to the mid-Victorian era with the meteoric rise of Grimsby and Hull and the unparalleled expansion of the fishing industry. The more distant trawling banks of the North Sea were successively explored and exploited. The early years of the twentieth century witnessed another great expansion of British sea fisheries. The herring fishery was revolutionized by the introduction of steam drifters and also by the modern practice of herring driving throughout most of the year. The advent of steam trawlers was responsible for another great advance. Since the fishing capacity of a steam trawler was equal to that of eight or ten smacks, it followed that the quantity of fish landed at the ports enormously increased. Trawling, in fact, ended by securing the lion's share of the industry.

Of the Channel fisheries, Brixham was the most important. To watch the red and tawny sails of the big fishing smacks gliding, score upon score, across the shining waters of Torbay in the early morning haze was an unforgettable experience of those pre-war years. The fishery bred some of the finest seamen in the British Isles. The hands were not paid wages but worked on shares. The majority of the trawlers were owned by men who had entered as apprentices and worked their way up. The previous decade had been the most prosperous which Brixham had ever experienced. In 1913 there were 140 large ketches in the port, besides a good many smaller craft. There were about 700 men engaged in the fishery, and several hundreds more in the ancillary industries. The Brixham fishing fleet subscribed to a private insurance system which was operated at a very low rate —only ¼ per cent.

There were still a large number of sailing trawlers working out of Ramsgate, and a fine fleet of luggers at Hastings. West of the Tamar, the principal fishing centres were Looe, Polperro, and

Mevagissey; Newlyn, and the other Mounts Bay ports; and 'round the land', St Ives and Padstow. The main Cornish fisheries were drifting for herring, mackerel, and pilchard; and the majority of the fishing craft were luggers of various types.

In 1914 the fishing and ancillary industries employed altogether some 350,000 men, of which the fishermen proper numbered well over 100,000. That our Government was fully alive to the importance of these fishermen as a reserve for the Royal Navy can be seen from the *Annual Report on Sea Fisheries* for 1913:

'The chief claim to the attention and support of inshore fisheries lies in the fact that they maintain a hardy, healthy population on our coasts which contributes to the Navy and the Royal Naval Reserve, and is an important asset to the general national physique. It is to the interest of every nation to maintain in being a country population engaged in country pursuits, and, in the case of an island Power, a population accustomed to the sea.'

The pay which the reservists received for their services in the R.N.R. was a much-prized addition to their earnings as fishermen. The younger generation enrolled in large numbers; it was 'the thing' for a steady young man, who was thinking of getting married, to belong to the R.N.R.; even quite small fishing places, such as Staithes in Yorkshire or Port Isaac in Cornwall, contributed a substantial quota of reservists.

In past centuries a high proportion of the trade of this country had gone by sea and river. Before the coming of the railways land transport was usually slow and often uneconomic. In the early years of the present century the coasting trade, despite the competition of the railways, continued, at any rate on certain routes and in respect of certain cargoes, to hold its own. The coasting trade was particularly important in serving the less accessible parts of the country beyond the reach of any branch line, and for transporting heavy and bulky cargoes. A considerable num-

ber of the coasters were still wooden sailing ships, and of no
great size.

These small, sturdy, wooden sailing craft were the common
carriers of the coast (a few of them, which had been built during
and even before the French Revolutionary and Napoleonic Wars,
were still afloat in 1914[1]), carrying coals, bricks, slates, timber,
china clay, and minerals to all parts of the country. Often they
would discharge their cargoes on open beaches, to be hauled
away by horse and cart.

'Their title to a living', declares Williamson, 'was low running
costs, achieved by small crews of hard-working mariners with
inherent knowledge of sails and gear and how to make the most
of them. In this respect the Thames barge was probably the most
efficient short-distance carrier ever evolved, with two men
able to deliver 200 tons of goods anywhere on the Channel or
North Sea coast or the nearer continent.'[2] In the river estuaries
and off the low, flat coastlands of Essex and Suffolk the Thames
sailing barge was a familiar sight; in the West Country ketches
and schooners carried bricks and other heavy cargoes to the ports
of the Bristol and English Channels, as well as to Ireland, and
smacks of 30 and 40 tons even brought groceries from Bristol to
the ports of the Bristol Channel; ketch-rigged billy-boys sailed
in large numbers from the north-east coal ports to the havens of
south-eastern England. Besides these, many larger vessels—brigs,
brigantines, and barquentines—plied up and down our coasts.

'Such ships were, for the most part, neither built nor manned
in the great seaports; they belonged to much smaller rural ports
and havens. They were financed by local capitalists, built by
local craftsmen and commanded and manned by local mariners.
They were as integral a part of rural England in many counties
as the village churches, the markets, the mills, the farm wagons
or the village smithies.'[3]

[1] One of the most famous of these veterans was the ketch *Ceres*, of Bude.
According to West Country tradition, the *Ceres* made her first voyage, in
1811, to the north coast of Spain with stores for Wellington's army. Thereafter
she was employed in the coasting trade. In 1900 she narrowly escaped being
embayed in Bude Bay, but just managed to struggle into Padstow. The old
ketch continued in the same trade until 1935, when she was wrecked off the
North Devon coast, though without the loss of any of her crew.
[2] J. A. Williamson, *The English Channel* (1959), p. 353.
[3] Michael Bouquet, *No Gallant Ship* (1959), p. 13.

Beyond the clustered spars of small, sturdy sailing coasters moored alongside the harbour walls were the establishments of the industries ancillary to the shipping — the shipyards, the foundries, the ropewalks, the premises of the sailmakers, block-makers, and sawyers, as well as the offices of the shipowners, merchants, and agents. Throughout the day there was heard the screech of straining blocks, the clink of mallets on caulking irons, and the recurrent clunk of the shipwrights' adzes; there was a compound odour of Stockholm tar, canvas, cordage, newly-sawn timber, coals, bilge, and seaweed. Up and down our coasts there were many such communities, for the most part self-contained and self-sufficing economic units. In the northern isles, Lerwick and Kirkwall; on the east coast, Peterhead, Scar-borough, Bridlington, Goole, Faversham, and Whitstable; on the south coast, Rye, Shoreham, Littlehampton, Poole, Bridport, Teignmouth, Topsham, Brixham, Dartmouth, Looe, Par, and Fowey; on the west coast, Newquay, Padstow, Appledore, Bridge-water, Gloucester, Portmadoc, Garston, Runcorn, Chester, Barrow, and Whitehaven.

A number of these ports, including Knottingley, Brixham, Dartmouth, Looe, Braunton, and Gloucester, had their own mutual insurance societies, which were conducted with admir-able efficiency and economy.

Besides the multitude of small sailing ships employed in the home trade there were large numbers of schooners from certain western ports plying to Newfoundland. Harbor Grace in those days was frequently filled with British sailing ships, many of them from Fowey and Portmadoc. The West Country schooners engaged in the Newfoundland trade included some of the fastest and most weatherly sailing vessels in the world.

It was not only in the purlieus of Whitehall, but up and down the coasts and seaports of 'peaceful England', that signs were not lacking that all this atmosphere of peace and carefree confidence was in some degree deceptive. In recent years there had been disturbing cases of espionage on both sides of the North Sea.

In one of his later essays Richard Jefferies has related how he was puzzled by an unaccountable far-off 'booming' which was occasionally heard in the silence of the summer woods. It was, he says, not unlike distant thunder—yet all the time the sky above was perfectly blue. It stole on the air as a tremor, rather than as a sound.

In something of the same way the profound peace and security —to all outward appearances complete and absolute—in which the inhabitants of these islands had been lapped for generation after generation, was disturbed by a sudden mysterious shock; so slight as to be scarcely perceptible, but impossible to shrug off as a mere figment of the imagination, when the solid earth seemed to tremble beneath their feet. Such a shock occurred, one fine day, in the summer of 1913.

A young naval rating was that day picnicking with his two small sons on the South Downs near the Hampshire border. Dozing off after the meal in the shade of some furze, he was presently awakened by the sound of guttural voices, which were certainly not those of Englishmen. Impelled by growing curiosity, he cautiously sat up and peered through the furze at the speakers. What he saw was two men, presumably Germans, manipulating an expensive-looking telescope — this was, he observed with quickening interest and concern, levelled at the coast, where lay Portsmouth Harbour.

Motioning the youngsters to keep silence, he crept off with them down the hill and informed the village constable. The latter was at first very unwilling to take action; until the rating told him plainly that, if he did not immediately warn his superiors, he, for his part, would report the matter to the naval authorities. The constable finally agreed to telephone the superintendent. The result was that the two strangers were caught and interrogated. After being detained for a while, they were released. The matter was not thought serious enough to warrant a prosecution —though the pair were required to leave the country.

A small thing, possibly. But straws show which way the wind blows; and one could scarcely imagine such an occurrence in the England of Disraeli and Gladstone. Just a passing tremor, just a momentary uneasiness. But—it served to show only too clearly how the peace, serenity, and unquestioned security of those golden Victorian summers had passed away for ever.

CHAPTER 11

Life in the suburbs

The immense spread of suburban development in the last quarter of the nineteenth century and in the early years of the twentieth was one of the major social consequences of the Industrial Revolution. It was closely associated with the expansion and increasing prosperity of the English middle class. Nearly every city and large town in the kingdom was surrounded by a fringe of suburbs. But by far the most extensive of these suburban accretions was centred around London.

From some parts of the high ground situated to the south of the capital it was possible to get a bird's eye view of this astonishing growth. Between the Surrey hills and those of Middlesex and Essex away to the north were full twenty miles of roof-tops. On the outer fringe were the extensive red-roofed suburbs which had sprung up during the last two decades, including those resulting from the great building boom of 1910-13; beyond, were belts of solidly-built villas of the 'eighties and 'nineties mingled with broad zones of old Victorian property, the latter gradually predominating as one's gaze travelled on towards the massed roofs of Bermondsey; still further north, beyond the slender spires of Wren's City churches, the suburbs started again, stretching on and away to the latest of the building estates on the outskirts of Finchley and Golders Green. Nothing like this vast acreage of roof-tops and chimney-pots existed anywhere else in the world.

The rapid extension of mechanical means of transport enabled more and more people to live further off from the centres of cities and towns. The railways (including, of course, the London tubes) were supplemented by electric trams and motor omnibuses. It was in fact the electric tramways which had largely fostered the development of Liverpool's outer suburbs, districts such as Everton, Mossley Hill, and Sefton Park. In the matter of electric trams Liverpool and Manchester had been notably in advance of the capital. But London's fleets of brand-new motor omnibuses were by far the most numerous in the country.

Even in the vicinity of the same city or town, there was usually a wide variety of suburban residential areas. Places like Finchley, Hampstead, Clapham, Wandsworth, Dulwich, Wimbledon, Croydon, Surbiton, Sutton, and Purley—to name only a few of the larger London suburbs—had their own distinct individuality. Some districts were reputed to be expensive and rather exclusive; others were regarded as cheaper to live in, and more free and easy in their way of life. After all, a fairly high proportion of the middle class were now living in a suburban environment; and within this class there existed gradations which were at once more numerous and which were taken far more seriously than they are today. Such considerations as a man's occupation, his social and financial standing, and the kind of education he had received largely influenced his choice of a home. There was a great gulf fixed between such desirable neighbourhoods as, say, Windmill Hill, Hampstead, The Pines, Putney, or the Rose Walk, Purley, and the myriads of streets of small red- or brown-brick villas, with their pocket-handkerchief-sized gardens, which comprised most of the suburban area.

Geography, also, gave character to a district. There were riverside suburbs like Twickenham, Kew, Putney, Chiswick, Hammersmith, Woolwich, and Greenwich. There were suburbs which had grown up beside open spaces like Hampstead Heath and Wimbledon Common. There were suburbs dominated by some commending local feature like the Crystal Palace. There were also a good many places in the outer suburbs which lay on the edge of the open country. For instance, neither Sutton nor Purley were suburbs in the same sense as Croydon, which unquestionably made part of London—while Sutton and Purley still remained separated from the vast, sprawling mass of the capital by several miles of farmland.

In a well-known book of this period, C. F. G. Masterman's *The Condition of England*, a rather gloomy impression is conveyed of the suburban outlook and mentality. According to

Masterman, among the leading characteristics of suburbia were 'contempt for the classes below it, envy of the classes above, and no desire for adventure or devotion to a cause or an ideal'. And elsewhere he observes: 'Suburban life has often little conception of social services, no tradition of disinterested public duty, but a limited outlook beyond a personal ambition'.

There was a good deal of exaggeration, to say the least of it, in these assertions. The contempt and envy singled out for reprobation undoubtedly existed in the suburbs—but so they did all over the country. As for the charge that there was no desire for adventure, in all probability that is something it would be equally hard to prove or disprove. (It is to be noted in passing, however, that one of the most daring and successful secret agents of the First World War was born and bred in Dulwich.) That the denizens of the suburbs were indifferent to a cause or an ideal is another of those sweeping generalizations which are difficult either to sustain or to refute. Philanthropic societies such as the R.S.P.C.A. had plenty of suburban subscribers. A great many territorials hailed from the suburbs. The constitutional as well as the militant suffragists had a large suburban membership. There was no lack of workers for both political parties at suburban elections. (The Croydon by-election in March 1909, involving the dreadnought issue, had been one of the hottest contests since the turn of the century.) A 'tradition of disinterested public duty' such as existed among the squirearchy was, admittedly, not to be found in the suburbs. It would scarcely be reasonable to expect to find such a tradition which usually went with the possession of land and a substantial income. In suburbia such inherited wealth did not exist, or only very rarely.

Masterman is, however, much nearer the mark when he describes the inhabitants of suburban London as being devitalized and cut off from the realities of life. The lives so many of them led were excessively narrow and restricted. The outlook of suburbia was unquestionably tame and colourless compared, for instance, with that of a Cornish fishing port or a Highland crofting community. Thus there was a smugness and artificiality about the life of the suburbs which did not manifest itself to the same degree in the cities and towns, and still less in the country and on the coast, where the environment was more stimulating, and where the various social classes lived in closer and more continuous contact. In these placid, prosperous suburban households the children could and often did grow up in almost total ignorance of any other way of life and any other background than their own.

'Divorced from the ancient sanities of manual or skilful labour, of exercise in the open air, absorbed for the bulk of his day in crowded offices adding sums or writing letters, each a unit in a crowd which has drifted away from the realities of life in a complex, artificial city civilization, he comes to see no other universe than this . . . '[1]

The women as well as the men tended to lead somewhat narrow, empty, artificial lives. They were not compelled to do so from necessity: but in consequence of a snobbish convention which had come down to them from the Victorian era that it was 'ladylike' for those in comfortable circumstances to be idle, or, at any rate, to do as little domestic work as possible. A century before, women of higher social standing than theirs had been accustomed as a matter of course to supervise and assist their maids in the work of the kitchen and still-room. But in a well-to-do suburban household of the early twentieth century it often happened that all the housework was done by servants. Even in quite a modest establishment a good cook-general did most of the work. The consequence was that the mistress of the house was frequently left with more time on her hands than she knew what to do with. She went in for much visiting and being visited. She was an avid reader of the kind of journals which specialized in 'society' news. On occasion she would invade the West End in such numbers as to attract the notice of the newspapers. She also engaged in current fads and crazes. The type of suburban female immortalized by George and Weedon Grossmith in *The Diary of a Nobody* as 'Mrs James of Sutton' was certainly not peculiar to the London suburbs; but it is not to be denied that she occurred there in considerable numbers.

But, despite the belittling influences of this environment, there was much that was sound and praiseworthy in suburbia. Nearly always the types and tendencies noted above were the exception rather than the rule. There were a great many homes

[1] C. F. G. Masterman, *The Condition of England* (1912), p. 84.

where both husband and wife led active, useful, and sufficiently contented lives and brought up their children to do likewise. The political strains and stresses of those years have always to be viewed against this steady, sober, workaday background. The suburban housholder would read about the storm that was gathering up across the Irish Sea with a feeling of comfortable detachment. His wife would follow the latest developments in the Votes for Women campaign with interest and amusement, but without any desire to emulate the suffragettes.

One of the chief advantages of living in the suburbs was that it was possible with even a medium-sized house to possess a comparatively large garden. In a good-class district many of these properties included a small orchard in addition to the kitchen garden, and sometimes there was a tennis court. Gas was in general, and electricity in common, use in most districts.

In these pleasant, comfortable residences there might be one, two, or several maids; one or more gardeners; and sometimes a chauffeur, for in such neighbourhoods there were usually a few, though no more than a few, motor-cars. Where there was a young family a children's nurse was often employed. One of the familiar summer sights in suburbia was Nanny in her white apron and neatly arranged coif wheeling a perambulator along the sunlit pavements with two or three small children and probably a dog trotting beside her. Nanny was a *somebody*. When she remained in the same household for several years, as she frequently did, she was a friend as much as a servant.

The children as a rule were educated at fee-paying schools, starting at a kindergarten. A small but increasing proportion of the boys were sent first to a preparatory, and later to a public school. Their sisters usually attended day schools, though boarding schools for girls as well as for boys were now springing up in large numbers along the south coast. By this time Girls' Public Day Schools had been established in many parts of the London area and at many places in the provinces. The education they offered was comparable with that provided by the cathedral and grammar schools for boys.

That there was a certain sameness about the daily round in the suburbs could not be disputed. Breakfast, and the morning paper: walk to the station: train to the City: office, with break for luncheon: then office again until the early evening:

and finally, train home, with the evening paper. There were the same faces in the train; the same colleagues at the office; the same greetings and jests exchanged. With the exception of Sundays, Christmas, and certain other public holidays — and, of course, the annual fortnight or so at the seaside—all this went on, week in, week out, throughout the entire year.

In a contemporary novel about suburban life, Keble Howard's *The Smiths of Surbiton*, young Mrs Smith put the question to her husband:

' "Doesn't it get rather monotonous?"
'Ralph shrugged his shoulders.
' "It might, perhaps, if I were a restless sort of chap. Luckily for me, I'm fairly placid." '

Yet, granted the monotony of this daily round, the time was coming, and it was coming quite soon now, when many of these office workers would have given practically all they possessed to be back again in those quiet, orderly roads, in those peaceful, humdrum offices, and in those comfortable armchairs by the fire at the conclusion of the day's work, and would be dreaming of all those once familiar things as an unattainable paradise.

Some householders were fortunate in the possession of some hobby or other outside interest which gave colour and savour to life. Gardening, stamp-collecting, photography, natural history, model railways, and wireless telegraphy all had their devotees. There were football, cricket, croquet, and bowling clubs, amateur dramatic and music societies. The children were often boy scouts and girl guides.

The country was much nearer to London in those days than it is now, and when one got out there it really *was* the country. Primroses, violets, cowslips, bluebells, kingcups, honeysuckle, and wild roses were to be found at no great distance from town. Nightingales still sang in certain secluded valleys which now hear their song no longer. Wild strawberries and other fruits flourished on the Kent and Surrey hills. Large numbers of Londoners regularly frequented the many hundreds of miles of rural lanes and footpaths within easy reach of their homes.

Though cycling was no longer the fashionable pastime that it had been, it had become immensely popular. On almost every

Sunday in the year droves of cyclists set out, singly, or in small parties, or in clubs, down the main highways leading to the country and the sea. Outside certain favoured hostelries on the Canterbury, Brighton, and Portsmouth roads one might see the serried ranks of machines piled up on the grassy verge awaiting the return of their thirsty owners. At the top of steep inclines like Reigate Hill cyclists would line the banks in dozens and scores watching the ascending traffic. The passage of the seasons was marked by the drooping bunches of primroses, bluebells, buttercups, moon-daisies, scabious, and other flowers strapped to thousands of handlebars.

The trim, well-kept roads and lanes of the suburbs seldom saw anything that was unusual or exciting. In the winter there might be the muffin man with his bell; and in the summer the sweet, melancholy cry of the lavender woman might occasionally be heard. Other possible visitors were the organ-grinder or other street musician (sternly prohibited in the more select thorough-fares), the geranium seller ('Three pots a shilling!'), the rag-and-bone man, and, in the poorer districts of the town, the Punch and Judy show, which was enjoyed by grown-ups as well as children. From time to time a tinker would appear at the back door and inquire if there were any buckets to mend or scissors to grind. Sometimes the visitors would be gipsies (they were not so welcome), with their birchbrooms, brushes, and other oddments. The older folk could recall the periodical appearance of the Green Man and dancing bear.

A notable event in the summer, especially in a very hot summer like that of 1911, was the appearance of the watercart. In those days a great many roads, even in the inner suburbs, were not made up; and choking clouds of dust would rise up at the lightest breeze. Hence the watercart.

'The smell of that water on the dust', recalls Macqueen-Pope, 'was one of the best things of the time and an ineffaceable memory. They don't use watercarts now. There is no need. It may be better or it may be worse, but one of the best summer scents has gone, and the stink of petrol does not make up for it.

Nothing so fresh, so clear or so vitally of the true earth can be smelt today.'[1]

One of the great thrills of everyday life in that period, and perhaps the greatest, was the dramatic onset of a fire engine. From somewhere away in the distance the insistent clanging of a bell would be heard. Then, as passers-by stopped to listen, the clamour rapidly increased. Shouts of 'Fire! Fire!' were heard; and presently round the corner dashed a pair of fine, powerful horses drawing the fire engine, the traffic scattering in all directions to make way for its headlong passage. The firemen with their shining brass helmets and brass shoulder-straps sat along either side of the engine; while one of them vigorously rang the bell. When it had hurtled past, the normal life of the streets went on again—apart from small groups of people who still stood staring after it, the clamour receding in the distance, and the usual crowd of excited youngsters who were scampering along, as fast as their legs would carry them, in the direction of the conflagration. In the more go-ahead boroughs the horse-drawn fire engines were gradually being ousted by motor vehicles. The latter went faster, of course; but they did not evoke the same thrill as the old horse-drawn fire engines.

There were also certain red-letter days in the year which stood out against the rest. The Fifth of November—Guy Fawkes' Day —was associated with the grey skies, falling leaves, damp earth, and early twilight of approaching winter. For a week before-hand hordes of 'Guys' had perambulated the parish in hand-barrows, or confronted the passer-by at street corners and other strategic points, soliciting tribute. The Fifth was essentially a family festival. Fireworks were let off in innumerable back gardens, to the huge delight of the children of the house and their friends, under the supervision of fathers and uncles. There was the usual difficulty in getting the catherine-wheels to revolve properly, and sometimes the set-pieces—the most expensive part of the entertainment—were hardly a success. But the glittering shower of golden rain (a firework one could hold in one's hand), the hiss of the rockets, the splutter of the Chinese crackers, and, above all, the thrilling, all-pervading, acrid smell of gunpowder made up for any disappointments on the Night.

[1] W. Macqueen-Pope, *Twenty-Shillings in the Pound* (1948), p. 155.

Queen Alexandra's Day, which came towards the end of June, was redolent of summer scents and sunlit pavements. It had been instituted in 1912 to celebrate Queen Alexandra's arrival in this country fifty years earlier. On a glorious day of cloudless blue skies, light breezes, and radiant sunshine, bevies of pretty girls in flowery dresses and wide-brimmed hats sold artificial wild roses from trays adorned with pink satin ribbons, the proceeds being given to the hospitals. From a very early hour in the morning these girls were on duty, parading the streets, standing at cross-ways, and invading railway stations, clubs, hotels, and restaurants (and even the Old Bailey!) with trays full of roses and small rose-coloured collecting-boxes. By midday the streets were full of men, women and children wearing these wild roses.

But the outstanding occasion of the whole year in the southern suburbs was Derby Day in the late spring. For several hours in the morning, and for several hours in the evening, the quietest and staidest thoroughfares which lay anywhere near one of the routes to Epsom Downs suffered an upheaval of the first order. The customary segregation of suburbia was rudely broken down; and for one day, at least, the inhabitants were summarily reminded of the fact that 'There is a world elsewhere'.

By 1914 the majority of the spectators at the Derby were accustomed to proceed to Epsom Downs by train or motor-car. The volume of horse-drawn traffic was constantly diminishing. Nevertheless a great deal of the latter still remained, and in 1914 the range of diversity of the conveyances streaming down the road to Epsom were greater than had been the case for many a year. It appeared that every known variety of vehicle had been pressed into service for the great London holiday: in short, anything and everything that went on wheels, 'and some conveyances', as the *Globe* observed that evening, 'of a composite nature that would defy description'—the sort of vehicle which only seemed to see the light of day on Derby Day, and on Derby Day alone.

The sun shone down on all this merry throng bowling down the leafy Surrey lanes on the way to Epsom, though a cold wind blew and the air was chilly: automobiles of all sizes and ages, including hundreds of London motor-buses that had been chartered for the day by private parties; victorias, landaus, brakes, charabancs, governess-carts, and wagonettes in large numbers; donkey-shays loaded with 'Arrys and 'Arriets in all their gala finery; picturesque gipsy caravans; furniture vans, milk-floats, costers' barrows, and every kind of tradesman's cart with the family snugly ensconced in chairs that had been taken out of the house for the occasion. The lively *tarantara! tarantara!* of the posthorns mingled with the clopping of horses' hooves, the merry jingle of harness, the ceaseless exchange of cheerful repartee, the raucous hooting of innumerable motor-horns, and the shrill cries of urchins turning hand-wheels by the dusty roadside. Many of the conveyances were decorated with ribbons and roses, and the drivers of the horse-drawn vehicles not infrequently had whips which were adorned with the colours of favourite runners. It was an engaging medley of aristocracy and democracy. Peer and coster rode wheel to wheel, each good-humouredly taking his turn in the swelling stream of traffic that choked all roads and lanes between Westminster and the race-course on the Surrey downs. There were welcome halts at such favourite hostelries as the Horns at Kennington and the Cricketers at Mitcham, 'to wet the whistle', 'to lay the dust', and 'to give the little 'oss a rest'. So the variegated procession of vehicles streamed hour after hour through Merton, Morden, Ewell, and into Epsom.

The return from the racecourse, that same evening, was one of the sights of a lifetime. Notwithstanding the natural disappointment of many of the racegoers—for the Derby was won that year by the American-owned Durbar II, a rank outsider, and became known as 'the Silent Derby' on account of the gloomy silence born of stricken hopes—the roads leading to South London presented, from six to ten o'clock, an amazing and never-to-be-forgotten spectacle. All along the route from Epsom through Ewell, Morden, Merton, Balham, and Clapham the inhabitants had turned out in their thousands to share in the fun. Children squeezed between their elders to the edge of the pavement, crowded in doorways and at windows, or perched upon walls, balconies, and at other vantage-points to watch the return from the Derby. Not only were many of the more fantastic vehicles gaily caparisoned with paper streamers, ribbons,

The Suffragette demonstration outside Buckingham Palace, May 21st

Police and Suffragette prisoners after the demonstration

8. *Haymaking scene*

Cyclists on the Epping road

and flags, but even the horses, ponies, and donkeys which drew them wore paper plumes and, occasionally, paper bonnets. (Sometimes the owner of one of the 'shays', in accordance with ancient custom, would attire his donkey's fore-legs in an outsize pair of woman's drawers.) There was an endless exchange of witty ripostes between the travellers and the crowds lining the route. Many of the catchwords then so popular were continually being evoked by the chance encounters and frequent misadventures of the occasion—as at the sight of some elegant, long-haired Nut ('Git yer 'air cut!'), or dilapidated, broken-down donkey-shay with no springs ('Wot-ho, she bumps!'), or unlucky motorist in difficulties ('Git out and git under!'). From time to time bands of ragged urchins raced alongside the traffic with cries of 'Chuck us out a copper luk'a lidy!' There were hearty choruses to cornet or concertina accompaniment. In some of the shays and wagonettes the sexes had ceremoniously exchanged headgear—often with quite startling results. There was a certain music-hall classic with characteristic Cockney wit and a lilting refrain which seemed to enshrine the very spirit of those joyous hours:

> Las' week down our alley came a toff,
> Nice old geyser with a nasty cough,
> Sees my missus, takes his topper off,
> In a very gentlemanly way . . .

> 'What cheer!' all the neighbours cried.
> 'Oo are yer goin' to meet, Bill?
> 'Ave yer bought the street, Bill?
> Laugh? — I thought I should ha' died
> When I knocked 'em in the Old Kent Road.

The memory of that return from the last Derby of the peace is attended by a certain quiet happiness, recalling the long journey homeward in the gathering dusk; the steady rumble of wheels and clop-clop of horses' hooves along the white dusty highway; the occasional bray of some coster's old 'moke' in the friendly twilight; the frequent libations; the snatches of song and chorus; the abounding *camaraderie* and exuberant spirits; the tireless badinage, the long vista of twinkling lamps, and the fragrance of mayblossom in the darkness.

F

CHAPTER 12

The Fight for Home Rule

The first week of May was also Budget week, the introduction of the Budget that year having been postponed on account of the gun-running affair and Lloyd George's throat trouble. For days City men in the suburban railway carriages had been anxiously discussing dreadnoughts and old age pensions, education, medical services, and income-tax. Particularly discussing income-tax!

The imminence of the Budget cast a gloom over many a British breakfast table. Mother, who knew the symptoms of old, would warn the children to be extra-careful not to bother their father in any way during Budget week. Deeper and deeper would grow the frown on that unfortunate parent's brow—until, on his return from town on the fatal day, and knowing the worst, he would give utterances to a final despairing groan and announce, with a kind of ghastly gaiety, that it would probably mean the workhouse for them all . . . after which he would feel better and begin to cheer up.

Lloyd George rose shortly after three o'clock in the afternoon of the 4th and spoke for two and a half hours.

His Budget speech was uninspiring, dull, rambling, and at times, incoherent—like the speech in which he introduced the famous Budget of 1909. He indulged in no rhetorical flights and for once he was not personal. As the *Daily Telegraph* remarked, 'He attacked incomes freely but not persons'.

Notwithstanding the defects of the actual speech, however, he held the close attention of the House, for personal as well as public reasons; for many of the members around him were men of substance, and in some cases of considerable wealth; and the Budget proposals touched them closely.

The Budget of 1914 followed the general trend of modern Liberal legislation. There were comprehensive plans for slum clearance; for the welfare of necessitous children; for the encouragement of higher education; and for the provision of more hospitals and nurses. An important feature of this particular Budget was that it provided a substantial measure of relief for ratepayers and for further exemption of parents from income-tax.

Owing to both these far-reaching social reforms and the heavy naval shipbuilding programme insisted on by the Board of Admiralty, Government spending was to be increased to an astronomical degree. To provide the wherewithal, there was to be a corresponding increase in taxation. There was a heavy

The Citizen's Reward.

FIRST VOICE:—" Wot, workin' 'ard! Let's 'eave 'arf a brick at 'im."
SECOND VOICE:—" Wot, succeedin'! Let's 'eave a 'ole one."
["*Pall Mall Gazette*" *leading article of yesterday.*

graduated increase in income-tax; the scope of super-tax was extended, and unearned incomes were to pay much more. There was a swingeing increase in death duties. It was apparent that the burden of the new taxation would fall entirely on the rich and well-to-do commercial and professional classes.

While the Chancellor of the Exchequer was still speaking, one of the Radical members came out into the Lobby and said gleefully, 'He's flinging millions about as if they were half-crowns, but he's doing it all right. He's taking money from the people who have it, and giving it to those who haven't. That'll fetch 'em at the next election!'

Though they were not unexpected, these increases in taxation came as a severe blow to the comfortable classes. The Budget proposals were welcomed by one side for precisely the same set of reasons that they were condemned by the other. 'The Budget was well received by the Liberal and Labour parties', the *Annual Register* declared, 'chiefly because of its expected furtherance of great social reforms.' 'Our Budgets', observed the *Westminster Gazette*, 'become year by year a process of social adjustment.' 'His latest Budget', said the *Morning Post*, 'is simply a promise to tax the few for the benefit of the many.' (The *Standard* put it rather differently: 'The privilege of paying is still to be confined to those whose numbers are sufficiently small to make them of little account in the matter of voting power'.) 'What Mr Lloyd George openly sets before the nation', summed up the *Daily Telegraph*, 'is a system of providing new and numerous benefits for one part of the community entirely at the expense of another. That system is elaborated to an intolerable degree by the proposals for increased taxation now put forward. They will bear with great severity upon the hard-working professional men and men of business, who are the mainspring of the economic life of a nation such as this. They aim at nothing less than the destruction of the landowning class, especially by means of the increased and reorganized death duties.'

On one thing, at least, everyone was agreed. From the time-honoured Liberal policy of Peace, Retrenchment, and Reform, the item of Retrenchment appeared to have been expunged for ever. Lloyd George had become the author of the first two-hundred-million Budget. 'As Chancellor of the Exchequer', the *Daily Telegraph* observed sombrely, 'his pride is to wallow in millions in the spirit of a man who has broken the bank.'

That the new social services were badly needed and did an immense of good is indisputable. The lot of the poorer classes, especially of the very poor, was thereby made more tolerable. What is not nearly so well understood, however, is that the heavy increases in taxation necessitated by these measures also did harm. It was not only the rich who were mulcted by the present Budget. As Austen Chamberlain had lately remarked, 'On incomes between £700 and £1,000 a tax of 1s 4d in the pound in peace time was a tremendous burden'. The more moderate scales of taxation in former years had made it possible for quite modest households to aspire to a relatively high standard of living and had also enabled people in many different walks of life to 'get on' and to make adequate provision for their old age. As a case in point, it might be mentioned that the career of the distinguished novelist, H. G. Wells, would scarcely have been possible if that writer had happened to be born one or two decades later.

Moreover, it had been customary in the higher strata of the social pyramid to shoulder all kinds of burdens and responsibilities (such as providing generously for their dependants—maybe some old butler, or coachman, or children's nanny—in their declining years) which would no longer be possible when their incomes were thus drastically diminished. Much of the ferocious hostility shown to the Liberal Government in those days is to be attributed, not so much to their Irish Home Rule policy or to their Welsh Disestablishment Bill, as to the threatened overthrow of an agreeable, easy-going, and accustomed way of life.

As the year advanced, the difficulties of the administration progressively increased. Lloyd George and several others in the Cabinet had lost much of their former prestige. The Chancellor of the Exchequer was still under the shadow of the Marconi scandal; his Land Campaign had not unfairly been described as 'an all-round fizzle'. A serious rift was opening between the Liberals and the Labour members. The Opposition was stronger and more formidable than ever before. A number of by-elections had been lost, and there was talk of a General Election towards the end of July. Labour unrest was again becoming very serious, and the threat of catastrophic strikes loomed ahead. (The ominous phrase was frequently heard, 'Wait till the autumn'.) The railwaymen's union had sent in their ultimatum to the companies demanding official recognition of their trade union, with a forty-eight-hour week and an all-round increase by five shillings a week. The long-drawn-out building strike showed no signs of ending and there was the further prospect of a nation-wide lock-out. It is hardly too much to say that had not an immeasurably greater calamity intervened, the General Strike might well have taken place twelve years earlier than it did.

Worst of all, the Irish imbroglio was reaching a climax. As the time approached for the Home Rule Bill to become law under the operation of the Parliament Act, the drift to civil war continued with ever-increasing momentum. In north-eastern Ireland there were impressive parades of the Ulster Volunteers and every indication that the loyalists would resist Home Rule *à l'outrance*. The hopes of the Opposition rose as they realized that there was at last a good fighting chance of the defeat, not only of Home Rule, but also of the whole current range of Liberal legislation. In the Commons angry scene followed angry scene. The debates and exchanges on Irish affairs were now carried on with out-bursts of asperity and rage unprecedented in modern Parliamentary history.

There was an outstanding passage of arms on the 21st, when the House assembled for the Third Reading of the Home Rule Bill. No agreement had been reached about the exclusion of the Ulster Unionists; the Prime Minister had refused to reveal the provisions of the Amending Bill, which was presently to be introduced in the Lords; and, in a tense and crowded chamber, Lord Robert Cecil opened the debate with a motion that the debate be adjourned. When Asquith rose to reply, he was com-prehensively 'barracked'. The motion to adjourn the debate was defeated, but the Opposition back-benchers joined in the cry:

'Adjourn! Adjourn!'

The shouts quickly swelled to a deafening roar:

''Journ! 'Journ! 'Journ!'

While the tumult was at its height, the Leader of the Opposition sat silent and motionless in his place, making no attempt to restrain his followers. For his part, the Prime Minister sat calmly confronting the Opposition front bench; while the angry Unionists kept up their chorus, until in the end the Speaker rose and the uproar momentarily subsided.

THE SPEAKER: I would ask the Leader of the Opposition whether it is with his assent and approval——
LORD WINTERTON: Do not answer!
BONAR LAW: I would not presume to criticize what you consider your duty, Sir, but I know mine, and that is not to answer any such question.

As Bonar Law, pale and tense, resumed his seat, the Unionists shouted, bawled, yelled, and howled their approval of this tart rejoinder. Many of them rose in their places and triumphantly waved their handkerchiefs and Order papers. The Speaker, who had risen, actually had to wait until the uproar subsided before he could make himself heard.

THE SPEAKER: Having invited the right hon. Gentleman to assist me in obtaining order, I have been disappointed in that [A shout of *Hurrah!*] and there is nothing open to me except, under Standing Order 21, to suspend the sitting of the House, which I do until tomorrow.

The Serjeant-at-Arms came forward to remove the mace, which was the outward and visible sign that the sitting was ended. The Tory members crowded round Bonar Law, shaking his hand and clapping him on the back, while Lord Winterton and John Ward skirmished in the wings; and then, as the Speaker was leaving the chamber, one of their number—by this time livid with rage —moved purposefully over to the Treasury Bench and stood gesticulating and shouting abuse at the Prime Minister, who, for his part, surveyed him with a placid and untroubled smile; until finally the frenzied member, having yelled himself practically voiceless, followed his colleagues out of the chamber.

The Third Reading of the Home Rule Bill, which had thus been shouted down by the Opposition on the 21st, was again attempted on the 25th. On this occasion it was carried by a large majority; but, bearing as it did no relation to the realities of the situation in Ireland, the Bill was really no more than an empty form.

'No doubt', observed the *Morning Post* sourly, 'this puppet show was enacted in order to satisfy the Radicals and the Nationalists.' 'As far as we can see', the *Northern Whig* had stated a week earlier, 'the only barrier between the nation and civil war at this moment is the Crown.'

Throughout these critical weeks the King had, in fact, been using all his influence to bring about a peaceful settlement of the Irish question; and with the same object Asquith had been patiently negotiating behind the scenes with Bonar Law and Carson. But the discussions hung fire. It was all too apparent that there were those in the opposite camp who entertained hopes that by die-hard tactics they might, perhaps, wreck Home Rule as a whole; and as the difficulties of the Government increased these irreconcilables redoubled their efforts to overturn it altogether. The Ulster Covenant had allowed of no concession to Home Rule in any part of the province—even in those counties where there was a substantial Catholic majority; and during this time the Ulster Unionists, with increasing suspicion of the Government, were reverting to their original position. For county option and the time limit, which Asquith had proposed, the permanent exclusion of Ulster was substituted. 'Let us have done', urged their leader, 'with six-year limits; let us have done with county limits, as if men in one county are going to abandon men in another county just because there may be a majority here or a majority there.' In fact, no suggested alternative could divert Carson from his demand for 'a clean cut' of exclusion for Ulster. The Government's Amending Bill, introduced in the upper house on June 23rd, improved the concessions to the Ulster Unionists; it was, however, so altered by the Lords on July 8th as to change the nature of the Bill completely. 'It is', declared the *Manchester Guardian*, 'part of a policy quite deliberately devised and pursued, for wrecking the Government, destroying Home Rule, and along with it destroying the Parliament Act.' Once again there was deadlock.

After a brief lull in their campaign of violence, the militant suffragists had, in the spring and summer of 1914, resumed their destructive activities. Sir Edward Carson having repudiated a promise made some time previously that, if ever the Provisional Government came into existence, the women of Ulster would receive the vote, militancy had appeared in Northern Ireland.

Country houses in various parts of the province went up in flames; and the county councils, in accordance with Irish law, had to bear the cost. Antrim alone was obliged to pay out more than £90,000 in compensation. London was also harassed by their depredations. In March a suffragette called Mary Richardson seriously damaged the Rokeby Venus in the National Gallery. 'I have tried to destroy the picture of the most beautiful woman in mythology', she declared, 'because the Government are destroying Mrs Pankhurst—the most beautiful character in modern history.' A few weeks later Sargent's portrait of Henry James was remorselessly slashed with a chopper. Damage was being deliberately done to all kinds of property—private houses, railway stations, seaside hotels and piers, and grandstands; an old country church was burned to the ground, and a bomb placed under the Coronation Chair in Westminster Abbey.

To his secret indignation, not even the King was immune from the attentions of the suffragettes. On May 11th, at a gala performance at the Royal Opera House, at which he was present with the King and Queen of Denmark, King George was actually shouted at by some of these women. On the 21st—contrary to all constitutional usages—they sent a deputation, headed by Mrs Pankhurst, to Buckingham Palace to protest against forcible feeding. The police at once formed a cordon round the area and forbade them access. The Suffragettes never saw the King (in point of fact he was away from home); but those looking on from the Palace windows saw some very ugly scenes, as a struggle took place between the women and the police in the presence of a jeering crowd. Mrs Pankhurst was arrested and carried bodily by a huge inspector to a nearby motor-car. The Suffragettes tried hard though unsuccessfully to drag the mounted police off their horses. Policemen were bitten and scratched, and some of the women knocked down. A good many arrests were made, and the prisoners marched across St James' Park to Cannon Row Police Station. The following day, at a charity matinée of *The Silver King* attended by their Majesties, a woman stood up and reviled the King as 'a Russian Tsar'; another was later found chained to her stall (and had to be removed, stall and all), while others in the galleries showered down suffragette leaflets on the heads of the audience. The famous incident at the Court on June 4th is related elsewhere.

A week or so later, at Ascot, the police took no chances. All applications for tickets for the Club enclosure were most carefully scrutinized; many were turned down, and everybody was hustled off the course before the Royal procession arrived. During the whole of this period the National Gallery, the Victoria and Albert Museum, Hampton Court Palace, Windsor Castle, and many of the other famous sights of London were either closed down altogether or open to the public under certain rigid restrictions.

Though the Suffragettes were making themselves an unmitigated nuisance to many of the leading men on both sides of the House, the latter from time to time managed to turn the tables on their persecutors. One of the militants who had long harassed Asquith at length transferred her attentions to Carson. She used to waylay him as he entered or left his house in Eaton Place. On several occasions she was removed by the police. She next resorted to the favourite Suffragette stratagem of padlocking herself to the railings outside the house. In Carson, however, she met her match.

'When the butler reported to his master what had happened, Carson conceived an ingenious and amusing device for ridding himself of this embarrassing manifestation. Anticipating the demands of nature, Carson told the butler to take a jug of water and distribute its contents so as to form a trail from the enchained lady along the pavement to the road. There is nothing which kills like ridicule, and having heard the pointed and irreverent comments of the crowd which soon collected on the spot, the suffragette soon unchained herself and shamefacedly made off.'[1]

As the year advanced the W.S.P.U. intensified their campaign of violence. Mrs Pankhurst's hold over her followers was never greater than in this final phase of militancy. During the last few months she had been in and out of prison; and she now changed her former slogan, 'They must do us justice, or do us violence!', to one more ominous, 'They must give us freedom, or give us death!' The more brutality was meted out to them by the police, the more converts were gained by the W.S.P.U. and the more

[1] Ian Colvin, Carson (1953), p. 368.

money flowed into their treasury. If the 'Cat and Mouse Act' permitted the authorities to pounce on ex-prisoners at will and haul them back again into jail, it also enabled the militants ruthlessly to 'cash in' on their sufferings. Haggard, ailing women on stretchers were paraded round from meeting to meeting with the object of whipping up wrath and fury against the Government. All attempts by the authorities to suppress the militant journal, the *Suffragette,* had failed; despite all obstacles it continued to be published and distributed every week. In June the Home Secretary, speaking in the House of Commons, declared that in the militant movement they had a phenomenon 'absolutely without precedent in our history'.

There was also trouble and strife within the Established Church. The Kikuyu controversy had broken out afresh towards the end of July; and the Archbishops of Canterbury and York had held prolonged interviews with the combatant Bishops. As before, much was said; but nothing was settled.

It would, indeed, be scarcely too much to say that the whole trend of our public affairs, throughout that hectic spring and summer of 1914, appeared to be imbued with the crazy, topsy-turvy logic of *Alice Through the Looking Glass.*

Within the peaceful settlement of the Balkan Wars the international outlook during the early half of 1914 appeared deceptively tranquil and hopeful. Though the British proposal for a naval holiday in the armaments race had fallen through, in certain other respects relationships between Germany and Great Britain had materially improved. The personal goodwill and earnest desire for peace of the new German Ambassador, Prince Lichnowsky, had played no small part in promoting better relations between the two Governments. In Western Europe, at any rate, the old quarrels and bitterness appeared temporarily in abeyance. The apprehensions entertained by President Wilson's private and unofficial, but highly influential, emissary, Colonel House, who had recently returned from a visit to Germany, were discounted by Grey and his subordinates. 'As the year advanced the belief of our Cabinet that the dangers were passing away grew steadily', testified Churchill. 'Even the vigilant watch-dogs of the Foreign Office were at ease. Both Houses of Parliament comported themselves as if foreign affairs did not exist.'

Towards the middle of June, William II visited his friend, the Archduke Francis Ferdinand, the heir to the throne of Austria-Hungary, at his palace of Konopischt. The magnificent rose gardens were at the height of their beauty, and the Emperor remained there for four days. A week later he was on his way to Kiel for the annual regatta, while the Archduke went off to the Army manoeuvres in Bosnia. The two men were never to meet again.

For weeks to come the international barometer continued to register 'Set Fair'. 'In the matter of external affairs', Lloyd George told the bankers at the Mansion House on July 17th, 'the sky has never been more perfectly blue.' On the 23rd, the very day that Austria presented her ultimatum in Belgrade, the same speaker, addressing the House of Commons, urged the advisability of economy in our armaments expenditure in view of the 'altogether better feeling' prevailing between Great Britain and Germany; and he went on to argue that the points of co-operation between the two countries were 'greater and more numerous and more important than the points of possible controversy'.

June saw the naval visits to Kronstadt and Kiel.

The 1st Battle Cruiser Squadron, under the command of Rear-Admiral David Beatty, arrived at Kronstadt, after visiting Riga and Reval, on the 20th. There ensued ten days of continuous, if exhausting, festivities.

On the 23rd Beatty and his captains lunched with the Imperial family at their country palace of Tsarskoye Selo. They were taken out to the palace in gilded coaches with coachmen and footmen attired in golden livery and cocked hats. (Beatty's flag-captain said he felt like Cinderella going to the ball!) On the 25th the officers of the Squadron were entertained by the Mayor of St Petersburg at a sumptuous banquet held in the Town Hall. Beatty, on returning thanks for the magnificent gifts presented to him on the previous day, proceeded to empty a brimming beaker of champagne at a single draught—a feat which evoked the unstinted admiration of all those present.

Two days after Nicholas II and his family visited 1st Battle Cruiser Squadron in Kronstadt harbour and lunched with Beatty on board his flagship. The ships of the Squadron were dressed overall in honour of the Imperial visit and saluted the Tsar of All the Russias with thirty-one guns. At his own request the Tsar was shown all over the *Lion*, visiting the gun turrets, magazines, and shell rooms in turn, and displaying the greatest interest in all he saw. He was followed around the ship, at a discreet distance, by his four young daughters, the Grand Duchesses, in white frocks and black sashes—each girl with an equally youthful midshipman in attendance, who had been thoughtfully assigned to them by the Admiral.

On the night of the 27th a grand ball and supper were given on board the *Lion*, whose upper decks—transformed almost out of recognition by bowers of flowers, festoons of flags, and even fountains playing—were encased by red and white striped awnings. The *New Zealand*, moored alongside for the occasion, put on a Maori war dance, which was much admired and enthusiastically applauded. The company that night numbered nearly two thousand.

As a fitting finale to the visit, on the departure of our Squadron from Kronstadt at the end of the month the battle cruisers manoeuvred in close order at 25 knots in the presence of the Tsar in the Imperial yacht. It is safe to say that the Russians could never before have seen these evolutions carried out at such a speed by capital ships. On his return to England Beatty was created a K.C.B.

The arrival of the 2nd Battle Squadron and of the 2nd Light Cruiser Squadron in Kiel Bay on June 23rd greatly impressed the Germans. It was a remarkable exhibition of seamanship. Declining the aid of tugs, the ships stood in to the land and made fast to their special moorings practically simultaneously. Five of the latest German dreadnoughts were moored close to ours, their light grey colouring contrasting with the darker grey of the British ships. There followed one long round of official receptions, banquets, balls, and other entertainments.

On the 25th William II arrived at Kiel in his yacht, the *Hohenzollern*. He came through the Kiel canal, and the bows of the Imperial yacht cut the silken ribbons suspended across the entrance to the new docks, the most spacious in the world, which were thus formally declared open. The significance of this ceremony was not lost upon the British officers. The widening of the canal, now brought to completion, allowed the largest dread-

noughts to pass swiftly from the Baltic into the North Sea.
Immediately on his arrival, the Emperor received Sir George
Warrender and his captains together with the German admirals.
The 25th also saw the start of the regatta, and the last banquet
ever to be held on board the *Hohenzollern*.

The festivities of Kiel Week were now in full swing. There
were yachts and their owners from all over Europe. During the
day-time there was the racing, and in the evenings there were
dinner-parties and dancing. The great Hamburg-Amerika liner,
the *Viktoria Luise*, was the evening rendezvous of the fashionable world during Kiel Week. The British ships were objects of
lively curiosity to the Germans—especially our light cruisers,
since the Germans had nothing like them. The officers and men
of both nationalities spent much of their time in one another's
wardrooms and messes.

Sunday, the 28th, was a very beautiful day. In the afternoon
a gay *thé dansant* was in progress on board one of the German
battleships. At about five o'clock the band suddenly stopped
playing by order of the Captain who announced that the party
must break up, news having been just received of the assassination of the Archduke Francis Ferdinand and his wife at Sarajevo.
That was the end of the festivities at Kiel. The Emperor was out
sailing when he learned of the death of the friend with whom
he had been staying scarcely a fortnight before. He came ashore
in great agitation and immediately left Kiel. The *Viktoria Luise*
received orders to proceed the following day to Hamburg. At the
same time the British vessels prepared to return to England. As
on the 29th the 2nd Battle Squadron and the 2nd Light Cruiser
Squadron steamed out of Kiel Bay, Warrender dispatched a
farewell message to the German Commander-in-Chief by wireless:

Friends in past and friends for ever.

CHAPTER 13

The last season

On Monday, April 20th, before a large and distinguished audience which included King George and Queen Mary, the great crimson curtain of the Royal Opera House, Covent Garden, rose on the first act of Puccini's *La Bohéme*. The part of Mimi was taken by Melba and the orchestra was conducted by Albert Coates—the first Englishman ever to conduct in International Grand Opera. The occasion marked the opening of the London season, ushering in an endless round of receptions, balls, dances, dinner and garden parties, operas, plays, concerts, levées, Courts, regattas, race meetings, horse and flower shows, and other functions such as no other capital in the world could offer. The year 1914 saw the gayest and most brilliant of these seasons—and the last.

The same evening also saw the first performance of a memorable new revue at the Palace Theatre, *The Passing Show*, with music by Herman Finck, which was an immediate and outstanding success. Among the most popular turns in this revue were a rather cruel burlesque by Nelson Keys of Granville Barker in the latter's production of *A Midsummer Night's Dream*; a hilarious scene depicting the Cabinet attired as a troop of ballet girls (with Arthur Playfair as Asquith and Nelson Keys as Lloyd George) dancing, under the direction of John Redmond, to the music of the *pas de quatre*; Basil Hallam, immaculate in grey top-hat and morning coat—the personification of the Nut of the period with his famous song, 'Gilbert the Filbert'; and Gwennie Brogden singing 'On Sunday I walk out with a soldier'—destined, not many months later, to become, perhaps, the best known recruiting song of all time:

> On Sunday I walk out with a soldier,
> On Monday I'm taken out by a Tar.
> On Tuesday I'm out with a baby boy scout,
> On Wednesday a hussar.

On Thursday I gang out wi' a Scottie,
    On Friday, the captain of the crew—
But on Saturday I'm willing,
    If you'll only take the shilling,
To make a man of every one of you.

But the great success of the evening was unquestionably the accomplished young American actress, Elsie Janis, with her graceful dancing, her brilliant mimicry, and a charming song entitled, 'I've got everything I want but you', which she sang with Basil Hallam.

Half a century afterwards these gay, lilting melodies from *The Passing Show* are still familiar in our ears, and Herman Finck's music, 'that sparkled like champagne', is as evocative of the fateful year 1914 as are the nostalgic waltzes of Joyce or Baynes or some of the short stories of H. H. Munro, the incomparable 'Saki'. Basil Hallam's celebrated song, 'Gilbert the Filbert', enshrines something of the spirit of this vanished era, and has immortalized the last of the *jeunesse dorée*, the elegant 'stage door Johnnies', the 'Bloods', who were so soon after to perish, like the singer himself, on the battlefields of Flanders.

April also witnessed, at His Majesty's Theatre, the first performance of a new play by George Bernard Shaw, *Pygmalion* (recently revived as a highly successful 'musical' with the title of *My Fair Lady*). *Pygmalion* was really a modern version of the old story of Pygmalion and Galatea, and told how a certain Professor of Phonetics, Mr Henry Higgins, determined, for a bet, to make a fine lady out of a poor flower-girl, Eliza Doolittle. The Professor was played by Sir Herbert Beerbohm Tree, and Eliza Doolittle by Mrs Patrick Campbell, who was ideally suited to the part. The play became famous for a startling innovation. In the third act the ex-flower girl, reverting to the uninhibited discourse of her youth, flounced out of a Chelsea tea party with the ringing rejoinder 'Not bloody likely!' on her lips, to the huge delight of the audience. It was the first time that this rather forceful epithet, so common 'among the working class and in the senior common-rooms of the older universities', had been heard on the London stage.

With the return of the King and Queen from Paris, on the 24th, the season was fairly under way; already the first influx of visitors from abroad had arrived in town, and the hotels were filling up. The bright spring weather had brought on the flowers in the parks and squares, and there was an unusually fine display of daffodils, narcissi, hyacinths, and tulips. The gravel walks were newly raked, and the breezes brought the fragrance of new-mown grass.

The streets, too, appeared to be *en fête* for the season. The display of striped awnings and gay window boxes overflowing with flowers that adorned the fronts of so many houses in the spring and summer was a perennial delight to our visitors from the Continent and North America. In some parts of the West End there were whole streets which seemed to be ablaze with flowers.

The season was remarkable for the number and brilliance of the balls and dances that were given—both large and small affairs, from the magnificent entertainment held in one of the great historic houses and graced by the presence of royalty, to the small, select party given at some hotel by a country squire and his wife who had come up to town in order to allow their young daughter a few weeks of the season.

One of the most notable private parties of the season was the Venetian masquerade given by Mrs Alec Keiller at her house in Hyde Park Gardens. The terrace at the back of the house had been flooded to represent a Venetian canal, which was traversed by a bridge whose lanterns were reflected in the water below, on which floated Venetian boats with tawny-brown sails. There was also a Venetian Banqueting Hall, which was thronged with guests dressed in Venetian costume, who entered whole-heartedly into the spirit of the carnival.

Another brilliant spectacle was the ball given by Sir Alfred and Lady Mond on May 1st to celebrate the *début* of their daughter, Miss Eva Mond, at their town house in Lowndes Square. The garden at the side of the house had been transformed into an open Roman court surrounded by a colonnade of white columns linked together with chains of laurel; in the background were groves of flowering hawthorns, and the whole was sur-mounted by a vast marquée, painted dark blue to simulate the sky. The dancing floor, which was made of hardwood, with all the appearance of black and white marble squares, had been laid over the modern lawns and flower beds; and in the centre of this floor a fountain in the form of a small bronze 'boy with dolphin' played in a marble basin, illuminated with coloured lights, which rose out of a miniature lake, in which water lilies were growing. Around the colonnade there were raised seats for those who did not dance. The guests, who totalled nearly 800, included the Prime Minister, who was accompanied by his wife and Miss Violet Asquith, practically the entire Cabinet, many of the Corps Diplomatique, and a large contingent of leading actors and actresses.

One reason which had been given for the unprecedented dancing 'boom' of 1914 was the vogue of ragtime, which now took up about half the time at the average dance. It had become phenomenally popular. Some of the more exotic transatlantic importations of previous seasons had, indeed, been frowned upon by London hostesses[1]; but ragtime, in 1914, was danced any-where and everywhere, from Earl's Court to the great houses of Mayfair and Belgravia, and was vociferously applauded and almost invariably encored.

Not ragtime, however, but the tender and entrancing melodies of the Viennese and English waltzes of the period best recall the memory of those last few magical weeks of peace. To the witch-ing strains of the 'Blue Danube' and the other waltzes of the great Johann Strauss; of the well-loved waltzes from Franz Lehar's *Merry Widow* and *Gipsy Love*; and of our own Archibald Joyce's 'Dreaming', 'Song d'Automne', and 'The Vision of Salome', Charles Ancliffe's 'Nights of Gladness', and—most nos-talgic of all—Sidney Baynes' new and haunting waltz, 'Destiny', the young men and women of that doomed generation glided over the polished floor, heedless of anything but the pleasures of the moment. Night after night the strains of waltz or ragtime might be heard coming from the brilliantly lighted windows of

---

[1] This distaste on the part of the more fastidious spirits is reflected in a letter written by Edward Marsh (who was certainly no puritan), dated July 1913: 'I can't tell you how glad I am the Season is over, it got bloodier and bloodier—the onestep—turkeytrot—bunnyhug or fishwalk or whatever you choose to call it—carried all before it, and my general dislike of its vulgarity, combined with my particular dislike of being on the shelf as a nontrotter—hugger—or walker, worked me up into a fine frenzy of disgust and socialism. . . . A few more such evenings and I shall have no noble and picturesque Toryism left for you to explain away. The negrification of Society will soon be complete—and black faces will be an essential part of evening dress.' [Q. Hassall, *Edward Marsh* (1959), p. 238].

some mansion in street or square, while outside on the pavement were gathered small groups of deeply interested passers-by, who from time to time would catch glimpses of a richly carpeted staircase, of a gleaming chandelier, of bowers of beautiful roses and carnations, of footmen's liveries, and—a revelation to the round-eyed Annies and Maudies looking on from below — of the exquisite gowns of the women who came out on to the balcony for a moment to rest and to drink in the cool evening air.

It has sometimes been suggested that it was almost with a sense of premonition, with a sort of subconscious feeling that they were having their last fling before the world as known to them toppled to ruins all around, that the leisured classes in this land flung themselves into the headlong pursuit of pleasure. This may have been so in some cases; but it is most unlikely that these apprehensions were at all general. The truth is that among the well-born and well-to-do in England there existed such a conviction of complete and lifelong security that it would scarcely have occurred to them to doubt that this comfortable and well-ordered existence which they had enjoyed for so long was part of the natural order of things.

There had been changes, of course—but how much of the old and familiar remained! To the silk-hatted strollers about town, the London they knew was, externally, very much the same London as their forebears had known before them. Some of the most fashionable thoroughfares of the West End had remained but little altered for generations. The graceful curve of Nash's Regent Street, the historic buildings of St James's Street, and much of Piccadilly were just as they had been in the days of their fathers and grandfathers. So were the famous clubs in Pall Mall and its vicinity—clubs which had no counterpart in any other capital in Europe; so were the town houses of the higher nobility — houses which might well have been described as palaces — Londonderry House, Devonshire House, Grosvenor House, and the rest; so were quite a number of the shops, restaurants and hotels—Fores's windows filled with sporting prints and paintings, Sotheran's with its rich store of antique books, Berry's the wine merchant's, Lock's the hatter's, Verrey's with its old and romantic associations, and Brown's Hotel, so little changed from decade to decade.

Among the inhabitants, too, there still remained some celebrated survivals of a bygone age. The tall, distinguished figure of Lord Ribbesdale might sometimes be seen strolling along Piccadilly on his way to Brook's or The Turf. That wayward genius, Wilfrid Scawen Blunt, occasionally came up to town from his Sussex manor. Lady Dorothy Nevill, the friend of the great Disraeli and many other eminent Victorians, had died only the previous spring.

There were the same familiar scenes in Hyde Park, the same crowds of upper, middle, and lower-class people who instinctively frequented their own particular parts of the Park and tended to avoid those resorted to by the others. There was still the regular gathering of Society after church on Sunday morning for the traditional parade near the Achilles statue. There was still the fashionable concourse in the early evening in the corner of Stanhope Gate—while outside, beyond the railings, a ceaseless stream of limousines and carriages rolled down Park Lane, past the great houses with their green sunblinds and window boxes ablaze with scarlet and pink geraniums. The volume of motor traffic had greatly increased in the last few years; but there were many landaus and victorias passing to and fro in which ladies bowed to their acquaintances on the pavement, and there were a fair number of horse-cabs among all the fleets of taxis; and though in the Row the horsemen and horsewomen were not nearly so numerous as they had been a generation earlier, there were plenty of young ladies, followed by grooms, and children riding Shetland ponies, escorted by their nurses.

In spite of Lloyd George and all his works, the social pyramid was still, to all outward appearances, solid and secure. The tempo of life was quickening; but much of the old grace and elegance survived. Never had London appeared gayer and more prosperous. Never had there been so much that was worth doing, and seeing, and hearing. Neither the old nor the young had any suspicion that what they were witnessing, during that incomparable season of 1914, was, in fact, the end of an era.

In the great town houses of the higher aristocracy was exercised an almost princely hospitality. At evening receptions their doors were thrown open to an immense throng of guests, who, one after another, slowly ascended the wide staircase to where the host and hostess stood to receive them: to exchange handshakes and a few brief words of conversation with them before passing on into the great corridors and spacious rooms, adorned with banks of the most beautiful flowers and foliage, where exquisite gowns and jewels, uniforms and orders, and ribbons and stars, glowed in the blaze of electric light, and everyone there seemed to know each other. The presence of leading men from both Houses of Parliament, members of the Corps Diplomatique, and the usual sprinkling of celebrities from the world of art and literature added greatly to the brilliancy and interest of the scene. These 'crushes', as they were called, played a vital and integral role in the conduct of home and foreign politics; for in the period under review society, politics, and diplomacy were all closely linked.

That staunch democrat, the American Ambassador, had very quickly come to appreciate the great qualities that lay behind the glittering façade of pomp and privilege. Page reported to President Wilson:

'The aristocracy is here and it isn't effete by a long shot. If it prove to be teachable, it will rule for many a long year. On some sides it seems dense. But if you take a peer to be a fool, you'll find out your mistake in a day or two's talk at the short range in a country-house party. He'll tell you more than you know about artists and cows and foreign lands and chemistry and rainfall in India, and he'll beat you riding, shooting, golfing, or at tennis and—in the evening at poker, if you wish; and after intelligent talk about theology, he'll swear at Lloyd George in a way that a cowboy would admire.'[1]

The English aristocracy seldom affected false modesty; they did not pretend to be other than what they were, and the outside world could take them or leave them, just as it pleased. Thus, on being introduced to an elderly Duke, one of Page's countrymen had exclaimed enthusiastically: 'Say! I'm real glad to meet your Grace.' 'So I should damn well think you ought to be!' rejoined the old gentleman simply. That imperious lady, the Marchioness of Londonderry (once likened by E. F. Benson to 'a

[1] B. J. Hendrick, *Life and Letters of Walter H. Page*, III, p. 67.

highwaywoman in a tiara') was as natural and unselfconscious as a child in her frank enjoyment of the glory of riding in the family State coach to the opening of Parliament, or of standing at the head of the great staircase in Londonderry House to welcome her guests.

A striking feature of this season of 1914 was the ever-widening chasm that was the outcome of the savage party war-fare of recent years. London society, as has been said, was riven to a degree without parallel since the Home Rule Bill of 1886. The quarrel had spread from the debating chamber to the dinner table and drawing room. There were fears, indeed, that politics would ruin the season. As it was, several Easter house parties had practically broken up as soon as the guests saw one another. Ducal diehards had sworn to walk out of any gathering con-taminated by the presence of any of his Majesty's Ministers. When Lord Curzon gave a great ball which was attended by the King and Queen, the King's first Minister, his wife, and his daughter were pointedly excluded. Every dinner party was made up with strict reference to the politics of the guests. Leading Tory hostesses rigidly barred all the Liberal magnates and reli-giously 'cut' their womenfolk. The American Ambassador recorded in June:

'At dinner tonight (only Conservative guests besides Mrs Page and me) I sat next the Countess of H——, a good-natured, culti-vated woman who has seen much of the world.
' "I've dropped all my friends in that crew", she said. "Not one would I invite to my house."
' . . . The ferocity of this contest passes belief. The privileged classes know that they are fighting for their lives and they are scornful and desperate to the last degree.'

A few weeks later he wrote:

'The bitter feeling becomes more bitter all the time. . . . Two nights ago the gibes of the two parties came near to a fist fight as the members were going out of the House—all of which means that the revolution is making progress but that it is meeting desperate tactics by the opposition and the tension is indescribable and—painful.'[1]

Occasionally the strained relations between the rival factions had its amusing aspect, as in an incident recorded by a well-known hotelier of that era, the late Harry Preston, which occurred at the Café Royal:

'The political chieftains of the day often used to dine at the Café Royal. Mr Lloyd George was dining there one night with Winston Churchill, Sir Edward Grey, and one or two other members of the Liberal Government. It was a time when political passions ran high, and Lloyd George was the *bête noir* of the Tories. At a nearby table a Tory M.P. was dining. He called a waiter, and said audibly: "You see that little man with the long hair sitting next to Winston Churchill?"

' "Yes sir. That is——"

' "Don't tell me who he is! I know. Poison him, and I'll give you £5,000."

'And with that he returned to his steak.'[2]

It was, however, principally those who took an active interest in politics, as well as the more fanatical supporters of either side, that carried matters to such extremes. Despite all the wild talk of late at Westminster, life throughout the country went on much as usual.

The essential and underlying solidarity of the nation was strikingly displayed, on May 27th, in the record crowd—it was estimated at something like 400,000 people—which assembled on Epsom Downs for the Derby. There was no sign here of the searing racial and religious hatreds which might suddenly and appallingly flare up, even at a football match, in Scotland or Ireland. The spirit of Derby Day was typically and essentially English. The vast conglomeration of encampments, booths, stands, tents, coaches, caravans, charabancs, omnibuses (they were there in hundreds that year), and every other conceivable type of vehicle; and the surging, seething, jostling, roaring mass of humanity, with its endless vagaries of grouping and colour—

[1] B. J. Hendrick, *Life and Letters of Walter H. Page*, III, pp. 59, 118.
[2] H. Preston, *Leaves from my Unwritten Diary*, pp. 62-3.

dukes and dustmen, gentlemen and gipsies, dowagers and
Donahs, 'bloods' and 'bobbies', together with all the riff-raff and
rascality of the turf—presented a spectacle which was to be seen
nowhere else in the world. As a Frenchman had once observed,
'This is not a crowd, but a nation'.

Whitsun brought three days of perfect spring weather: warm
sunshine, deep blue skies occasionally flecked with fleecy white
clouds, and light breezes. It was a time of general holiday, and a
good many people from the towns went down to the seaside or
out into the country. Whitsun also provided a breathing-space
for those engaged in the strenuous round of the London season.
The lovely old country-house gardens in which England then
abounded were in the height of their spring-time beauty. Quite
a number of the self-imposed exiles took advantage of this respite
from the rigours of the season to return, if only for a brief while,
to the glades and bowers of home. In the London parks the lilacs
and laburnums of May gave place to the roses and rhododendrons
of June.

Ascot Week, also, was fine. June 18th—Cup Day—was baking
hot. The sun blazed down out of a cloudless sky, and the occasional breezes, when they came, were very welcome. The sparse
patches of shade cast by the trees in the paddock were much in
demand, even during the races. An immense crowd lined the
course, and—a sign of the changing times!—it was noticed that
cars greatly outnumbered the horse-drawn vehicles.

There came a sound of distant cheering, as far down the New
Mile the Royal Procession, emerging from the avenues of
Windsor Great Park, swept swiftly and noiselessly over the
short turf of the course. The gleaming State landau carrying
the King and Queen was drawn by four bay horses, preceded
by scarlet-coated outriders, and followed by seven landaus
containing their Majesty's guests, each drawn by two bays.
Outlined against the green turf and the fresh spring foliage
of the neighbouring woods the jingling, glittering cortège was
a splendid and stirring spectacle. The applause swelled to a
mighty roar of welcome as the procession approached the Royal
enclosure, and presently, amid the crashing strains of the

National Anthem, the King and Queen entered their flower-decked box.

The lawns below were thronged with a brilliant and distinguished company. In this glorious setting of smooth green turf, glowing flower-beds, spring woodlands, and hazy meadows, with the strains of a military band coming from behind the grandstand, and the profusion of beautiful summer frocks and parasols —the predominant shades in the enclosure that year were black and white—and all the top hats and tail coats, and the gossip and the laughter, the scene on the sunlit lawns was more like a Royal garden party than a race meeting. Ascot Week marked the climax of the London season.

For the last time the aristocracies of Europe basked in the sunshine. The world of fashion paid little heed to national frontiers. Foreigners were there in force. Among the visitors from the Continent were the Grand Duke Michael and his daughter, the Countess Zia Torby, and the Marquis de Soveral, the 'Blue Monkey'. Queen Alexandra was there with her sister, the Empress Féodorovna of Russia, and also the ex-King of Portugal. It was long since so many foreign royalties were seen together at Ascot.

It has often been said that opera in London was a social, rather than a musical, function. This is to some extent an exaggeration; but it is probably true enough to say that opera was essentially a mixture of both. Under the patronage of Edward VII and Lady de Grey much had been done to revive the former glories of Covent Garden; opera had in fact become an integral part of the London season, and the greatest singers of the day now appeared there. Early in 1914 Wagner's sacred music-drama, *Parsifal*, was performed at Covent Garden. Later, in the spring and summer, there was a full programme of Wagnerian and Italian works. This was the last year that Caruso sang at Covent Garden.

If the season of 1914 had been notable for no other reason, it would have been singled out as remarkable for the dazzling succession of Russian operas and ballets produced by Sir Joseph Beecham at Drury Lane. No fewer than ten operas and fourteen ballets were announced—five of the former and four of the latter entirely new to England. Great as had been the success of the Diaghileff Company in 1913, it was destined to be even greater in 1914. Such was the demand for seats that the theatre was almost sold out for the entire season even before the company had arrived in England. Never before, perhaps, had the historic Theatre Royal held such splendid audiences as those which flocked to these Russian operas and ballets. Night after night, notwithstanding the heat, the great theatre was crowded. To those who were young these marvellous productions were a revelation—the memory of which would be treasured to the end of their lives.

The Russian operas began, on May 29th, with Moussorgsky's masterpiece, *Boris Godounov*, portraying one of the darkest and most tragic pages in Russian history. The extraordinary dramatic power of Féodor Chaliapine as Tsar Boris, the gorgeous colouring of the scenery and costumes, the superb pageant of the Tsar's coronation, the kaleidoscopic effect of the crowd scenes, the splendid choruses, the tender and pathetic music of the nursery scene, and, above all, the terrible finale in which death puts an end to the unbearable sufferings of the conscience-stricken usurper, made a profound impression on the crowded audience.

On June 8th, another great night, Chaliapine appeared in Borodin's *Prince Igor*. It was the first time that the opera had ever been heard outside Russia. A never-to-be-forgotten experience was the wild, barbaric choruses and the war-dance of the Tartar warriors by the light of torches and camp fires. The scene was the limitless expanse of the South Russian steppes, with the low, squat tents of the nomadic Polovtzi silhouetted against a red and tawny sky. The great stage of Drury Lane was crowded with figures. The magnificent colours of the Tartar costumes glowed superbly in the golden light. The chanted chorus swelled to a tremendous crescendo. The Tartar tribesmen danced as if possessed. Wave after wave, leaping, shouting, chanting, wildly brandishing their bows above their heads, they hurled themselves forward to the very edge of the stage and there sank to the ground. The curtain fell to deafening applause.

June 15th saw the first night of Rimsky-Korsakoff's *Coq d'Or*, a glorious, exotic, dazzling spectacle which created the sensation of the season. Another unforgettable spectacle was *Scheherazade*, also by Rimsky-Korsakoff, a ballet founded on a famous episode in the *Arabian Nights*, with a gorgeous setting by Bakst. The sheer beauty of the stage pictures and the magical effect of the entrancing music held the great audience spellbound.

The season ended on July 25th with Stravinsky's *Petrouchka*, amid scenes of unprecedented enthusiasm, loudly acclaimed speeches from the stage, and shoals of bouquets.

The Court of June 4th, 1914, was a notable one for several reasons. In the first place, it was one of the most brilliant Courts of modern times. Seldom had there been a larger or a fairer assemblage of *débutantes*—the Queen herself is said to have remarked on this. Secondly, it coincided with a period of extreme political and social tension. Thirdly, it was one of the two last Courts to be held in Buckingham Palace on the eve of Armageddon, before the old order of things was swept for ever into limbo.

For the young girl of the upper class, her presentation at Court marked a metamorphosis that was both dramatic and sudden. Emerging from the sheltered, ordered life of the schoolroom— and the regimen in a good many schoolrooms, even as late as 1914, was still fairly Spartan—she was launched, as it were, at one stroke, into the grown-up world.

It was a ceremony that in most cases was looked forward to with excitement mingled with apprehension. There was the heart-shaking moment when, on the great night, she first beheld herself in her new Court dress in the mirror, crowned with her headdress of white ostrich plumes. There was the long-drawn-out delay in the Mall as the endless line of vehicles crept inch by inch towards the Palace through a continuous avenue of curious sightseers gazing in at the embarrassed occupants. There was the sudden, dazzling blaze of light and colours in the great red-carpeted Hall, thronged from wall to wall with hundreds and hundreds of *débutantes* and their mothers accompanied by fathers and brothers in uniform or Court suits of black velvet with steel swords. As in a dream she would ascend the grand staircase adorned with beautiful red and white roses, where the Yeoman of the Guard stood, with halberds in their hands, as still as statues. Then on past the throng in the Picture Gallery and the three great drawing-rooms. There was a long vista of glittering chandeliers and gleaming parquet flooring.

Punctual to the moment, the King and Queen appeared, followed by their Pages and the Royal Family. They advanced slowly through the densely crowded drawing-rooms to the Ballroom; and, as they passed, the ladies on either side sank to the ground in a deep curtsey.

So the Court began.

It was, perhaps, the outstanding example, at the very apex of the social pyramid, of the intimate mingling of society, diplomacy, and politics to which reference has already been made. From first to last the whole thing was most admirably planned, prepared, and stage-managed. The American Ambassador, who was present at this Court with his family, later described it as the 'best-managed, best-mannered show in the whole world'.

There was an echoing roll of drums from the band concealed in the gallery above. The whole assembly rose instantly to their feet as, preceded by the Lord Chamberlain's procession bowing low over their white wands of office, their Majesties entered the Ballroom; then, as the final chords of the National Anthem died away, the King and Queen slowly ascended the dais, where they stood before the Thrones to receive the Corps Diplomatique. The other members of the Royal Family also took their places on the dais, under the great canopy which had been brought over from the Durbar. The ladies of the Corps Diplomatique ranged themselves on one side of the Thrones and the Duchesses on the other. Not until the last of the Ambassadors and their ladies had made their bows and curtsies did the Sovereigns seat themselves upon the Thrones.

The orchestra played softly while, one after the other, in a long single file, the ladies who were to be presented passed slowly before their Majesties. The music and the procession continued for nearly two hours.

It was a glorious, magnificent spectacle which will never again be seen. A brilliant mêlée of uniforms, orders, stars, white and black feathers, beautiful Court gowns, waving fans, and softly shimmering tiaras. Here in the vast Ballroom were to be seen almost every known uniform in the British Empire; Chamberlains in white and gold; scarlet-clad Pages; foreign Attachés; jewelled Rajahs and Ranees; Gentlemen-at-Arms, Yeomen of the

Guard, and the King's Indian orderlies drawn up by the crimson-carpeted dais. In the ranks of the Corps Diplomatique, 'all gaudier than gold and colours ever before made man—all but me in my distinguished waiter-black', stood the American Ambassador, enjoying himself thoroughly. His amused glance fell presently on the stalwart figure of the President of the Board of Trade. 'Old John Burns stands just across the way in more gilt than any but a strong working man could carry.' Meanwhile the apparently endless procession filed on past the Thrones.

'All the men and the ladies of no high rank stand for two mortal hours while the stream of *presentées* flows by—in trains and with feathers and jewels, every one making her obeisance. The King and Queen nod—that's all. . . . The uniforms and the jewels make any opera-scene pale into sheer make-believe; the tiaras and the coronets sparkle everywhere, and the "creations" of all the great frock-makers flow along.'[1]

To the left of the dais the Ambassadors carried on a murmured conversation with one another and the gentlemen-in-waiting and the Royal Princes. The Master of the Horse offered to make a bet with Page that the American polo team would defeat the British. But at this point there came a startling interruption. One of the young girls filing past the Throne suddenly dropped on her knees before the King, and, with outstretched hands, exclaimed: 'Your Majesty, for God's sake . . . '.[2] Thereupon two gentlemen-in-waiting took her firmly by either arm and marched her hurriedly out of the Ballroom. The King gave no sign of having either seen or heard: but Queen Mary had turned very red. The long procession continued to file past; and it would appear that a good many people in the Ballroom were quite unaware that anything untoward had occurred.

At last the final presentation was made, and the ceremony ended. Once again the hidden orchestra played 'God Save the King'. The King bowed to the Ambassadors and to the Ambassadors' ladies, and the Queen curtsied—afterwards to the

[1] B. J. Hendrick, *Life and Letters of Walter H. Page*, pp. 57 et seq.
[2] 'Your Majesty, for God's sake stop torturing women!' The suffragette was the daughter of an eminent British architect, whose wife was in another part of the Palace at the time. When this unfortunate lady heard what had happened, she fainted. That night the outraged monarch wrote in his diary, 'I don't know what we are coming to'.

Duchesses, and lastly to the Ministers. The King took the Queen's hand and the Pages took her train. Preceded by the Lord Chamberlain and his satellites stepping backwards before them, the Royal Family slowly retired through the drawing-rooms to their own apartments.

Gradually the great Ballroom emptied. The Corps Diplomatique and the Court officials adjourned for supper to one room, and the general public to another. Soon the guests began to make their way back to the Hall. Another Court was over.

As the American Ambassador and his family drove out through the Palace gates at midnight, his son drew a long breath and observed contentedly:

'Mother, it comes hard on Daddy . . . but that show's worth all it costs!'

CHAPTER 14

Sarajevo and after

It is unlikely that the whole truth about the murder of Francis Ferdinand will ever be known. There had been more than one attempt on his life that day. Others besides the Pan-Servian fanatics wanted him out of the way. Nor was the Archduke, properly speaking, merely the chance victim of a brutal and senseless outrage. There was more to it than that. Francis Ferdinand's visit to the capital of Bosnia, on that particular date, was a direct challenge to Slav national feeling. 'It was deliberately timed for Serbia's national day,' Taylor observes, 'the anniversary of Kossovo. If a British royalty had visited Dublin on St Patrick's Day at the height of the Trouble, he, too, might have expected to be shot at.'[1] On the other hand, the responsibility of Servia for the crime was much greated than is generally appreciated. There was bitter resentment in Austrian official circles and among the general public at the ruthless and persistent agitation carried on by the Pan-Slav societies. It is significant that, after the crime, the weeks went by and the Serbs took no adequate steps to satisfy Austria's reasonable demands; and to this day the assassin, Gavrilo Princip, a Bosnian student, is honoured as a national hero in Jugo-Slavia. During this time the British press was practically unanimous in upholding Austria's right to take all steps necessary to prevent a recurrence of such an outrage. Still less were the crowned heads of Europe disposed to sympathize with Servia, whose troubles were largely of her own making. 'All kings', as the *Manchester Guardian* was later to observe, 'have a strong trade unionist, as well as a personal objection to regicides.'

On June 30th the Prime Minister after question time formally expressed the 'indignation and deep concern' of the House at the Sarajevo murders and of their 'profound sympathy with the Imperial and Royal family' of the Dual Monarchy. The murders

[1] A. J. P. Taylor, *The Struggle for Mastery in Europe*, p. 520, n. 2.

he described as 'one of those incredible crimes which almost make us despair of the progress of mankind'. And there for several weeks the matter rested. The truth was that it was domestic rather than external affairs that were occupying the attention of Parliament and people at this moment, just as they had done during the past two years. 'Parliament', observed the *Nation*, 'gave nearly as much time on Monday to its annual survey of the foreign affairs of a world-wide Empire as it bestowed on the municipal dispute between Purley and Croydon.'

When the subject of the assassinations was brought up after dinner, over port, at the Prime Minister's country house, Asquith asked one of his guests, the son of the Russian Ambassador, what he thought about it; and young Benckendorff replied that he believed that this time his country intended to stand firm. Several of the other guests vociferously disagreed, and a ferce argument ensued. 'The interminable and acrimonious discussion raged for so long', Benckendorff declared, 'that the most attractive guests, dispatched at last by Mrs Asquith to persuade us to join the ladies, had every difficulty in fishing us out of the dining-room.'

During practically the whole of July the House of Commons was too much taken up with the Irish controversy to have any thought for the possible consequences of Sarajevo. Matters in Ireland had gone from bad to worse with the ceaseless drilling and organizing of the Ulster Volunteers, who continued to dominate the north-eastern counties. Moreover, as a result, firstly, of the Government's inability to enforce its will in Ulster, and secondly, of the recent gun-running at Larne, the recruitment of the newly-formed National Volunteers in the Catholic parts of the country received a powerful stimulus. Though they numbered barely 2,000 at the beginning of the year, they had increased by June to over 100,000. From his Sussex manor the rebel squire, Wilfrid Scawen Blunt, wrote grimly approving of this new development:

'I confess it rouses me to hear talk again of physical force. I never believed much in the Union of Hearts without a reserve of the other, and a long experience of British Imperial ways has taught me (if I may be allowed the bull) that in dealing with British Governments, the best sort of moral force is always

Harvesting under Chanctonbury Ring, Sussex

team at Exceat, Sussex

The coastguard

Children in
sailor suits of
the period

Old skippers yarning
on the quayside

Fisherman

material force. Our people cannot be trusted to go straight without two strong incentives, money in front of them (like the
carrot in front of an ass) and a big stick behind. The Irish
National Volunteers must be the big stick.'[1]

Public apprehension increased with the approach of the 224th
anniversary of the battle of the Boyne. The 'Twelfth' this year
falling on a Sunday, the commemoration had to be transferred
to Monday, the 13th. It was certainly the greatest and most
spectacular celebration of the Boyne that had ever been seen; it
was feared that the thunder of the Orange drums, reacting upon
nerves already overstrained by the long-drawn-out crisis, would
inflame ancestral passions to explosion point; however, to everybody's relief, it all passed off peacefully. Arrayed in their blue
and purple sashes, with thousands of banners flying, and accompanied by hundreds of bands playing the Orange battle hymns,
'The Boyne Water', 'Dolly's Brae', 'The Sash my Father Wore',
and 'Derry's Walls', more than 70,000 Ulster stalwarts marched
out from Belfast to the central gathering at Drumbeg. There,
taking as his theme the ancient watchword, *No surrender!* Sir
Edward Carson made a powerful speech.

'But don't let us be under any delusion when we use the words
"No surrender". At the present moment it means to us something
very grave, and something very perilous. It means, if it is to have
any reality at all, that you are prepared to do now within the
next few weeks, if it is necessary, what your forefathers did
upon the day you are now celebrating, when King William
crossed the Boyne, and when, behind the walls of Derry, the
British connection was maintained, and your civil and religious
liberties were secured. . . . I tell the Government that in a very
short time, unless they are prepared to leave us alone, we will
recognize the Provisional Government and no other Government. . . . Give us a clean cut for Ulster or come and fight us.'

Amid a tornado of cheering Carson moved towards his peroration.

'I say it is a cruel thing at the present hour to find these men
[1] W. S. Blunt, *My Diaries* (1932), p. 838.

G

in Downing Street or Whitehall or Limehouse, or wherever they live (loud laughter), not plotting to leave us alone, but plotting to take away as much as they can from us, fighting over bits and corners of Ulster here and there, whether they might take some and leave more as a kind of sop for John Redmond and his cattle drivers and boycotters.'

In spite of the intransigent claims of the Irish leaders, the question had by now been narrowed down to the consideration of the precise area of Ulster to be excluded from the Home Rule Bill. 'There is thus but a small difference between the two disputants', noted Sir Almeric Fitzroy on the 16th, 'though, as everybody knows, the reduction of the area of difference often means an intensification of the hold which each maintains on what is left.' In a last endeavour to overcome these difficulties the King on the 18th summoned a conference of Party leaders—Liberal, Conservative, Nationalist, and Ulster Unionist — at Buckingham Palace. The conference opened on the 21st in the Council Room looking out on the Palace gardens. After an introductory speech by the King, the Speaker was called upon to take the Chair. The discussions lasted for three days; neither the Nationalist nor the Ulster representatives were really the plenipotentaries of their respective parties; and, having accomplished virtually nothing, the conference was wound up on the 24th.

As far back as October 1913 the Admiralty had arranged for a test mobilization to be held in the following year, instead of the usual summer manoeuvres. The decision was taken mainly on the grounds of economy. On July 15th the test mobilization began at Portsmouth and other depots. It was on a scale unprecedented in history. The whole operation had been most thoroughly prepared and was executed with clockwork precision. By the fifth day all three Fleets were fully manned; 20,000 naval reservists were mustered, medically examined, kitted up, and marched on board their allotted ships, which then coaled and sailed for Spithead, where, at the end of the week, a great review was held.

This was incomparably the most numerous and most formidable assemblage of fighting ships ever concentrated in British waters, marking the culmination of the past ten years' unremitting and intensive preparation for war. Covering an area about seven miles in length and two miles in breadth, the Fleet lay in eleven lines stretching from a point eastward of Spitbank Fort almost as far westward as Cowes. The long lines of warships were strikingly set off by the thickly wooded slopes of the island in the background. There were eight battle squadrons consisting of 59 battleships, 24 of them dreadnoughts. In addition to the battle-cruiser squadron, there were twelve squadrons of cruisers and light cruisers. There were thirteen flotillas of 187 destroyers, and nine flotillas of 59 submarines. The whole of this tremendous force was under the command of Admiral Sir George Callaghan, flying his flag in the new 25,000-ton super-dreadnought, the *Iron Duke*, which lay at the head of the line of battleships.

On Saturday the 18th it was fine summer weather, and exceptionally clear. Portsmouth and Southsea were *en fête* for the occasion. From the early forenoon vast crowds had gathered along the entire sea front from the old sally port to beyond the South Parade. Innumerable pleasure craft of all types and sizes, packed with spectators, cruised in the broad avenue of water between the battleships and the cruisers. During this day the cadets from the Royal Naval College at Osborne and Dartmouth were taken on board the vessels of the First and Second Fleets until the following Monday in order that they might gain some insight into the conditions of life afloat.

Delayed in town by the Irish crisis, the King did not reach Portsmouth until the late afternoon, to the disappointment of the waiting crowds; but shortly after midday Admiral Sir Hedworth Meux, the Commander-in-Chief at Portsmouth, arrived in his barge, accompanied by the First Lord and Admiral Lord Fisher, to inspect the seaplanes.

Immediately the King's arrival was signalled, a royal salute was fired by the *Victory*. It was at once taken up by the *Iron Duke*, and, before the echoes had died away, it was followed by the thunder of the guns all along the lines of anchored ships. The royal yacht entered the lines between the *Iron Duke* and the *King George* V; and the King proceeded to carry out an informal inspection of the Fleet.

At daybreak on the last day of the review, Monday, the 20th, the weather was heavy and overcast. The night had been wet, and a cold easterly wind swept the grey, rain-blurred sea. The Spithead forts and the hills of Wight were half hidden in haze.

From an early hour that morning volumes of dense black smoke had been rising from the hundreds of warships getting up steam, and a heavy smoke-cloud overhung the anchorage. At 8.30 the King, who was accompanied by the Prince of Wales, was joined by the First Lord and other members of the Board of Admiralty. At 9.0, in obedience to a signal from the *Iron Duke*, the whole armada, led by the royal yacht, steamed eastward out of the Solent. The First Fleet alone formed a line about fourteen miles in length, so that when the leading vessels had disappeared in the distance the rearmost had scarcely left the anchorage. Watched by tens of thousands of people assembled on the Esplanade and piers, and on all the beaches from Gosport to Littlehampton, the First, Second, and Third Fleets steamed out into the misty Channel. From Selsey Bill the spectators could see the whole horizon, as far as the eye could reach, covered with warships. By noon the roadstead was empty.

Later in the morning the weather cleared up. It stopped raining, and the sun, which had for some time been struggling to break through the clouds, at last appeared. The mists dispersed, and there was another brilliant July day.

When the royal yacht anchored off the Nab, there began the most impressive spectacle of the whole review. Down the great waterway glided an endless column of ships. First, the dreadnought battle-cruiser squadron in single line ahead, headed by the *Lion*, followed by the *Queen Mary, Princess Royal*, and *New Zealand*. Then in stately procession, the latest and most powerful of our battleships in two parallel columns, consisting of four battle squadrons, led by the *Iron Duke* and *King George* V : *Colossus, Hercules, Ajax, Centurion, Bellerophon, Superb, Collingwood, Marlborough; Temeraire, Neptune, Audacious, Orion, Conqueror, Monarch, Thunderer, St Vincent, Dreadnought.* Astern of the battle fleet steamed the cruiser squadrons of the First Fleet, and in their wake fifty-six torpedo-boat-destroyers in divisions of fours.

The Fleet came on past the *Victoria and Albert* in single line ahead, with mathematical precision, at 11 knots. As each ship approached the royal yacht, her band played the National

Anthem; the marines brought their rifles to the present, and the ship's company broke into hearty cheers. The sun blazed down on the blue and scarlet tunics and gleaming bayonets of the marines drawn up on the quarter-deck. The King stood on the bridge of the royal yacht with the young Prince at his side, acknowledging the salutes.

Following the First Fleet, after an interval, came the Second Fleet, comprising the 5th and 6th Battle Squadrons: the 8 *Formidables*; the *Lord Nelson*, the 5 *Duncans*, and the *Vengeance*; and the Third Fleet, comprising the 7th and 8th Battle Squadrons; the 6 *Canopus's* and 9 *Majestics*—together with their attendant cruiser squadrons and auxiliaries. The last of the torpedo-boats brought up the rear.

It took more than six hours for this immense line of warships to pass, with bands playing, seamen cheering, and marines presenting arms, before the *Victoria and Albert*.

Towards the conclusion of the review a squadron of sixteen naval seaplanes flew out from the shore towards the Nab End buoy, and, circling the royal yacht, dipped in salute; after which they sped back over the Isle of Wight to their station at Calshot.

One after another the grey ships faded away in the distance beyond the Nab.

CHAPTER 15

The ultimatum to Servia

On the afternoon of Friday, July 24th, the Cabinet was once again revolving the Irish question. The Buckingham Palace Conference, which had opened on the 21st, had finally broken down. The Nationalists refused point-blank to concede anything beyond the terms of the Amending Bill. The Unionists insisted on the 'clean cut' — that is, the permanent exclusion of the whole province of Ulster. 'Nothing could have been more amicable in tone', Asquith noted in his journal, 'or more desperately fruitless in result.' The deliberations of the last few days had turned chiefly on the geographical demarcation of the area to be excluded from the operation of the Home Rule Bill. Above all, it had been found that there were exceptional and intractable obstacles in the case of Fermanagh and Tyrone—two counties in which the rival political and religious factions were inextricably intermingled. The delegates had failed to come to any kind of agreement, as Asquith had stated in Parliament, 'either in principle or in detail'.

With the breakdown of the conference the last hopes of a peaceful settlement seemed to be vanishing. The anger and bitterness engendered by the long-drawn-out Irish quarrel were at their peak. The *impasse* was total and absolute. Government were at the end of their resources; the situation was desperate, constitutional measures had wholly failed, and civil war was expected to break out at any moment. The thoughts of Cabinet, Parliament, and people alike, it is safe to say, were centred on Ireland. What happened next has been described, in a memorable passage, by Winston Churchill:

'The discussion had reached its inconclusive end, and the Cabinet was about to separate, when the quiet grave tones of Sir Edward Grey's voice were heard reading a document which had just been brought to him from the Foreign Office. It was the

Austrian note to Servia. He had been reading or speaking for several minutes before I could disengage my mind from the tedious and bewildering debate which had just closed. We were all very tired, but gradually as the phrases and sentences followed one another, impressions of a wholly different character began to form in my mind. This note was clearly an ultimatum; but it was an ultimatum such as had never been penned in modern times. As the reading proceeded it seemed absolutely impossible that any State in the world could accept it, or that any acceptance, however abject, would satisfy the aggressor. The parishes of Fermanagh and Tyrone faded back into the mists and squalls of Ireland, and a strange light began immediately but by perceptible gradations, to fall and grow upon the map of Europe.'[1]

Though the Austrian ultimatum came as a shock, it was not wholly unexpected. Quite early in the month there had been angry demonstrations in Austria, not only against Servia, but also against Russia. For some time a violent press campaign had been raging on either side of the Austro-Servian frontier. In the middle of July there had come disturbing rumours, but nothing certain; on the 14th there was a stock exchange panic in Vienna, and prices had also slumped in Berlin. Nevertheless, life on the Continent had gone on much as usual. Cambon had felt such little concern about the matter that he arranged to go on holiday in the latter half of the month. William II departed for his cruise in the Norwegian fiords. Helmuth von Moltke, the German Chief of Staff, was staying at Karlsbad with his wife and daughter. Grand Admiral von Tirpitz had departed to a Swiss spa. Both the German and Austrian Ministers of War were also away on holiday. In central Europe many thousands of families had already left the towns for the seaside or the mountains; while, less fortunate than they, millions of peasants toiled in the harvest fields under the blazing July sun—among them a good many youngsters released from military service under special harvest furlough.

But on July 7th the Crown Council of the Dual Monarchy, encouraged by an unconditional pledge of support from William II, had resolved to settle accounts with Servia once and for all. The war party had been given a free hand. The German Govern-

[1] W. S. Churchill, *The World Crisis*, I, p. 193.

ment approved of their Ally's note to Servia without ever having
seen it. ('What it amounts to,' the British Chargé d'Affaires later
told the German Foreign Minister, 'is that you have given
Austria a blank cheque.') It would appear that this decision was
largely influenced by the belief which prevailed in high official
circles in Germany that Russia dared not march.

'I still hope and believe even now', von Jagow wrote to Lichnowsky on July 18th, 'that the conflict can be localized. . . .
The more resolute Austria shows herself, the more energetically
we support her, the more likely Russia will be to keep quiet. . . .
We shall not fail to hear some blustering in St Petersburg, but
fundamentally Russia is not yet ready to strike.'[1]

This was an error. The present military strength of the
Russian Empire was rated far too low in German official circles.
Their Foreign Ministry was seriously misinformed about her
preparedness for war and the consequent risk of embroilment
over Servia.

The secret of the ultimatum was well kept. Berchtold pur-
posely arranged for the Austrian note to be held back until after
the French President's visit to St Petersburg. Still, despite this
precaution, there was a feeling of uneasiness in the air. Shortly
before the delivery of the ultimatum, Lichnowsky informed Grey
that Austria was about to take some step, and that he regarded
the situation 'as very uncomfortable'.

Immediately the Austrian ultimatum became known, the
alarm bells began to ring furiously in all the chancellries of
Europe, and the newspaper offices hummed with rumours. Not
only were the Austrian demands of unprecedented severity but
they had to be accepted unconditionally within forty-eight
hours. Failing this, Austria would march.

'No one could say what is going to happen in the East of
Europe', Asquith wrote in his journal on the 26th. 'The news
this morning is that Servia has capitulated on the main point,
but it is very doubtful if any reservation will be accepted by
Austria, who is resolved upon a complete and final humiliation.
The curious thing is that on many, if not most, of the points
Austria has a good and Servia a very bad case, but the Austrians
are quite the stupidest people in Europe. There is a brutality
about their mode of procedure which will make most people

[1] Q. Wolff, *The Eve of 1914*, p. 437.

think that this is a case of a big Power wantonly bullying a little one. Anyhow,' he concluded grimly, 'it is the most dangerous situation for the last forty years.'[1]

Servia's reply to the ultimatum was virtually to accept the terms proposed; making various reservations in respect of a few points only. Notwithstanding her submissive attitude, however, Austria, on the expiration of the forty-eight hours time limit, broke off diplomatic relations with Servia and ordered her Minister to quit Belgrade.

Directly it was known that the Servian reply had been rejected and that war was imminent, the people of Vienna went wild with delight. Immense crowds paraded the streets and chanted patriotic songs until the small hours of the morning. The rowdy demonstrations in Vienna and many other of the principal cities of the Dual Monarchy showed how popular the idea of war with Servia had become. 'The language of the press this morning', the British Ambassador, Sir Maurice de Bunsen, telegraphed from Vienna, 'leaves the impression that the surrender of Servia is neither expected nor really desired.'

On the 25th there were warlike demonstrations in Berlin also. A great procession marched down Unter den Linden, the van chanting 'Die Wacht am Rhein' and the rear the Austrian national hymn, 'Gott erhalte'. Other processions marched from the Imperial Palace to the Brandenburg Gate, and from Bismarck's monument to the Austrian Embassy. There were angry cries of 'Nieder mit Serbien! Nieder mit Russland!' Next day the Berlin demonstrations took on a semi-official aspect, as the Guards' band marched out and played the Austrian national hymn amidst fervent applause. Meanwhile the financial and commercial interests of the Continent took fright and the stock exchanges of Berlin, Vienna, Paris, and St Petersburg were severely depressed.

On the 25th our Ambassador in St Petersburg called on the Russian Foreign Minister and urged him to exercise caution. 'I said all I could to impress prudence on the Minister for Foreign Affairs,' observed Sir George Buchanan, 'and warned him that if Russia mobilized, Germany would not be content with mere mobilization, or give Russia time to carry out hers, but would probably declare war at once.'

[1] Earl of Oxford and Asquith, *Memories and Reflections* (1928), II, pp. 5-6.

On the same day the German Foreign Minister discussed the matter with Theodor Wolff, the editor of the *Berliner Tageblatt*, who had returned in haste to the capital from a holiday on the Dutch coast. Wolff spoke of the danger of a general war. Von Jagow did not agree; he believed that the diplomatic situation was very favourable for the Central Powers, as neither Russia nor France desired war. The Russians, as he had already informed Lichnowsky in London, were not yet ready to strike—in two years' time, added the Minister, the danger would be far greater than it was at present.

'As I left he said: "I do not regard the situation as critical"— still with his soft voice and the little smile that seemed limited to his rather melancholy lips and no true index to his real feelings.

'At the door, on the point of leaving, I asked him one more question:

' "So far, we have only talked politics: one personal question —I have left my family behind at Scheveningen; ought I to bring them home?"

'He hesitated a moment and then answered:

' "There is no necessity, really no necessity." '[1]

Grey was under strong pressure from both senior officials at the Foreign Office and his Ambassadors in Paris and St Petersburg to stand firm on the side of the Entente. Buchanan telegraphed from St Petersburg that if we failed to do so, whatever was the issue of the war, we should find ourselves without a friend in Europe, and our Indian Empire would be under threat of attack by Russia.

On the 27th the British Ambassador in Vienna expressed his opinion that the Austro-Hungarian Government were determined on war with Servia and that they considered their position as a Great Power to be at stake. 'This country', declared Sir Maurice de Bunsen, 'has gone wild with joy at the prospect of war with Servia, and its postponement or prevention would undoubtedly be a great disappointment.' To that end Berchtold deliberately held back the Servian note accepting most of the Austrian demands for three whole days; and in fact did not pub-

[1] Wolff, *The Eve of 1914*, p. 451.

lish it till the evening of the 28th, which was the day on which
Austria declared war on Servia.

On the night of the 26th angry and excited crowds filled the
streets of Vienna, St Petersburg and Belgrade, and alarming
headlines appeared in the evening editions of the Sunday newspapers. The next day saw a violent press campaign launched
against Germany in France.

As usual all the Ministers left town for the week-end. On
Saturday Churchill went down to his house at Overstrand, near
Cromer, where his wife was seriously ill. In order that he might
be in continuous touch with the Admiralty he had had a special
operator installed in the local telegraph office. That afternoon
the news reached him that Servia had submitted to the Austrian
ultimatum; and he recalls that when he went to bed that night
he felt that the trouble might blow over. But on Sunday the
news was bad. Warlike passions were rising in nearly every
capital in Europe. Twice Prince Louis warned him over the telephone that the situation was rapidly deteriorating. Churchill
went down to the shore with his children and spent the morning, as he has related, damming the rivulets which streamed
down the sands in the wake of the ebbing tide. (Irrigation
schemes were to be a lifelong 'ploy' of Churchill's.) It was on
the sands that a telegram reached him from the *Daily Mail*,
emphasizing the increasing gravity of the crisis. After his second
telephone conversation with Prince Louis, he resolved to return
to town.

Meanwhile in the almost deserted Admiralty the First Sea
Lord had come to the conclusion that the Fleet must not be
allowed to disperse; and that afternoon on his own responsibility
he drafted and dispatched the telegrams cancelling the
Demobilization Orders. 'When the Ministers hurried back late
that evening they cordially approved of my action', Prince Louis
observed, 'and we had the drawn sword in our hands to back up
our urgent advice.' The Fleet was thus ordered to 'stand fast';
and next morning the following notice appeared in all the
newspapers.

NO MANOEUVRE LEAVE
We received the following statement from the Secretary of the
Admiralty at an early hour this morning.

Orders have been given to the First Fleet, which is concentrated at Portland, not to disperse for manoeuvre leave for the present. All vessels of the Second Fleet are remaining at their home ports in proximity to their balance crews.

On the evening of the 25th, leaving Nicolson in charge at the Foreign Office, Grey had gone down to his fishing cottage in Hampshire. It was radiant summer weather. In the rays of the westering sun he crossed the fields behind Itchen Abbas and followed the familiar way past the ancient avenue of limes to the little, low-roofed lodge half hidden in the trees. Here, where some of the happiest hours of his life had been passed, Grey enjoyed a momentary respite from the troubles that were crowding upon him. Next day, Sunday, was one of the finest days of that beautiful summer. The air was fragrant with the scent of meadowsweet, lime-blossom, and sweet briar, and murmurous with the cooing and crooning of doves and the hum of myriads of bees. The small green lawn before the cottage looked down on the swiftly flowing Itchen, fringed with beds of sedges and reed-mace, on a wide expanse of water-meadows where some short-horns, knee-deep in the high grass, were grazing in the shade of the old spreading oak-trees, and on the thickly wooded slopes across the valley. Most of the birds that had nested in spring in the bushes round the cottage and in the nearby chalk-pit were silent now; but the wrens and greenfinches sang on, and throughout the hours of sunshine there was the busy boom of the bees gathering honey from the lime-blossom.

It had been agreed between Grey and Nicolson that if things got worse and no one else moved the four Powers who were not directly concerned in the quarrel should mediate in unison between Austria and Russia. These were Germany and Italy, of the one group; and France and Great Britain, of the other. Pending the result of the Conference, the four Powers were to ask the Governments of Austria, Russia, and Servia to suspend all warlike preparations. During Grey's absence the situation that was developing so alarmed Nicolson that he hurriedly summoned his chief back to London and dispatched the proposal for a Conference.

At first the response of the Powers appeared entirely favourable. First, St Petersburg approved, then Paris, then Rome. Lastly, on the 27th, Lichnowsky informed Grey that his Government accepted in principle the plan of mediation between Austria and Russia by the other four Powers, 'reserving, of course, their right as an ally to help Austria if attacked'. For a moment the tension was relaxed.

At the outset of the crisis Grey had laid it down that, so long as the dispute concerned Austria and Servia alone, he did not feel called upon to intervene; but that, directly it was a matter between Austria and Russia, it became a question of the peace of Europe and therefore a matter of general concern. Grey's anxious endeavours to preserve the peace were, however, severely handicapped by his reluctance to take any step which might be unfavourably interpreted at St Petersburg.

On the 27th the Russian Ambassador informed Grey that in German and Austrian official circles the impression prevailed that in any event Great Britain would stand aside; and he deplored the effect that such an impression must produce.

'This impression ought', Grey hastened to reply, 'to be dispelled by the orders we have given to the First Fleet, which is concentrated, as it happens, at Portland, not to disperse for manoeuvre leave.' At the same time he added that this statement should not be taken to mean that anything more than diplomatic action was promised.

An hour later he was trying the effect of this argument on the Austrian Ambassador, Count Mensdorff.

'I feared', said Grey, 'that it would be expected in St Petersburg that the Servian reply would diminish the tension, and now, when Russia found that there was increased tension, the situation would become increasingly serious. Already the effect on Europe was one of anxiety. I pointed out that our fleet was to have dispersed today, but we had felt unable to let it disperse. We should not think of calling up reserves at this moment, and there was no menace in what we had done about our fleet; but, owing to the possibility of a European conflagration, it was impossible for us to disperse our forces at this moment.'

When Cambon visited Grey on the 28th he expressed strong

approval of the Admiralty's decision to hold the fleet together at the conclusion of the recent exercises. For, he declared, 'if once it were assumed that Britain would certainly stand aside from a European war, the chance of preserving peace would be very much imperilled'.

The net effect of these affirmations and reservations, however, was that Germany and Austria still expected Great Britain to remain neutral, while Russia and France evidently counted on her active support. At this point Lichnowsky in London did his utmost to warn the German Government of the dangers of the situation. On the 27th he wired to Berlin: 'If it comes to war in these circumstances we shall have England against us'.

Grey's policy now suffered a double reverse. The German Government, suddenly changing their mind, refused point-blank to take part in the proposed Conference, on the grounds that it would be in the nature of a court of arbitration which (they averred) could only be convened at the request of Austria and Russia. St Petersburg, too, favoured direct negotiations with Vienna; and Germany supported this suggestion. Lord Samuel recalls that, happening to enter the Cabinet room a few minutes before one of the meetings, he discovered Grey sitting in his place alone. Samuel says that he would never forget the passion in his colleague's voice as he exclaimed—'There's some *devilry* going on in Berlin!' Grey himself has related in his memoirs that from this time on the situation rapidly degenerated.

'After the refusal of a Conference one blow to the prospects of peace followed after another. I do not suggest that I thought them the direct consequence of the refusal of a Conference; they were rather like the deliberate, relentless strokes of Fate, determined on human misfortune, as they are represented in Greek tragedy. It was as if Peace were engaged in a struggle for life, and, whenever she seemed to have a chance, some fresh and more deadly blow was struck.'[1]

It will be remembered that Austria had held back the Servian reply to her ultimatum for three days, which was sufficient time to enable the smouldering fires of warlike passion in Austria and Germany to grow into a conflagration of such magnitude it

[1] Grey of Fallodon, *Twenty-five Years* (1928), II, pp. 174-5.

would be impossible to control. So, indeed, it came to pass. After
reading the placatory Servian note, William II declared there was
no longer any cause for war; a resounding diplomatic triumph
had been gained without a shot fired; and his Government now
endeavoured to restrain their ally. But it was too late. On July
28th Austria declared war on Servia, immediately following this
up with a bombardment of Belgrade, and thereby set off a chain-
reaction which, within a matter of days, effectually exploded
the banked-up powder magazine of Europe.

Great Britain was already preparing for war. On the 27th was
held the first of the Cabinets on the European crisis which continued daily and, later on, even twice a day. Every day the
Cabinet met at 11 a.m. and on several days sat for hours. Grey
laboured desperately but in vain: first, to preserve the peace of
Europe, and, when that finally proved impossible, to stand firm
by the Entente. The First Lord was in his element; he was firmly
resolved that, if the worst came to the worst, the Fleet must be
ready. The significance of these measures was not lost on the
German Naval Attaché, who, on the evening of the 28th,
telegraphed to Berlin:

'Admiralty are not publishing ships' movements. 2nd Fleet
remains fully manned. Schools closed in naval bases; preliminary
measures taken for recall from leave. According to unconfirmed
news 1st Fleet still at Portland, one submarine flotilla left Portsmouth. It is assumed that Admiralty is preparing for mobilization on the quiet. . . . In the naval bases and dockyards great
activity reigns; in addition special measures of precaution have
been adopted, all dockyards, magazines, oil tanks, etc., being put
under guard. Repairs of ships in dockyard hands are being
speeded up. A great deal of night work is being done. . . .
Movements of ships, which are generally published by the
Admiralty, have been withheld since yesterday.'

On the same day the decision had been taken at the Admiralty
to dispatch the First Fleet to its war station in the Orkneys.
Churchill relates that he considered it inexpedient to bring this
matter to the notice of the Cabinet. He therefore informed only
the Prime Minister. 'To him alone I confided the intention of
moving the Fleet to its war station on July 30th. He looked at

me with a hard stare and gave a sort of grunt. I did not require anything else.' At 5 o'clock that afternoon the Admiralty telegraphed to the Commander-in-Chief, Sir George Callaghan:

'Tomorrow, Wednesday, the First Fleet is to leave Portland for Scapa Flow. Destination is to be kept secret except to flag and commanding officers. As you are required at the Admiralty, Vice-Admiral 2nd Battle Squadron is to take command. Course from Portland is to be shaped to southward, then a middle Channel course to the Straits of Dover. The Squadrons are to pass through the Straits without lights during the night and to pass outside the shoals on their way north. *Agamemnon* is to remain at Portland, where the Second Fleet will assemble.' [1]

At daybreak on the 27th, the 2nd, 3rd, and 4th Battle Squadrons — as well as the 2nd and 3rd Cruiser Squadrons — had already sailed for their home ports to give leave. They were recalled by wireless, ordering them to return immediately. In pursuance of these orders, they were steaming at full speed up-Channel in the early morning of the 28th, when they were sighted by Hilaire Belloc in his yacht, the *Nona*, off Start Point.

'Nothing was further from my mind than war and armament as the sun rose on that glorious July morning, right out of a clear horizon, towards which the wind blew fresh and cool. It was a light but steady wind of morning that filled my sails as I sat at the tiller with a blanket about me, and laying her head to the north.

'We had just rounded the Start at dawn. . . . Immediately after its rising a sort of light haze filled the air to eastward. . . . In this loneliness and content, as I sailed northward, I chanced to look after an hour steering or so, eastward again towards the open sea—and then it was that there passed the vision I shall remember for ever, or for so long as the longest life may last.

'Like ghosts, like things themselves made of mist, there passed between me and the newly risen sun, a procession of great forms, all in line, hastening eastward. It was the Fleet recalled.

'The slight haze along that distant water had thickened, perhaps, imperceptibly; or perhaps the great speed of the men-of-

[1] Q. W. S. Churchill, *The World Crisis*, I, p. 212.

war buried them too quickly in the distance. But, from whatever cause, this marvel was of short duration. It was seen for a moment, and in a moment was gone.

'Then I knew that war would come, and my mind was changed.'[1]

On the 29th Churchill secured from the Cabinet the authority to put into force the 'Precautionary Period' regulations. The emergency measures so carefully conceived and prepared by the Committee of Imperial Defence were now set in motion, as the arrangements prescribed in the War Book successively came into operation. Naval harbours were quickly cleared, ports, docks, and bridges guarded, and ships boarded and examined; police leave was stopped, and coast-watchers patrolled the shores. Also flotilla precautions against any possible surprise attack were developed.

As Balfour was strolling in Cockspur Street on this day he met Lord Fisher, who informed him that 'Winston' had just ordered the Fleet to its war station. Years after, Balfour recalled that late that night he was walking home after dining with a friend 'and looking at all the people in the street going along happily, and saying to myself that I knew that war was coming upon them'.

By this time the two crises—the domestic and the European— were running neck and neck. Earlier in the week events had taken a grave turn in Ireland. In Dublin Sunday, indeed, had not passed so peacefully as in Itchen Abbas or Cromer.

Some time before a group of leading Irish Nationalists had managed to purchase on the Continent a large number of rifles, which in due course were transhipped, off the Ruytingen Banks, from a German tug to Erskine Childers's 30-ton cutter, the *Asgard*, and also to a slightly smaller cutter belonging to Conor O'Brien, the *Kelpie*. Like Childers, O'Brien was a skilful and experienced yachtsman; with him on this cruise he had his sister (who acted as his mate and emergency cook) and several others, of varying capabilities. Long afterwards O'Brien related, with much interesting and amusing detail, the story of their

[1] Hilaire Belloc, *The Cruise of the 'Nona'* (1925), pp. 149-50.

adventurous passage to Ireland with the contraband cargo. How off St Margaret's Bay a division of dreadnoughts, suddenly looming up out of the mist, swept past them, in line abreast, on their way to the review at Spithead. How day after day the cutter sailed on, sometimes close in with the shore, sometimes far out in the Channel, or lay becalmed. How after rounding the Lizard, a thick fog came on, and (having by this time run out of bread) O'Brien anchored in Gwavas Lake off Newlyn, out of sight of the land, and secretly sent a boat in, which in due course returned with the loaves and newspapers. (It was then that they learned of the European crisis.) How, after bucketing through Bardsey Sound, they transhipped their cargo to the *Chotah*, which was equipped with an auxiliary engine. Finally, on Sunday morning they sailed across St George's Channel, and that night assisted the crew of the *Chotah* to unload the rifles in Wicklow harbour.

The *Asgard* had arrived off Howth shortly after midday. A body of 3,000 National Volunteers had earlier marched out from Dublin and occupied the little port in force. A motor-boat was supposed to have been waiting to signal to the *Asgard* that the coast was clear—but, owing to the weather, it had not arrived, and it appeared that none of the Volunteers cared to trust themselves to a sailing vessel. Punctually at 12.45 the *Asgard* stood into Howth harbour between the piers; Childers having decided to chance it without waiting for the signal. The cutter was moored to one of the piers and the disembarkation of the rifles began. The Volunteers each took a rifle and the rest were hurried away in motor-lorries.

As soon as the arms had been landed, the *Asgard* sailed away and the Volunteers set out on their return journey. But the assistant commission of police in Dublin, a certain Mr Harrel, had already been warned by telephone of what had been going on at Howth and had called out both the police and the military. After a savage scuffle on the Howth road between the troops and the Volunteers, the latter managed to get away with most of their rifles. Some time later, on their return to the city, the troops were set on by an infuriated crowd, which presently booed and stoned them. Exactly how it happened has never been satisfactorily ascertained—but on their arrival in the centre of the city, at Bachelor's Walk beside the Liffey, the soldiers suddenly turned about and fired on the crowd. Several persons were killed and many more wounded, half of them seriously. A number of the victims were merely passers-by and in no way concerned in the row with the troops; for the firing had been indiscriminate, and among those shot down was a youth cycling across a bridge at some distance.

The news of the shootings spread swiftly throughout Catholic Ireland and a fierce cry of wrath arose. Whatever explanation or defence might be attempted by the authorities, there could be no question that, for all practical purposes, there existed one law for the Ulster Volunteers and another for their Nationalist opponents. As one of the Irish leaders had pointed out to the police on that Sunday, there could be no possible offence simply in carrying arms, 'since the right that had been allowed in one Irish city clearly could not, a week later, become an offence in another Irish city'. The tottering prestige of the British Government in Ireland was dealt a blow from which it was destined never to recover. At the same time a powerful impetus was given to the Nationalist volunteering movement. Last but not least, the news of the Howth gun-running and its sequel confirmed the belief held in Berlin and other foreign capitals that for the time being Great Britain's hands were tied and that consequently she would be unable to intervene on the Continent.

CHAPTER 16

'The officers are going'

The month of July, which had opened in a blaze of heat, continued for the most part to be warm and sunny. Conditions of drought had prevailed for months: now root crops were badly affected. Day after day the corn ripened in the torrid sunshine—everything presaged an early harvest; the broad fields of rippling wheat were speckled and streaked with scarlet poppies, which love the heat; the hedgerows lining the dusty white lanes were fragrant with woodbine and wild roses. The Kentish cherry orchards had borne a record crop—there seemed to be more cherries than leaves. By the middle of the month the second crop of hay was ready for mowing. These hot July days brought out the butterflies in abundance. Clouded yellows fluttered over the surface of the clover. In a few favoured localities one of the rarer British butterflies, the purple emperor, was to be seen soaring round the tops of the tallest oaks. An occasional swallow-tail was reported from the fens. The nightingale had been silent this month and more in the woods and spinneys of southern England; but the chur of the nightjar and the sharp rattle of the corncrake were sometimes to be heard, afar off, in the warm summer dusk.

With the season of flower shows approaching, the cottage gardens were looking their best. Farm labourers took great pride in their fruit, vegetables, and flowers; and there was generally keen rivalry between cottage and cottage, and village and village. The cricket season was also in full swing; and here again there was great enthusiasm for the local team, whose fortunes were followed with intense interest. In the higher circles of the community there was the usual crop of July weddings, with the 'big house' crowded with guests, general rejoicings in the village, and schoolchildren strewing rose-petals before the happy bride as, with her attendant maids, she emerged into the sunlit church-yard.

212

Already the season of harvest and of 'harvest home' was approaching. After that there would be the ploughing match, and not many weeks later it would be Christmas again. So the country year went by—so certain, so stable, so secure. Would it ever change?

Meanwhile, London sweltered in the heat. The temperature on the first day of the month, at noon, reached eighty-six degrees in the shade. The fleets of red motor omnibuses blazed in the sunshine. Straw hats and parasols were everywhere. The 'flappers', who were young damsels who had not yet put their hair up, paraded in their gayest frocks. Many of the children—girls as well as boys—were dressed in cool white sailor suits. Strollers in the parks sought the shade of the trees, or lingered beside the plashing fountains. The itinerant ice-cream vendors attracted eager crowds of customers. In the streets and squares the torrid air shimmered above the tarred wood-blocks. Sunblinds and awnings redoubled in numbers. The water-carts were out in the oven-like suburban ways, and soon the plaintive cry of the lavender sellers began to be heard:

Will you buy my sweet blooming lavender . . .

One of the best known and loveliest of all our English street cries, *Will you buy* is evocative of those serene summers of long ago as is the sound of the muffin man's bell of bygone winter fogs and frosts.

At Wimbledon the finest players from both sides of the Atlantic were competing for the lawn tennis championships. In the warm summer nights the grounds of the White City and Earl's Court Exhibition, scintillating with myriads of many-coloured lights, were thronged with visitors. The people sat in the little green chairs around the bandstands and listened to the strains of the new waltz, *Destiny*, without any inkling of the tragic significance which that melody would hold for them in years to come. The parks and other open spaces had never been so popular.

One of the commonest topics of conversation at this time was whether a foul blow had been struck in the fight between Carpentier and Gunboat Smith. Some said it had, and some said it hadn't. Hardly anyone evinced much interest in the news that a certain Russian mystic named Grigorieff Rasputin, who was reputed to exercise an unwholesome influence over the Imperial family, had been stabbed, in an obscure village affray, somewhere on the other side of Europe.

The Court mourning for the deaths of the Archduke and his wife had for the time being stopped the dancing; but the opera houses had benefited, and, despite the heat, there were packed houses nightly at both Covent Garden and Drury Lane. A good many women wore black, but with diamonds and pearls the mourning note was materially relieved. The tragedy made little impact on London society as a whole, though only a few months before the murdered Archduke had been a guest of King George and Queen Mary at Buckingham Palace.

Henley Regatta opened on Wednesday, July 1st, in this brilliant summer weather. In the phenomenal heat which was making life a burden on baking pavements and in airless rooms in town it was pleasant enough on the water. A thunderstorm which threatened towards midday happily blew over. There was a remarkably large attendance that day, which included considerable numbers of foreigners (French, German, and American voices could be heard on all sides); for there was nothing quite like Henley anywhere else in the world, and the regatta was an international event.

The setting was the broad straight reach, stretching northward from Henley between an avenue of lofty poplars, with the temple on Regatta Island in the distance gleaming white in the sunlight, against a background of densely wooded hills. A whole armada of punts, skiffs, and canoes lined the booms on either side of the long stretch of sunlit water which was the course. Never before had Henley presented such a scene of vivid and variegated colours — the gay summer frocks vying with the brightly coloured Japanese paper sunshades, which the men as well as the women carried. Hour after hour the sun blazed down remorselessly on the cool muslins and embroidered lawns, on the straw hats and flannels, on the scarves and blazers, and on the bunting and awnings fluttering lazily in the breeze.

English national pride suffered some rather painful shocks in

the course of the next few days. On the 2nd, in all four heats of
the Grand Challenge Cup, a foreign eight was matched against
an English one; and in all four heats the English eight was
defeated. The most thrilling race on the 2nd was between
Leander and Harvard. The two boats were rowing in ding-dong
fashion until they reached Fawley, at which point the English
crew held a quarter-length lead — then Harvard, suddenly
quickening their stroke and rowing with tremendous dash and
determination, took the lead, and arrived at the winning-post a
length ahead of their rival.

Friday was dismally wet and dull; but on Saturday, the 4th,
the radiant summer weather returned and rowing conditions
were practically ideal. It was a day of blazing sunshine, tempered by a cool, refreshing breeze. Once again a great crowd
lined the booms. On the 4th, in the most exciting race of the
whole regatta, Italy won the Diamond Challenge Sculls. The
English sculler, C. M. Stuart, got away to a good start, largely
through the mishap of his Italian rival, Sinigaglia, in grazing a
pile, which left him nearly two lengths astern. But Sinigaglia
rowed with such skill and *élan* that Stuart's lead was gradually
reduced, and, after passing Fawley, the boats drew almost level.
Then the heavier man's weight told decisively; and in the end
Stuart just rowed himself out and Sinigaglia finished alone.
Saturday also saw the final heat for the Grand Challenge Cup
between the two American crews, the Union Boat Club of
Boston and Harvard. (It was the first time on record that England
failed to have a crew in the finals.) Boston got away to a good
start and gained a quarter of a length. But Harvard, rowing
magnificently, quickly drew level and were leading at Fawley;
after which they rowed right away and won the race by a good
length, finishing amidst a hurricane of applause—above which
rose, triumphantly, the strident Harvard 'yell'.

It was some consolation for the English spectators that
Leander beat Mayence, the German four, in the Stewards' Cup
final. Mayence led all the way until, at Fawley, they were a
length ahead; then the Leander stroke, rowing at the top of his
form, made one of the spurts for which he was famous. The
spectators became frantic with excitement. The German stroke
attempted to spurt too; but his crew were unable to respond, and
their lead was rapidly reduced. Only 100 yards from the finish,

when they were still a few feet ahead, the German four, completely exhausted, 'cracked' and stopped rowing.

On July 10th the radiant weather drew an exceptional throng for the Eton and Harrow match. There must have been something like 20,000 people present that Friday — perhaps the largest and most distinguished audience on record. The new boxes as well as the grandstand boxes were packed with spectators, and the space reserved for the coaches was crowded to the last inch. The stands were gay with colour—garden-party frocks, silk hats and white waistcoats, blue cornflowers in buttonholes, and light blue tassels on walking-sticks and umbrellas. A notable feature of this day's attendance was the unusually large number of young children who had been brought to view the match. The Duke of Devonshire's box was crowded with excited youngsters waving large flags of light blue whenever Eton scored. It was a grilling hot day, with light breezes occasionally fluttering the red and white awnings which hung above the coaches.

The Eton and Harrow match was one of the principal events of the London season and the greatest society cricket match of the year. But for the boys the play outweighed the social aspect of the occasion. Several hundred pairs of keen young eyes watched every ball, every stroke, and every smart bit of fielding. Dark blue handkerchiefs were jubilantly waved by the Harrovians whenever an Eton wicket fell. (In this connection the *Times* correspondent observed: 'The yell that announces the fall of a wicket can never be mistaken; there is a strident brutality about it that is never roused by the biggest hit'.)

Harrow, who went in first, were in a strong position at the end of the first day's play. But in their second innings, on the 11th, notwithstanding the fine stand made by their captain, G. W. Wilson, and W. K. McClintock, who scored 64 runs in 70 minutes, their batting broke down badly on a good wicket and they failed to follow up their advantage. The overthrow of the Harrovian batsmen was largely due to Foster, who, bowling from the Nursery end, in five overs succeeded in taking four wickets for 16 runs. McClintock was finally bowled out and Wilson caught. The consequence was that Harrow were all out just before the luncheon interval for only 144.

At a quarter past two Eton set to work in good heart to get 231 to win. Just as Foster's bowling had saved the day for Eton in the morning, so did the fruitful partnership of Hambro and Crossman (who between them put on 73 runs) set them on the road to victory. Some time later, with 43 runs still needed, T. S. Hankey and F. Anson, batting pluckily and well, rose to the occasion; with the result that, just before six, a drive to the boundary won the match for Eton by four wickets.

The excitement during the last hour of play had been intense —just before the end, the shouting and counter-shouting between the overs seemed to die away into a tense and breathless silence.

Immediately Eton's victory was declared, the two Etonian batsmen ran for their lives towards the pavilion in order to evade the somewhat overwhelming congratulations of their supporters; at the same instant the crowd swarmed over the ropes and flooded the field; and a more than usually exciting scrimmage ensued between the rival factions assembled to cheer outside the pavilion.

The scene of the final 'rag' was the Earl's Court Exhibition, where a large number of the boys and their families spent the evening after the match. At first all was order and decorum. At the Welcome Club—the social centre of the Exhibition—there was a Guards' band playing during dinner, and afterwards the boys started dancing with their sisters. Later on the fun began. As the twilight descended and the lights were lit in the Exhibition grounds, one lot of boys inside the Clubhouse began to chant 'E-ton!' and another lot replied with 'Harrow!'

Before long there was a general exodus from the Clubhouse and the 'rag' began in earnest. The representatives of the rival schools, with light blue or dark blue scarves tied round their silk hats, paraded the grounds and galleries of the Exhibition in large bodies; and soon the gardens of 'Sunny Spain' rang with the opposing war-cries, 'E - e - e - ton!' 'Harr - o - w!'

The scrimmage that had begun outside the pavilion at Lord's a few hours earlier was joyfully renewed whenever these roving bands happened to meet. Shining silk hats were hurled high into the air; blue-tasselled umbrellas, brandished like shillelaghs, were cracked down upon their opponents' headgear (an operation generally known as 'tile-tapping'); large numbers of top hats were irretrievably ruined. These sorties were made and sustained with the utmost good humour, they were all part of the 'rag'.

Many of the boys, accompanied by their parents, sisters, and cousins, had invaded the numerous sideshows at the Exhibition, and sampled in succession the Giant Coaster, the Half Twist, the Bowl Slide, the Helter Skelter, the Water Chute, and the Joy Wheel. It was at the last of these that a party of Etonians managed to grab the end of a rope from the men who were operating the mechanism of the Wheel, and a spirited tug-of-war ensued. Another Etonian had got hold of a fireman's brass helmet. By this time not only the boys, but also a good many of their fathers and uncles, had wholly abandoned themselves to the spirit of the 'rag'. 'The tug-of-war on the Joy Wheel', relates an eye witness, 'had convinced an Old Etonian that he was a boy again, so he pinned a bit of light blue silk on his tall hat and shouted "Eton" with the best of them.'

While the fun was at its height the young Prince of Wales appeared on the scene, and seemed greatly to enjoy himself. Another of the distinguished visitors that night was a Russian grandee, the Grand Duke Michael (one rather wonders what he thought about it all!). Finally, after what was probably the best —as it was certainly the last—of all the Eton and Harrow nights at Earl's Court, the tired but happy youngsters proceeded uproariously homeward in taxis and motor-cars.

On July 16th, as a magnificent wind-up to the Court festivities of the season, a State Ball was held at Buckingham Palace. Some 2,000 guests—members of the Corps Diplomatique, Government and Opposition; Dukes and Duchesses, Marquesses and Marchionesses, Earl and Countesses, Viscounts and Viscountesses, Lords and Ladies, Baronets, Knights, Gentlemen, Ladies, and Misses; officers of the Navy and Army — took their pleasure among the wealth of beautiful flowers which transformed the galleries and chambers of the Royal Palace into a garden of enchantment on Court Ball nights. The air was scented with summer fragrances, and the glittering chandeliers blazed down on a shimmering, dazzling scene of ever-changing colour and movement. The following was the programme of dances that night:

Quadrille	Methusalem	Strauss
Waltz	Gold and Silver	Lehar
Quadrille	Zigeunerbaron	Strauss
Waltz	Seduccion	Cremìeux
Waltz	Donauweibchen	Strauss
Waltz	Nights of Gladness	Ancliffe
Polka	Sängerlust	Strauss
Waltz	The Cinema Star	Gilbert
Waltz	Destiny	Baynes
Waltz	Morgenblätter	Strauss
Waltz	Désir du Moment	Fortoni

The London season drew to its close. Among the last of the balls which had rendered the present season exceptionally brilliant was that given at the Speaker's House on July 15th, which was attended by a great many young officers, nearly all of whom were to fall in action within a few months. Three days later another important ball was given by the Marchioness of Salisbury at the family mansion in Arlington Street. The great house was filled with flowers sent up from Hatfield for the occasion; which, like the Court Ball already mentioned, belonged to an era whose death-knell was so soon to strike.

The end of the summer term brought the last of the Speech Day addresses, usually a blend of good sense and humour, altruism and realism, platitude and humbug. There were the stereotyped references to the classics, the place of organized games, the Officers' Training Corps, recent additions to the school's fabric, any outstanding successes achieved in University scholarship and other public examinations, the school's remarkably clean bill of health during the past term—and, of course, how well the Old Boys were doing all over the world.

The Headmaster of Harrow declared that classics would still be recognized as the finest foundation for English in all its applications; at the same time he strongly criticized 'the hampering attitude of the universities towards the modern side' in their requirements for Greek.

Speaking at Epsom College on prizegiving day, July 25th, Lord Rosebery—who had been prophesying disaster for the last ten years and more—declared that never, or hardly ever, had he seen the political horizon, both in Great Britain and Europe, so charged with clouds pregnant with thunder as was depicted today. The main subject of his address, however, was a very favourite one on Speech Days—namely, the formation of character. Developing this theme, Lord Rosebery said that he believed some germ of character was innate. 'He did not know whether this went counter to theological dogma, but he was firmly persuaded of the fact, and had noticed that the way a baby took to a bottle was a fine indication of character.' (Laughter.)

At Bedford Grammar School the guest of honour was Lord Roberts, the hero of the North-West Frontier and the South African War. The old Field-Marshal congratulated the members of the Officers' Training Corps on their soldier-like bearing. 'Not all of them could be soldiers,' he declared, 'but every able-bodied youth ought to have his place in the Territorial Force, or, as he should like it to be, the National Army.'

The visitation of the Governors of the Skinners' Company to Tonbridge School included the customary Latin oration by the Captain of the School, and a formal and ceremonial inspection of the birch bushes . . .

Speech Day at Uppingham School has been vividly recalled for us by Vera Brittain, who as a young girl was present at that ceremony and who was soon after to lose her brother, her lover, and almost all the male friends of her youth in the imminent carnage.

'Some of the masters, perhaps, were more prescient, but I do not believe that any of the gaily clad visitors who watched the corps carrying out its manoeuvres and afterwards marching so impressively into the Chapel for the Speech Day service, in the least realized how close at hand was the fate for which it had prepared itself, or how many of those deep and strangely thrilling boys' voices were to be silent in death before another Speech Day. Looking back upon those three radiant days of July 1914, it seems to me that an ominous stillness, an atmosphere of brooding expectation, must surely have hung about the sunlit flower gardens and the shining green fields. But actually I noticed nothing more serious than the deliberate solemnity of the Headmaster's speech at the prizegiving after the service. . . .

'I have written so much of Uppingham Speech Day because it was the one perfect summer idyll that I ever experienced, as well as my last carefree entertainment before the Flood. The lovely legacy of a vanished world, it is sketched with minute precision on the tablets of my memory. Never again, for me and my generation, was there to be any festival the joy of which no cloud would darken and no remembrance invalidate.'[1]

Goodwood Week opened on Tuesday, the 28th, under the darkening shadow of the crisis; a fact which was brought home to a large concourse of holiday-makers by the absence of the King. Though the weather was fine, a sultry haze overspread the Sussex countryside, with a presage of thunder in the heavy cloud-banks which presently drifted in from the Channel. The threat of thunder, however, receded as the day advanced, and it continued dry; though in the evening there were some rather heavy showers.

Cup Day, the 30th, was by tradition almost a regular holiday in this part of the country; and for miles around everyone who could possibly contrive to be present was on his or her way to the racecourse on the height of the Downs. Many a narrow, winding Sussex lane, which from dawn to dusk seldom saw more than an occasional farm wagon or pony trap during the remainder of the year, now swarmed with traffic. On foot, on horseback, and in every kind of conveyance, farmers and their families, farm labourers, and all sorts and conditions of country folk took the shortest route that they could find across country by by-ways, bridle-ways, and cart-tracks; up the chalky bostals over the Downs from the secluded villages and hamlets of the Rother valley; through the placid feudal town of Arundel, down Fairmile Bay Combe, through the great North Wood with its lofty beeches, and through Charlton Forest and its adjacent woodlands; past Chilgrove Manor, down the long white lane under Bow Hill, and past Kingley Vale with its ancient yew-trees; across the broad cornfields of the Chichester plain, where already the tawny wheat was standing in sheaves, and up the steep, winding road skirting Goodwood Park.

[1] Vera Brittain, The Testament of Youth (1933), p. 87.

From early morning, and from every quarter, there came a constant stream of vehicles—motor-cars, charabancs, carriages, wagonettes, cabs, taxis, dog-carts, traps, and bicycles—all converging on Goodwood. Though the motors were not quite so numerous as in the previous year (1913 had been *par excellence* the motorists' Goodwood), they roared in their hundreds up the steep ascent over Bury Hill and Duncton Down from Surrey and London, and along the Chichester-Midhurst road from Portsmouth, Bognor, Worthing, Brighton, and the neighbouring seaside towns. 'If the present state of things continues,' the *Times* declared, 'there will soon be no horses at Goodwood except on the actual racecourse.' The fine white dust stirred up by all this fast-moving traffic whitened the trees and hedgerows and grass verges along the roads. The route to the racecourse was marked by an almost continuous cloud of dust. The railways also were busy that day. The little single-track line in the valley below Goodwood, which linked these secluded Downland villages with the outside world, disgorged large numbers of racegoers at Drayton and Singleton; and several thousands more arrived in special trains from London to Chichester.

Below the Grandstand and the terrace the whole course was spread out before the spectators almost as on a map. All around rose the folds of the Downs with their wide stretches of bare turf and immense groves of beeches. It was one of the fairest landscapes in England. Away to the southward, beyond a checkerwork of meadows, coppices and woods, lay the fertile farmlands of the coastal plain, with the slender spire of Chichester cathedral arising in their midst, and, further off still, the glint of the distant Solent and the misty contours of the Isle of Wight.

The sun blazed down upon a kaleidoscope of colour and movement. The steep slopes of Trundle Hill, which forms a kind of natural grandstand, were thronged from early morning until late in the afternoon with thousands of holidaymakers, hailing for the most part from the surrounding countryside, bent on extracting the last ounce of enjoyment from their annual Goodwood picnic. The heat was tempered by occasional breezes from the distant Channel, which also bore snatches of the scent of heather and wild thyme. The ceaseless murmur of the multitude mingled with the strident clamour of bookies shouting the odds, the rattle of gypsies' tambourines, the raucous shouts of the hawkers, and the singing of larks. Far below the Trundle, the fashionable throng moved slowly to and fro across the grass between the Grandstand and the Paddock. The private luncheon tents were ranged in the shade of the great trees along the terrace. It was the last of the old Goodwood Cup days. There were some curious contrasts. Cheek by jowl with the 'upper ten', in fact directly outside the entrance to the Grandstand, the gypsies as usual had set up their motley encampment under the spreading beech trees. Here the gypsy women in their picturesque rags and tatters contentedly smoked their clay cutties and discussed the affairs of the company until their menfolk returned from their business on the course.

On the surface all was gaiety and carefree enjoyment. But the undercurrent of concern, which had been present from the opening day of the races, persisted. The King's horse won the first race that day; but the little white pavilion at the corner of the Grandstand enclosure was without its Royal occupant, and the Royal Standard did not float over Goodwood House as in former years. Presently a rumour ran like wildfire round the stands and private enclosures—'The officers are going'.

In the villages around life went on as usual. The peaceful passage of the seasons was of far greater consequence to the farmer and his men than any trouble on the Continent. Concern at what was happening abroad was as yet confined to the local 'big house' and the parsonage; it had not penetrated to the village pub, where the talk still centred on the flower show, the Sunday School treat, the harvest, and the curious scarcity of swallows. Morning after morning the blue haze over the distant hilltops gave promise of another fine day, and in field after field the subtle tinge of bronze in the wheat marked the progress of the harvest.

On the concluding day at Goodwood, Friday, the 31st, the weather was cooler and the sky overcast. The shadow of the crisis had perceptibly deepened. In the neighbouring countryside many pleasant house parties had prematurely broken up. Before the first race people stood about in small groups discussing, not the customary racecourse topics, but the grave tidings from the City and the possibility of a catastrophic war. Throughout the day conversation turned on the position in Europe—interest in the racing being quite secondary. The attendance was poor, even for the last day of the races. In the afternoon gaps began to show in the crowd which lined the paddock railings. On all sides there was whispered talk of officers having been recalled to their ships or depots.

Hyde Park in the season

veen the dances

Caruso as Canio in Pagliacci

12. *Sir Edward Carson driving through Belfast on the 'Twelfth'*

The 'Asgard' leaving Hamburg at the start of the gun-running expedition

CHAPTER 17

'Ready, aye, ready'

The news of the Howth gun-running and the shootings in Dublin for the time being effectively diverted public attention, both in England and Ireland, from the mischief that was brewing on the other side of Europe. Outside certain informed circles no one as yet was likely to get excited about such a familiar problem as trouble in the Balkans. But Ireland was a different matter. If in a train or 'bus anybody started the topic of the gun-running and its unhappy sequel, the talk at once became hot and angry.

And just as the eyes and ears of England were held by the Irish crisis, so in France little else was read and talked about that crucial week but the tragic Caillaux case. Not since the Dreyfus affair, twenty years earlier, had Parisians been so passionately absorbed in a comparable issue.

To compass the ruin of the brilliant radical leader, M. Joseph Caillaux, Minister of Finance, M. Calmette, editor of the Royalist *Figaro*, had last March resolved to publish his enemy's intimate correspondence—in consequence of which he was presently shot dead in his office by the outraged Mde. Caillaux. Caillaux was obliged to resign, and on July 20th the case against his wife opened before a Paris jury. The trial in the Palais de Justice was accompanied by amazing scenes of private and political rancour, the court being crowded to suffocation with 2,000 spectators, including large numbers of women. It was the most celebrated *crime passionelle* of the century. (A lifelike effigy of the lady had lately been installed at Madame Tussaud's.) Fierce faction fighting broke out near the office of the *Figaro*. With peace and war hanging in the balance, the one man who might have effectively resisted Poincaré's *revanche* policy was excluded from office. Mde. Caillaux was finally acquitted, and on leaving the court was assailed by the cheers and hisses of an enormous crowd.

When the House of Commons met on the 27th the prevailing mood was one of deep anxiety. Party passion flared up as long as the Irish affair was under discussion; when Lord Robert Cecil rose and sternly inquired how many men the Government wished to be killed in Ireland before they concluded a settlement, there ensued something like pandemonium; the bitterness and resentment which had possessed the ministerialist rank and file after the revelations of April 24-25th returned in full force during this last week of July; but when later the Foreign Secretary outlined his policy, with respect to the Austro-Servian dispute, the mood of the House underwent an extraordinary change and immediately became grave, calm, and collected. But the mood changed again, and as swiftly, while the gun-running episode was being debated.

In reply to a question from Bonar Law, Grey told a tense and silent House that he had dispatched his proposal for a Conference to the Powers concerned.

'To that I have not yet received complete replies, and it is of course a proposal in which the co-operation of all four Powers is essential. In a crisis so grave as this the efforts of one Power alone to preserve the peace must be quite ineffective. . . . It must be obvious to any person who reflects upon the situation that the moment the dispute ceases to be one between Austro-Hungary and Servia and becomes one in which another Great Power is involved, it can but end in the greatest catastrophe that has ever befallen the Continent of Europe at one blow; no one can say what would be the limit of the issues that might be raised by such a conflict, the consequences of it, direct and indirect, would be incalculable.'

In the evening the Leader of the Irish Party rose to move the adjournment of the House to call attention to the serious events that had occurred in Dublin. He drew a parallel between the gun-running incidents at Larne and Howth, and then contrasted the reaction of the authorities in both these cases. 'Who is responsible', he demanded, 'for this monstrous attempt to discriminate between various classes of his Majesty's subjects in Ireland?' He went on to launch a scathing denunciation against Sir John Ross, the Commissioner of Police, whom he described as 'a well-known political partisan'. 'I ask finally', he declared, amid the plaudits of the Irish members, 'that the law shall be administered impartially. Let the House clearly understand that four-fifths of the Irish people will not any longer be bullied, or penalized, or shot for conduct which is permitted to go scot free in every county in Ulster.'

The Austrian declaration of war on Servia, on the evening of the 28th, marked the end of the first phase of the European crisis. Russia thereupon prepared to mobilize against Austria; and the threat of a general conflagration loomed stark on the horizon.

During the 28th and 29th the Lobby talk was chiefly of the European situation; the usual nightly discussion of the Irish question receded into the background, and the thoughts of members centred more and more on the international crisis. Little groups of members collected in the smoking-rooms and lobbies; the evening newspapers were eagerly studied, and there was a steady stream of members to and from the tape machine in the corridor.

On the 29th the German Ambassador, Prince Lichnowsky, called at the Foreign Office.

The situation was very grave, Grey told Lichnowsky, though there was no question of Great Britain intervening if Germany were not involved, or even if France were not involved. But, he added, should the issue become such that we believed British interests required Great Britain to intervene, it would be necessary to intervene immediately and our decision would have to be very rapid—just as the decisions of other Powers had to be.

Yet only an hour before he had warned the French Ambassador that he must not draw any misleading conclusions from the recent orders to the Fleet. Great Britain was by no means wholly on the side of France as she had been in the case of Morocco when France appeared to be directly threatened by Germany. He must repeat that Great Britain had no obligations to France.

Cambon listened with a sinking heart.

About midnight a telegram arrived at the Foreign Office from the British Ambassador in Berlin. It appeared that the German Chancellor had sent for him and asked whether Great Britain would undertake to remain neutral in any conflict which might ensue, if Germany promised not to interfere with Holland and to take no territory from France but her colonies. At the same time the Chancellor had declined to give any pledge that Germany would not invade Belgium; but he promised that if she did invade Belgium, and providing the Belgians did not resist, no territory would be taken from them at the conclusion of hostilities.

Grey curtly refused to entertain these proposals. To make such a bargain with Germany at the expense of France, he declared, would be a disgrace from which the name of this country would never recover. The Chancellor had also, in effect, invited us to bargain away whatever obligation or interest we had in the neutrality of Belgium. The British Government could not entertain that bargain either. We must preserve our full freedom to act as circumstances might appear to us to require in any eventualities.

It was now impossible for the Government to proceed with their Irish Amendment Bill which had been awaited with intense interest and was to have been moved on July 30th. After consultation that morning with Bonar Law, Asquith decided that the Second Reading must be put off.

The Prime Minister's wife, who was watching the scene from the Speaker's gallery, observed the bewildered looks of many members when Asquith rose and made the announcement:

'I do not propose to make the motion which stands in my name, but by the indulgence of the House I should like to give the reason. We meet today under conditions of gravity which are almost unparalleled in the experience of every one of us. The issues of peace and war are hanging in the balance, and with them the risk of a catastrophe of which it is impossible to measure either the dimensions or the effects. In these circumstances it is of vital importance in the interests of the whole world that this country, which has no interests of its own directly at stake, should present a united front, and be able to speak and act with the authority of an undivided nation. If we were to proceed today with the first Order on the paper, we should inevitably, unless the Debate was conducted in an artificial tone, be involved in acute controversy in regard to domestic differences whose importance to ourselves no one in any quarter of the House is disposed to disparage. . . . We therefore propose to put off for the present the consideration of the Second Reading of the Amending Bill—of course without prejudice to its future—in the hope that, by a postponement of the discussion, the patriotism of all parties will contribute what lies in our power, if not to avert, at least to circumscribe the calamities which threaten the world.'

Both the substance of this statement and the gravity with which the Prime Minister had spoken deeply impressed the House. Up in the Peers' Gallery Lord Lansdowne listened with hand to ear, as if to catch every syllable. The sudden peril from abroad had momentarily stilled the voices of faction. While Asquith was speaking members sat tense and silent. When he sat down they stared at one another in consternation; and in the Speaker's Gallery the women crowded round Mrs Asquith and assailed her with questions.

' "Good heavens! Margot!" they said, "what can this mean? Don't you realize the Irish will be fighting each other this very night? How fearfully dangerous! What does it mean?"

'The Orange aristocracy, who had been engaged in strenuous preparations for their civil war and had neither bowed nor spoken to me for months past, joined in the questioning. Looking at them without listening and answering as if in a dream, I said:

' "We are on the verge of a European war." '[1]

On the afternoon of July 28th two young officers belonging to the new light cruiser, H.M.S. *Southampton*, after enjoying a substantial repast at a hotel in Lulworth Cove, were taking their ease on the heights overlooking Weymouth Bay and making their plans for their forthcoming leave, which they had arranged to spend together on the Continent. As they sat and talked, they became suddenly aware that thick, black columns of smoke were beginning to rise in the still evening air from the warships anchored below in Portland harbour; picket boats were busily dashing to and fro among them, and between the shipping and the shore, and searchlights were frantically flashing signals.

[1] Asquith, *The Autobiography of Margot Asquith* (1922), II, p. 161.

'Looks like a flap!' remarked one of the young officers to his companion. 'Perhaps we'd better get back!'[1]

It *was* a flap. The same evening naval pickets and police combed the town and its environs, scouring hotels, lodging houses, restaurants and public houses in search of officers and men on shore leave. Notices ordering their immediate recall were flashed on the screen at the local cinemas. At the Pavilion Theatre an announcement was made from the stage that everyone had to be on board by 10 o'clock. As the Navy men were streaming out of the house, the audience rose to its feet and broke into loud applause, while the orchestra resourcefully played 'Rule, Britannia'. Bar after bar was invaded by the masters-at-arms, pints were quickly drunk up, and with a hasty 'So long!' the men hurried off. In the gathering dusk the great harbour was alive with the scintillations of innumerable flashing signal lamps. Many people listening to pierrot shows on the beach heard the rising clamour on the promenade and promptly joined the throng hurrying to the pier.

For hours, while the naval patrols were busy in Weymouth and Portland, and the streets swarmed with bluejackets hurrying down to the waterside, coastguards and others were carrying the news to outlying villages and hamlets; and telegrams were dispatched to officers spending their leave at a distance. Ladies in evening dress drove down to the pier to bid farewell to their husbands and relatives. From all parts of the town endless processions of naval personnel and civilians made for the waiting boats.

All night long the harbour blazed with myriads of powerful lights as the ships' companies and workmen from the Yard toiled without respite to get the vital stores transferred on board, and the huge cranes along the coaling pier squealed and whined hour after hour, as the coal was hoisted into lighters for towing out to the Fleet. When at last the stars paled before the coming dawn, the work was still going on.

In the early hours of the 29th the Fleet weighed and put to sea. It was misty weather, with the sun trying fitfully to pierce the haze. The 1st, 2nd, and 3rd Battle Squadrons went out first, followed by the 1st Battle Cruiser Squadron and the 4th Battle

[1] Stephen King-Hall, *My Naval Life* (1952), p. 92.

Squadron, with the *Iron Duke*, flying the flag of the acting Commander-in-Chief, Vice-Admiral Sir George Warrender, bringing up the rear. The departure of the First Fleet from Portland harbour was an impressive spectacle. One after another the huge dreadnoughts, with their massive superstructures and distinctive tripod masts, glided majestically through the eddying mists towards the harbour entrance. As they steamed out some of the ships' bands were playing 'Heart of Oak', 'The Death of Nelson', 'Britannia, the Pride of the Ocean', and other favourite pieces. A large crowd had assembled about the pier to see them go. Away beyond the great convict prison on the island was a broad belt of sunlit sea. As each ship gliding, ghostlike, through the haze, emerged into that blaze of sunshine, the onlookers could descry every detail on their decks. The white ensigns streaming from their sterns were brilliant specks of colour. Some of the ships began to clear for action. Over the misty waters came the sound of a familiar melody—'The Girl I Left Behind Me'.

Scarcely more than a week ago, after what was, in fact, the last great naval review of the general peace, the First Fleet had steamed out to sea beyond the Nab. Then it had been on its way to summer manoeuvres. Now, once again, the same ships were disappearing into the mist. Innumerable Service families who had been eagerly awaiting their holidays together faced a bleak and uncertain future. . . . Of a sudden in the newspapers there had been this talk of wars and rumours of wars. Then, like a thunderclap, had come the official intimation, No *manoeuvre leave*. Now the ships were bound for an unknown destination. Things were looking bad! War scares there had been in plenty in the past, but, somehow, they had all blown over. This time, by all accounts, it was the real thing.

Silently hundreds of women gazed their last on the distant grey ships fast fading out of sight, and then returned, with sad and anxious faces, to their lodgings.

In accordance with the Admiralty's order of the 28th, course was first shaped to the south-westward until the Fleet was out of sight of land; and then a middle-Channel course was steered to the Straits of Dover. During the afternoon two French dreadnought battleships, the *Jean Bart* and the *Courbet*, steamed past them, at 20 knots, cleared for action and making for Brest. They also passed a German liner. Otherwise, apart from the coastguards on the southern headlands and various fishing vessels, few saw them go.

At dusk all crews went to night defence stations, and guns and searchlights were manned. Steaming that night through the Straits of Dover at high speed and without lights, the battle fleet, preceded by its cruiser screen, then steered north-north-east up the North Sea. Throughout the 29th and 30th the ships were preparing for action. The torpedoes had been fitted with war heads and the crews had gone into War Routine. 'The decks are a quaint sight,' wrote a young officer in the *Dreadnought*, 'being littered with hoses, cables, hazelrod fenders and derricks —all placed there so that they may be handy if required and if they escape destruction. Tonight we are again at night defence and all lights out.'

In the forenoon of the 31st the passengers on board the Orkney mail-boat beheld with astonishment the Moray Firth swarming with warships, stretching away to the far horizon, and all steering north. At noon speed was reduced from 17 knots to 10.

In the evening the Fleet arrived off the Orkney Islands. Division after division, it steered past Duncansby Head to port, and the barren Pentland skerries to starboard; in typical Orkney weather—grey skies, drifting mists, and a light drizzling rain— it steamed past Stroma and Swona and entered Hoxa Sound. To the westward were Flotta and Fara, with the mountainous ridge of Hoy in the background, and to the eastward was South Ronaldsay. Far away across the Flow lay the green levels of the Orphir shore on Mainland, backed by the heather-clad summit of Horton Head. The Fleet stood on across the Flow and anchored along the northern shore.

The Fleet began to coal at once, first the battle cruisers and then the light cruisers. The ships not engaged in coaling were darkened, and a force of light cruisers and destroyers was sent out to patrol the approaches to the Flow.

From its war station up in the Orkney Islands the Fleet could control the northern exit of the North Sea as formerly the

Western Squadron had covered the approaches to the Channel. The southern exit was to be secured by the Second Fleet (which was then assembling at Portland), composed of pre-dreadnought battleships stationed in the Channel. The strategic concentration of the battle fleet was one of the great decisive events of the impending struggle, and automatically denied Germany egress to the ocean.

CHAPTER 18

The gathering storm

It cannot be stressed too strongly that the state of opinion inside the Cabinet was divided up to the last moment. As the crisis intensified, the anti-war faction became at first more insistent and determined—though, in point of fact, there was never any open clash of opinion between the two groups. In the negotiations which were now being carried on from day to day with the Ambassadors of both Entente and Triple Alliance Powers, Grey was severely handicapped by this crucial fact. He was well aware that his colleagues would never authorize him to pledge the country to the support of France, and that even to press for such a pledge might well result in the break-up of the Cabinet. Moreover, the division in the Government reflected the state of opinion in the House of Commons and throughout the country. The British people as a whole were neither pro-French nor pro-German: but there was a widespread and vehement desire for peace.

From July 28th on, the Cabinet met daily, sometimes sitting twice in the day. The discussions were calm, Lord Samuel relates, 'but very tense and anxious'. Long afterwards Grey expressed his conviction that, if there had been a premature attempt to force a decision, it would not have availed to bridge these divergencies of opinion, but, on the contrary, would have brought them out and made them irreparable. On one point all were agreed; and that was in approving Grey's proposal to seek a peaceful solution of the crisis by mediation. But the crisis continued and grew daily more menacing; if diplomacy failed, there would certainly be war; and what was Great Britain going to do? France and Russia were doing all in their power to induce her to come in on their side, while Germany was trying her hardest to secure her promise of neutrality. The majority of the Ministers, while agreeing that Germany should be warned against reckoning on British neutrality in all circumstances, were, nevertheless, strongly opposed to giving France and Russia any promise of support. As early as the 29th, as the Cabinet was dispersing, Burns had pressed Morley's arm and whispered earnestly, 'Now, mind, we look to you to stand firm'. He repeated this on the 31st.

Grey's own policy was, first, to prevent a general war, and, if that should fail, to induce the Cabinet, Parliament, and the nation to enter the struggle on the side of France. From the outset his field of manoeuvre was seriously circumscribed by the existence, on the one hand, of a semi-secret understanding with the Entente Powers and, on the other, by the state of public opinion in Great Britain. In one sentence Grey put the matter in a nutshell—'The Cabinet as a whole knew that it was not in a position to pledge the country'. He was therefore unable to take a firm line when a clear and unequivocal declaration by Great Britain might have proved a decisive factor, and was obliged to proceed, with the greatest circumspection, by means of warnings, hints, and cautious reservations.

Again and again Cambon called on Grey at the Foreign Office; and like his colleague, Count Benckendorff, argued, urged, and pleaded with the Foreign Secretary, endeavouring by every means in his power to get a definite assurance out of him. Grey consistently refused to give him any such assurance.

Telegrams kept pouring in, in an unending stream, from our Embassies and Legations in every capital in Europe. The strain on Grey was immense. He was living at the time in his friend Haldane's house in Queen Anne's Gate. As things got worse, Haldane made arrangements for all dispatch boxes to be brought to him during the night so that he might unlock them and judge for himself whether it was necessary for Grey to be aroused from his sleep.

Morley relates that, a few days after the Austrian ultimatum to Servia, he awoke to the fact that the continued existence of the Government was in question. It was apparent that the issue could not be indefinitely postponed. Churchill was working energetically for intervention, while Harcourt was organizing opinion among his colleagues in favour of neutrality. The latter party, to which Morley himself belonged, appeared to be gaining ground. 'One of these days I tapped Winston on the shoulder, as he took his seat next me. "Winston, we have beaten you after all".'[1] But Churchill only smiled enigmatically — as well he might.

About the same time, according to Grey, he was approached in the lobby of the House of Commons by one of the most active members of the Liberal party, who, 'in the manner of a superior addressing a subordinate whom he thought needed a good talking to', informed the Minister that he wished him to understand that under no circumstances whatever should this country intervene in the war, if it came.

'I answered pretty roughly to the effect that I hoped we should not be involved in war, but that it was nonsense to say that there were no circumstances conceivable in which we ought to go to war. "Under no circumstances whatever", was the retort. "Suppose Germany violates the neutrality of Belgium?" For a moment he paused, like one who, running at speed, finds himself suddenly confronted with an obstacle, unexpected and unforeseen. Then he said with emphasis, "She won't do it". "I don't say she will, but supposing she does?" "She won't do it", he repeatedly confidently, and with that assurance he left me.'[2]

Another leading member of the Cabinet, the redoubtable Chancellor of the Exchequer, testified to the state of feeling in high financial, industrial, and commercial circles at this juncture. He informed the Cabinet that he had been in consultation with the Governor and Deputy Governor of the Bank of England, and a number of other City magnates, also iron, coal, and cotton interests in the North of England; and that all of them were horrified at the idea of Great Britain intervening in a European war—they believed that it would destroy the whole system of credit of which London was the centre, that it would undermine industry and commerce and depress wages and prices, and that very likely, when winter came, it would result in rioting and civil strife.

An ominous aspect of these divergencies, both in the House of Commons and throughout the country, was that they tended to assert themselves along party lines. The people were in danger of taking sides over the matter of intervention or non-

[1] John Morley, *Memorandum on Resignation* (1928), p. 5.
[2] Grey, *Twenty-five Years* (1928), II, p. 182.

intervention as they had previously done in connection with the budget, the veto of the House of Lords, Home Rule, and other burning domestic issues. At least half — probably more — of Asquith's colleagues were anti-war, while in the House of Commons and Great Britain as a whole the majority of the Liberal party were strongly opposed to intervention on the side of the Entente. Though there was a strong body of opinion among Conservative M.P.s in favour of supporting France and Russia, the Opposition was by no means unanimous. Only one thing, Bonar Law informed Grey, would produce an overwhelming majority in favour of war—and that was an assault on Belgium.

Meanwhile the situation was fast deteriorating. On the afternoon of the 29th the news that the Austrians were bombarding Belgrade roused Russian public and official opinion to fever heat. On the edge of the abyss the Governments of the Powers involved instinctively recoiled. The Tsar and William II addressed earnest appeals to each other while endeavouring to restrain their respective high commands. During the 30th and 31st the negotiations between Russia and Austria continued. The latter finally agreed to do the very thing which she had declined to do at the outset of the controversy, which was to discuss the whole question of her ultimatum to Servia. Russia requested the British Government to undertake the direction of these discussions. Hope revived; and for a few hours there actually seemed to be a chance of a peaceful outcome of the crisis.

'But', comments Churchill, 'underneath the diplomatic communications and manoeuvres, the baffling proposals and counter-proposals, the agitated interventions of Tsar and Kaiser, flowed a deep tide of calculated military purpose. As the ill-fated nations approached the verge, the sinister machines of war began to develop their own momentum and eventually to take control themselves.'[1]

At this point the quarrel entered upon its second and far more dangerous phase. Everything now hinged upon the all-important factor of mobilization. Russian assurances that they were not mobilizing against Germany were received, understandably, with incredulity in Berlin. For several days the German Great

[1] W. S. Churchill, *The World Crisis*, I, p. 201.

General Staff had been working feverishly. As early as the 26th there were rumours in Berlin of mischief brewing in St Petersburg. The Germans became increasingly alarmed about the progress of the Russian preparations; and the military pressure upon their Government was proportionately intensified. On the night of July 29th-30th the Tsar's order for general mobilization sped from end to end of the vast Russian Empire. Shortly after the Germans took corresponding action on their side. On the 31st a 'state of imminent peril of war', *kriegsgefahr*, was proclaimed; the notices appeared calling up reservists of all classes; and on the same day their Ambassador in St Petersburg presented an ultimatum to Russia, demanding that she should countermand her mobilization within twelve hours.

The truth was that neither Nicholas II nor William II could withstand the constantly increasing strain of military pressure. Negotiation virtually ceased when Russia mobilized. From this time on the military machine took charge in the Great Powers of the Continent.

At a meeting of the Cabinet on the 31st Burns in his most forthright manner denounced the warning to Germany not to attack the shores or shipping of France in the Channel—'not only because it was directly a declaration of war and was leading inevitably to a war on land, but mainly because it was the symbol of an alliance with France with whom no such understanding hitherto existed'.

In the afternoon Cambon called on Grey at the Foreign Office to get an answer to his inquiry of the 30th as to what Great Britain proposed to do if Germany attacked France. He received little satisfaction from his visit. The truth was, the Cabinet was still undecided.

Grey declared that it was quite wrong to suppose that we had left Germany under the impression we would not intervene; but he had to tell Cambon that it had been decided in the Cabinet that, being bound by no treaty or obligation to intervene on behalf of France, we were unable to give any pledge of support. Of course, he went on to say, further developments might so alter the situation that intervention would then be justified. The preservation of Belgian neutrality might well be an important factor in determining British policy.

Cambon again inquired if Great Britain would support France

if Germany attacked her. He urged Grey to think, not of our obligations, but of our interests; to consider what the position of Great Britain would be if Germany destroyed France and dominated Europe. To all this Grey had to reply that, at the present moment, he could not give any definite pledge to France.

Cambon left the Foreign Office in a state bordering on desperation.

Shortly after Grey addressed a request to both the French and German Governments for an assurance that each would respect the neutrality of Belgium, provided no other Power violated it. A similar request had been made by Gladstone's Ministry in the Franco-Prussian War in 1870. Both France and Prussia had then agreed to respect Belgian neutrality. On this occasion, however, France agreed, while Germany sent an evasive reply.

'Of course [Asquith recorded in his diary] everybody longs to stand aside, but I need not say that France, through Cambon, is pressing strongly for a reassuring declaration. Edward Grey had an interview with him this afternoon, which he told me was rather painful. He had, of course, to tell Cambon, for we are under no obligation, that we could give no pledges and that our actions must depend upon the course of events, including the question and the course of public opinion here.'[1]

In the House of Commons that day, as the members moved slowly to and fro between the chamber and the lobby, the excitement was intense. A large group gathered around the tape machine in one of the corridors. When the announcement of the closing of the Stock Exchange was made, a wave of pessimism swept through the lobby. The tension mounted. On all sides were heard gloomy predictions and speculations. In the expectation of some statement by the Government, the members presently took their places in the chamber. But the Cabinet was still sitting, and most of them returned to the lobby. Meanwhile the tape machine was still spelling out the bad news. *Martial law proclaimed in Germany. Russia mobilizing.* Anyone who had anything to say on the situation was swiftly surrounded and eagerly questioned by the others. The inexorable tape

[1] Earl of Oxford and Asquith, *Memories and Reflections* (1928), II, p. 7.

machine continued ticking. Shortly after three o'clock that afternoon came the biggest sensation of the day. *Bank Rate raised to eight per cent! Germany mobilizing!* A murmur of excitement swept round the crowded lobby. Later came a denial of the German mobilization: but it failed to lighten the general gloom. As the afternoon wore on, the prevailing pessimism grew darker.

To the man in the street, the murder of an Austrian archduke whose name he could scarcely pronounce and in a place he had never heard of signified merely another Balkan crisis. It was, surely, no concern of his. Admittedly the situation might appear dangerous for a while and there would be the usual war talk in the newspapers. But in the end, he felt sure, it would all blow over. These things always did. . . . It is fairly safe to say that the thoughts of the great majority of working folk in this country were centred rather upon the approaching Bank Holiday— the last public holiday before Christmas—than on the crime at Sarajevo.

Even to the 'classes'—apart from a well-informed but extremely small minority—the gravity of the situation was not apparent for an appreciable period. As a case in point, it may be observed that almost at the very end of July the Archbishop of Canterbury appears to have had no inkling that the Continent was on the verge of a general war; and even later than this Beatty bet his flag-captain a 'fiver' that there would be no war. After all, it had all happened very suddenly. The momentary excitement aroused by the crime of June 28th had largely subsided. Public attention had in fact been focused for months upon Ireland and the trouble that was brewing there to the exclusion of almost all other interests. To trace the gradations of national consciousness with any degree of certainty is an impossible task. Suffice to say, it was not till nearly the end of July— say, the 29th—that the average well-to-do, middle-class household was suddenly aware of the danger.

That morning when he opened the *Times*, paterfamilias could scarcely believe his eyes. Then, with a shock, he realized that for days past the news had been gradually getting worse. What had at first appeared a cloud no bigger than a man's hand now

cast its darkening shadow over the whole Continent. These were
the headlines which confronted him:

> *On the Brink of War*
> *Waning Hopes*
> *Close the Ranks*

The significance of what he read was not lost upon paterfamilias. *Close the Ranks*. So it was as bad as that! Now, as his
gaze wandered from those menacing headlines to his familiar
surroundings—the open window looking out on the carefully
tended lawn and the rose bushes beyond, his wife presiding over
the cheerful breakfast table, the children chattering among
themselves of the approaching seaside holiday, the maid bringing in the coffee—it was as if some dread portent had suddenly
appeared in the summer sky.

At Tunbridge Wells, the following morning, people were
beginning to assemble under the trees by the Pantiles to listen
to the band of the Royal Irish Rifles. At the very moment that
the band were preparing for the concert the bandmaster received
a telegram ordering their immediate recall. The public were later
advised that there was no cause for alarm; it was a purely precautionary measure, stated the official explanation. Nevertheless,
it was noticed by some people that quite a number of men in the
Army and Navy in the vicinity had suddenly had their leave cut
short by orders to rejoin their respective units.

On the same day, on the Brunswick Lawns at Brighton and at
other favourite rendezvous of the well-to-do, there was an
atmosphere of tension and anxiety. Concern among the ruling
class was steadily increasing.

The newspapers on both sides strongly supported the appeal
made by the *Times* to close the ranks: and *Punch's* cartoon that
week brought the danger unmistakably home to a wide circle—
it represented Servia in the guise of a bantam boldly squaring up
to the great Austrian eagle, with the huge Russian bear lurking
watchfully in the background; and it was entitled 'The Power
Behind'.

It has to be remembered that communications in the England
of fifty years ago were nothing like so comprehensive and highly
developed as they are today. Regional differences were far more

pronounced. The outlook of Manchester was in striking contrast, in certain regards, to that of London.

Between town and country, too, there was a great gulf fixed. In the more isolated parts of the countryside Hodge and his mates paid little heed to what was happening in the outside world. They were wholly absorbed in their own affairs. Consequently the topics usually under discussion in the local parliament—the village 'pub'—concerned the farms, crops, gardens, friendships, and feuds, of the locality, the state of the weather, the prospects of the local cricket team, and such important occasions as lambing, sheep-shearing, haymaking, club-day, the flower show, harvest, and the ploughing match.

There is an amusing and revealing instance of this intense pre-occupation with local affairs in the long-standing rivalry between two South Down villages, Slindon and Graffham, in the matter of garden fruits, vegetables, and flowers. The controversy continued for years in the *West Sussex Gazette* and, in these weeks of rising tension, was wholly unaffected by the imminence of Armageddon.

'July 9th. A broad bean, grown in Slindon, was gathered last week, measuring 14 inches in length. Slindon was lucky to have a nice shower of rain. It has made the heavy crop of apples shine on the trees. Many years have passed since there has been such a sight of red currants in Slindon.

'July 16th. Slindon has the hollyhocks, growing 10 feet in height, full of flowers. If you are short of apples, Graffham, Slindon will gladly give you some for a tart.

'July 23rd. Your ten-foot hollyhock, Slindon, is not good enough. Graffham has one nearly twelve feet in height.

'July 30th. Slindon has, Graffham, a Canterbury Bell, this week, seven doubles on one flower, at Mr Homes'. As regards your 12 feet hollyhock, Slindon can go higher. There are four different coloured hollyhocks in Slindon, 14 feet in height. The flowers are a grand sight. All kinds of stone fruit are on trees and wall trees. The apples and pears are a great sight. Come and see.'

Throughout this period of uncertainty the arguments used on both sides in the press debate were forceful, cogent, and well reasoned. A number of leading Liberal newspapers threw the whole weight of their influence on the side of neutrality. In reply to a favourite gambit of the war party, 'Honour bids us to go to war', the *Manchester Guardian* queried pertinently, 'Whose honour?'—and proceeded to answer that inquiry in terms that apparently went to the root of the matter. 'Not that of the Government, for if what the war party says were true, then what Mr Asquith and Sir Edward Grey said was false. . . . Whose honour, then? The honour of those who have led France to hope that we would undertake responsibilities which all the time they were anxious to conceal from Englishmen?' The *Daily Chronicle* also fought stoutly for non-intervention. 'This is after all a Continental war, and Britons may again thank God for their insular position.' 'Despite all signs to the contrary', declared the *Labour Leader,* 'there will, I believe, be no war.'

On the opposite wing of public opinion the *Pall Mall Gazette,* as early as July 29th, voiced the demand for intervention clearly and succinctly. 'We pray that this dread issue may be averted. But, if it be raised, our duty is clear. We must stand by our friends with the most prompt resolution, and with the whole of our might.' The following evening the same journal made a telling appeal to historic principles of British policy. 'Our most vital interests absolutely forbid us to run the risk of seeing France crushed or permit any violation of the neutrality of Belgium or Holland. Antwerp is not less a "pistol pointed at the heart of England" now than it was in Napoleonic times, but rather more.' The majority of the leading Opposition newspapers in fact insisted that our country must, *coûte qui coûte,* stand by France and Russia.

Almost to the last moment, as the doubtful struggle swayed, now this way, now that, the issue remained uncertain. There was a distinct limit to the guidance the newspapers could give in these circumstances, when so much was unknown and even unsuspected. Even those experts who were popularly credited with an inside knowledge of European politics did but reflect the tremendous debate that was going on from end to end of the country. In spite of all their specialized knowledge and experience, the experts did not really know what England would do. *England did not know herself.*

Meanwhile the City had experienced the blackest week in its history.

On the 27th, with Austria-Hungary and Servia on the edge of war, the foreign exchange market in New York suffered a disastrous collapse as a result of the excessive selling of securities by Vienna, Berlin, and Paris. The breakdown rapidly spread to other foreign exchanges, including London, and resulted in an international crisis. On the morning of the 28th there was a slight recovery; but shortly afterwards the crisis went from bad to worse. Everywhere the whole vast complex structure of credit, upon which modern finance, commerce, and industry vitally depended, appeared to be toppling to ruins. London, as the financial centre of the world, was peculiarly vulnerable to such a collapse. The oldest men in the City declared that they had never known anything to compare with the prevailing state of chaos. At Lloyd's all ordinary business was suspended; transactions were confined to war risks, and these were accepted only by a few underwriters and at exceptionally high rates. There was a complete paralysis of foreign exchange business; at the Stock Exchange a number of firms failed, and many more seemed likely to fail also.

On the 31st several events of the highest importance followed swiftly upon each other.

At the Stock Exchange, at about a quarter past ten, two or three of the attendants in their gold-braided silk hats emerged hurriedly from the Committee Room with papers which they proceeded to post on the doors. They were followed by a surge of members, who presently stared, amazed, at the notices.

'The Stock Exchange is closed!' The news spread swiftly through the crowd, and Throgmorton Street became a seething mass of members, some in the conventional silk hat, some in straw hats, and others with no hats at all, questioning one another, jostling one another, rushing here and there in agitation, and gathering in groups to discuss a situation which was absolutely without parallel. Never in history had the Stock Exchange been closed on a working day! Throughout the rest of the day a huge crowd hung about the street to read the unprecedented announcement.

'*Stock Exchange closed!*' Newsboys shouted the news in the streets, darting in and out of the traffic which was swollen by numbers of taxis, piled high with luggage, carrying the advance brigade of the holidaymakers to the railway stations.

That day the Bank Rate was raised from four to eight per cent; and a huge queue formed outside the Bank of England drawing gold. Presently the word went round the crowded City streets that at Lloyd's the Lutine bell had been rung—general mobilization had been proclaimed in Russia!

Later there was a conference of leading bankers with the Government. The outlook was sombre indeed. Commercial and financial interests in the City were closely linked with their counterparts in Vienna and Berlin. Already certain industries were suffering severely. Many cotton workers were on short time, and the worsted mills of Huddersfield had been hard hit by the cancellation of orders. On the same day Grey reported to the French Ambassador:

'The commercial and financial situation was exceedingly serious; there was danger of a complete collapse that would involve us and everyone else in ruin; and it was possible that our standing aside might be the only means of preventing a complete collapse of European credit, in which we should be involved. This might be a paramount consideration in deciding our attitude.'

For the last few days Fleet Street had been humming like an angry hive. What Kipling described, long ago, as 'the sacred call of the war trumpet' had touched off a feverish activity. Groups of anxious journalists gathered before large-scale maps, pored over reference books, and studied photographs and cablegrams. Special correspondents, press photographers, and other aspirants to a roving commission on the Continent tirelessly climbed up stairs and interviewed editors. Among those who heard and answered the summons of the war trumpet was the late Sir Philip Gibbs, who has recorded in vivid detail his departure for the Continent on the night of the 30th.[1]

On the morning of the 31st the *Daily Mail* bore the ominous headline, 'Europe Drifting to Disaster'; from time to time a fresh crop of posters testified to the rapid march of events at home and

[1] See Philip Gibbs, *The Soul of the War* (1915), pp. 12-13.

abroad; and the evening papers were full of grave news concerning the unfolding of the grim drama across the North Sea.

For some time ordinary men and women had been asking themselves and one another, What had it all got to do with us? A great deal, apparently! Already the more thoughtful part of the population were beginning to discern the shape of things to come. The news from St Petersburg was like a bombshell. What answer would Germany make to the Russian mobilization? And, if Russia were menaced from the westward, what action would be taken by her ally, France? And that led on to the shadowy, intangible, yet somehow unescapable bond of the *entente cordiale*. What exactly did it entail? What was the difference between an *entente* and an alliance?

Talk about the war was increasing. It was beginning to be a common topic in trains and buses. More and more newspapers were sold. Anxious groups gathered around the tape machines in their clubs and elsewhere. Large-scale maps of central and eastern Europe were on sale at stationers' and bookshops. Now, and not until now—seven days after the news of the Austrian ultimatum reached London—the significance of what was happening abroad was about to be brought home to the general public.

'As I was reading the evening newspaper on my way home', F. H. Willis, then a young hatter, recalled, 'I noticed a paragraph announcing that the visit of the burghers of Boulogne to Hastings had been cancelled "owing to the International situation". This was the first time I became aware that there was an International situation.'[1]

Nevertheless, the demeanour of Londoners generally on this Friday was in striking contrast with the situation in many foreign capitals, which by now were in a ferment of warlike excitement. Here and there one heard the crisis eagerly debated; but it was by no means a universal topic of conversation. Anything like real excitement about the war was confined to those restaurants and cafés which catered chiefly for foreigners.

The everyday life of London appeared to go on this evening much as usual—the hordes of office workers hurrying along the hot, dusty pavements on their homeward way and mingling with the lighthearted, chattering holiday crowds at the railway

[1] F. H. Willis, *London General* (1953), p. 190.

stations; buses, taxi-cabs, and private motor-cars, along with the still abundant horse-drawn traffic—carts, vans, wagons, drays, hansoms, and four-wheelers—flowing past in a steady stream, under the familiar posters and electric signs extolling the merits of Johnny Walker (Born 1820. Still Going Strong), Beecham's Pills, Veno's Lightning Cough Cure, Swan Vestas, Stephens Ink, Veritas Gas Mantles, Reckitts Blue, Sunlight Soap, Benger's Food, Bird's Custard Powder, Eno's Fruit Salt, Nestlé's Milk, Bovril, and Rinso.

The same cheery coteries assembled at the Criterion, Trocadero, Romano's, the Café Royal, and other restaurants and taverns. The same happy crowds gathered outside the pit and gallery entrances of the theatres and music-halls. At the New Theatre Cyril Maude was appearing in *Grumpy* (tomorrow would see that play's 500th performance); at the Duke of York's there was *The Land of Promise*, by the rising young playwright, W. S. Maugham; at the Lyceum there was the immensely popular *The Belle of New York*; at the Globe there was *Kismet* with Oscar Asche and Lily Brayton, and at the Kingsway Lillah McCarthy and Granville Barker were playing in Arnold Bennett's *The Great Adventure*.

At the Palace Theatre there was the melody, fun, and laughter of *The Passing Show*. Once again the audience rose at Elsie Janis as she sang, 'I've got everything I want but you'; and once again they clapped and cheered when Basil Hallam came on in the guise of a gay, insouciant young man about town—the 'Nut' of those days.

> I'm Gilbert the Filbert, the Nut with a K,
> The Pride of Piccadilly, the blasé roué.
> Oh, Hades, the ladies all leave their wooden huts
> For Gilbert the Filbert, the Colonel of the Nuts.

For far more many Londoners than the theatre and music-hall audiences the close of play scores and the racing results represented the chief items of interest in the evening papers. Seldom had the county cricket championship presented a more interesting situation than it did at that moment. Yesterday, after all but losing the match to Nottinghamshire, Kent had achieved a brilliant victory. Surrey had only just succeeded in defeating

Sussex at the Oval. Middlesex also had done very well in the last few months. The championship appeared to rest between three counties—Surrey, Middlesex, and Kent—who headed the table in the order mentioned. At Goodwood, to the chagrin of the punters and to the profit of the bookmakers, Kiltoi had, quite unexpectedly, won the Chesterfield Cup in a canter. The punters shrugged their shoulders, then turned hopefully to 'Today's Selections for Alexandra Park on Saturday'.

The evening of the 31st was, in fact, the last on which, for a substantial part of the population, such things as these mattered a great deal, and the international situation very little.

CHAPTER 19

Mobilization

In the afternoon of Saturday, August 1st, the German Ambassador in St Petersburg, Count Pourtalès, presented his Government's declaration of war against Russia.

The news spread throughout St Petersburg, and the following day a great crowd assembled outside the British Embassy, to cheer for England and to sing 'God Save the King' and 'Rule, Britannia'. In the afternoon an endless procession of splendid carriages drove across the Neva and entered the gates of the Winter Palace. Several thousand men, the greatest in the land, thronged the vast gallery of St George. In the midst of that brilliant assemblage the Tsar, laying his hand upon the Bible, and speaking slowly and impressively, repeated the oath made by his Romanoff ancestor in 1812: 'Officers of my Guard here present, I greet in you my whole Army and give it my blessing. I solemnly swear that I will never make peace so long as one of the enemy is on the soil of the Fatherland!'

With that the Tsar embraced the French Ambassador. From the square below, which was packed with people, came the sound of loud and sustained cheering. Presently the Tsar and Tsaritsa stepped out on the balcony. Enormous crowds had assembled on both sides of the Neva. At the sight of their Sovereign tens of thousands of Russians fell on their knees and began to chant the Imperial hymn:

God, the All-Terrible . . .

On the previous day, at 5.30 p.m., mobilization had been proclaimed in Berlin. Officers driving in open cars swept down Unter den Linden waving their handkerchiefs and swords and shouting 'Mobilization'. The cry was taken up by the people on the pavements, and spread rapidly throughout the city. Special editions of the newspapers were rushed to the principal streets in large motor-lorries, and flung, in bundles, to the excited crowds. Enormous throngs gathered in Unter den Linden and the

249

Potsdamer Platz. The patriotic demonstrations in the Lustgarten outside the Imperial Palace lasted throughout the evening. At half-past six William II and the Empress Augusta Victoria came out on the balcony of the Knights' Hall and received a tremendous ovation. To his wildly applauding subjects the Emperor declared:

'A dark day has today broken over Germany. Envious persons are everywhere compelling us to defence. The sword is being forced into our hand. I hope that if at the last hour my efforts to bring our adversaries to see things in their proper light and to maintain peace do not succeed we shall with God's help wield the sword in such a way that we can sheathe it with honour.'

These words were followed by deafening applause, followed by the singing of 'Die Wacht am Rhein' and 'Heil Dir im Siegerkranz'.

On the morrow, Sunday, a day of brilliant sunshine, the streets of Berlin were filled with long processions of men returning, after long years of civilian life, to the Army. Attired in their field grey uniforms, helmeted, and carrying rifles, accompanied in many cases by their wives and sweethearts, they marched to the railway stations, bound for the frontier.

Mobilization had also been proclaimed in France, about the same hour, on August 1st. An Englishman then staying at a small chateau in the heart of Normandy has described the deeply impressive effect of that nationwide summons to arms. He recalls the tawny wheat-fields, ripe for the harvest, the heavily loaded cider orchards, the mirror-still surface of the River Mayenne, and the densely wooded hills beyond—the whole rich Normandy landscape bathed in golden sunshine, and lapped in the calm silence of the countryside. Such to all appearances was the profound peace and serenity of that lovely summer afternoon in northern France half a century ago.

'Suddenly, from a distant church steeple, came two sharp strokes from a bell, then a pause, and then two strokes were repeated. The town we had just left rang out two louder notes, also followed by a pause. It was the *tocsin* ringing out its terrible message; and yet another steeple sounded its two notes, and

another, and another. The news rung out by those two sharp
strokes is always bad news. The *tocsin* rings for great fires, for
revolution, or, as in this case, for a Declaration of War. Before
us lay Normandy looking inexpressibly peaceful in the evening
sunlight, and over that quiet countryside the *tocsin* was sending
its tidings of woe, as it was from every church tower in France.'[1]

All over the country the local Maire, with the official tricolour
scarf tied round his waist, was reading the Decree of Mobilization to the assembled townsfolk. Within the next few hours
millions of men, young and middle-aged, were reporting at their
depots.

In Paris the announcement put an end to a long-drawn-out
suspense which was becoming intolerable. On the night before
many people had not gone to bed at all, but drifted restlessly
about the hot streets, or stood about in groups gossiping, or
gathered outside the newspaper offices reading the news.
Throughout the 31st Paris was a city of rumours. On the lips of
all were allusions to that time which the elderly and many
middle-aged could vividly remember — 1870, *l'année terrible*.
Thousands flocked to the shops to buy provisions as for a siege.
In the evening had come the news of Jaurès' assassination,[2] and
with it the sudden fear of a popular insurrection. In the warm
summer darkness the newspaper vendors raced down the boulevards with their bundles of papers crying, '*Jaurès, Assassiné!
Jaurès, Assassiné!*' The atmosphere was charged with dread and
foreboding. During the early morning, shortly before daybreak,
there was heard from time to time the regular, measured tramp
of marching men.

Soon after 5 p.m. on Saturday the windows of every post office
in Paris displayed a small square of yellow paper bearing the
inscription: 'General Mobilization Order. The first day of the
mobilization is Sunday, August 2nd.' Within an hour the
thoroughfares were almost deserted. Motor-buses disappeared
from the streets. Taxi-drivers refused fares and drove straight
home to don their uniforms. Even the busy little river steamers

[1] Lord Frederick Hamilton, *Here, There, and Everywhere*, pp. 274-5.
[2] Jean Jaurès, leader of the French Socialists, had just returned from a
gathering of the Socialist International in Brussels, convened in a supreme
endeavour to avert the threat of war. It was attended by Keir Hardie, Rosa
Luxembourg, Haase, and other leading Socialists.

had gone from the Seine. Many cafés were forced to put up their shutters, and many shops were doing next to no business. Round about the humble blocks and tenements where the poorer classes lived anguished farewells took place between husbands and wives, mothers and sons, young men and sweethearts. Many of the women were sobbing uncontrollably. The City of Light was lightsome no longer.

Gradually the streets came to life again. No sooner had the Yellow Paper appeared in the post offices than a procession carrying flags and chanting the 'Marseillaise' suddenly arrived on the scene, and groups began shouting in chorus, 'À *Berlin!'* The streets quickly filled with motor-cars and taxis carrying reservists and their friends to the railway stations, where crowds of conscripts mingled with bewildered tourists, laden with their bags and cases, trying desperately to get a train. Long queues formed outside the offices of Messrs Thomas Cook. From time to time columns of troops passed down the boulevards; as they marched they waved their *képis* while the people in the crowded cafés sprang to their feet and cheered. There were fervent cries of *'Vive la France!'* and *'Vive l'Armée!'*

That evening crowds of men marched arm in arm in procession up and down the principal thoroughfares of the city chanting the 'Marseillaise'. At the head of each procession was borne the republican tricolour. Suddenly, as one of these columns was passing, a man dashed out of a shop with a large red ensign and fell into step beside the bearer of the tricolour—a gesture which evoked a roar of applause.

During the next few hours the Russian, French and British national anthems were sung with enthusiasm. On Sunday Englishmen were everywhere cheered in Paris. For, as the *Echo de Paris* had predicted, Frenchmen were confident that the British Government would never allow Germany to over-stride the Continent; and France and Russia would certainly see England on their side in the not so distant future.

At the Gare du Nord there were scenes of indescribable confusion. With so many thousands of tourists endeavouring to leave *en masse*, it was as if half Paris were trying to escape from the city. Early in the afternoon, when there was a rush to catch the two o'clock train, the crowd outside was so dense that it was impossible for a cab to get within a quarter of a mile of the station. Inside there were no porters to be had: mountains of heavy luggage piling up by the weighing machines — and vehicles unloading still more luggage: wholesale cancellation of trains, and a wild struggle for seats and standing room in the few of them that ran. Hotels and boarding houses had suddenly been bereft of their chefs, waiters, and porters; lifts had stopped operating, and beds were practically unobtainable. It was impossible to change a note anywhere, to send a telegram, or to buy a railway ticket. Immense quantities of costly luggage had to be abandoned by the owners in their desperate anxiety to escape from France.

The trains were packed to suffocation point. Compartments, corridors, and lavatories even were crowded. It is said that during these days one of the passengers, a young girl who had suddenly been taken ill with appendicitis, actually died on her feet, standing jammed in the corridor.

The steamers from the Channel and North Sea ports were loaded with several times their normal complement of passengers. The vessel from the Hook of Holland arrived at Harwich with *nearly eight times* its regular number of passengers. The outgoing steamers were crowded with foreign reservists. Early on Sunday morning a crowd of 1,200 worn and weary travellers stood on the quay at Calais. At sunrise they were taken off in the English cross-Channel steamers. In the afternoon the long-awaited express from Paris arrived—the last train out, so it was said. Exhausted, famished, and dishevelled, the passengers swarmed across the quay. All their heavy luggage had been left behind in Paris. The only clothes they had were the clothes they were wearing. The only luggage still in their possession were the grips and hand-bags they were carrying.

'There's a party of twenty-five of us,' a well-to-do young American declared, 'and the last we saw of our belongings was a pile of twenty-five suitcases in the road outside the Gare du Nord.'

On the same day when the boat train arrived at Dieppe there were already 2,000 people waiting on the quay—and a Channel steamer, packed to overflowing, was backing out of the harbour before their eyes. The crowd on the quay, now increased to at least 3,000, was obliged to wait until midnight for another vessel; and when at last it arrived it could only take 1,000 out of the

3,000. Even so, the fortunate ones who got aboard were packed like sardines—there were passengers standing on the staircases and even sitting in the boats. It blew fresh from the south-west; there was a high sea running, and the night was wet. Scores of people lay about on the open deck drenched by the sprays which continually broke over the side. At 3.30 a.m. they arrived at Newhaven.

At Boulogne, on the previous day, a steamer had similarly put to sea leaving a large crowd of travellers stranded on the quay. When some time later an extra steamer was brought round there was a fierce struggle among the many Americans to get on board —they were shoving and heaving and almost pushing one another off the gangway into the sea. When the exhausted passengers reached Folkestone, they found there was no accommodation to be had in the town, and the station buffets were completely sold out. They had to pass the night as best they could lying about in the comfortless waiting-rooms and offices and on the platforms.

Early on the 3rd a small steamer with 1,200 passengers crowded on her decks reached Dover. They spoke breathlessly of the pandemonium on the quay at Ostend, of people fighting and struggling to get on board the last steamer, and of families separated in the mêlée.

'Passengers, 603. Pieces of luggage, 223', was the expressive announcement posted up at Victoria Station before the midday Folkestone train came in, three and a half hours late. It seemed an accurate summary of the situation.

An English girl, returning home during these last days of peace from a finishing school in the environs of Paris, later related her experiences.

'A . . . had so much luggage', she declared 'that it took all our change to pay for it. We had notes, but no one would change them. We could only buy one ham sandwich, and had nothing else from the time we left Colombes at seven o'clock until we arrived at Dover—and the boat was crowded and ever so late, and we *were* so hungry.'[1]

[1] C. S. Peel, *How We Lived Then* (1929), p. 15.

Meanwhile on the other side of the Channel the islanders were pursuing the accustomed tenor of their way. While on the Continent the troop trains rumbled day and night towards the frontier and millions of men were hurriedly getting into uniform, while the capitals of the combatant Powers resounded with the war-chants of ferocious nationalism—'God, the All-Terrible' 'Gott erhalte, Gott beschütze' — 'Deutschland, Deutschland über Alles'—'Allons, enfants de la Patrie'—'Zum Rhein, zum Rhein, zum deutschen Rhein'—people in England were calmly preparing . . . to go away. For this was Bank Holiday week-end; it was something they had all been looking forward to for weeks; and in this, as in former years, they intended to make the most of it.

'The rush to the seaside during the next few days', observed the *Daily Mirror* on August 1st, 'is likely to be the biggest in living memory.' Yesterday, Friday, the crowds at the principal London termini had been enormous. Moreover, the bookings to the Continent had apparently been unaffected by the crisis— until the 1st tourists had been streaming across the Channel in thousands. With the prospect of fine weather for the week-end, the man in the street was fully determined to take his holiday, whatever might be happening abroad; and at an early hour on Saturday morning people were pouring out of town by train, bus, tram, motor-car, or cycle, all bound for the seaside or the country.

There was, however, noticeably less laughter and chaff and high spirits among these holidaymakers than was usual on such occasions. In spite of all the bustle and cheerful anticipation, there was a certain 'something' in the air this day . . . it revealed itself in the many anxious faces and subdued conversations. At the railway stations passengers, up to the very moment of departure, were feverishly buying up the latest editions of the morning papers; and, as soon as they took their places in the train, became completely absorbed in them. Parties of young office workers out for the day anxiously conferred among themselves. What had the *Daily Mail* said about the crisis? They read and quickly knew—and derived little solace from that knowledge. Things were about as bad as they could be. Further up the train, in the first-class compartments, their elders and betters gravely pondered the headlines in the *Times* and *Morning Post*.

Public interest in the Home Rule issue, the Welsh Disestablishment Bill, and the Kikuyu controversy languished . . .

Throughout the whole day the hunger for news grew and grew. It was in fact not only the passengers, but also the guards and engine drivers, who were avid for the latest report and rumour. When the trains stopped at wayside stations, almost always there were small groups of people standing about the platforms engaged in earnest conversation. Passengers got in and out. fresh discussions started up; newspapers were compared. The endless arguments and exchange of news went on all over the country from dawn till late at night.

The chastening effect of the war news made itself felt even among the holiday crowds at the seaside. Fathers building sand-castles with their children or looking on at the pierrots or a Punch and Judy show would hear a newsboy's shout in the distance or catch sight of a fluttering poster up on the promenade and immediately run off to buy a paper.

Even the weather reflected this mood of *Stürm und Drang.* A morning of blue skies and radiant sunshine was followed by a gloomy and threatening afternoon; and the glass was falling. Next day the south-westerly wind had freshened to gale force and a high grey Channel sea was running.

Many clubmen and others, reluctant to leave town at such a time, remained within easy reach of the tape machine, the special editions of the morning and evening newspapers, and the latest report concerning the ebb and flow of discussion in the Cabinet. As the hours went by, the fateful news of that Saturday reached the anxious citizens—the raising of the Bank Rate to ten per cent, the mobilization of Austria, Germany, and France, and the German declaration of war against Russia.

That night the conflagration all but spread to the streets of London. Thousands of young Frenchmen and young Germans were preparing to rejoin their regiments and had worked themselves up to a state of high patriotic fervour. One of the many parties of Frenchmen roaming the streets had begun to chant their National Anthem, 'Allons, enfants de la patrie . . . ' when there came an answering roar from across the way, as a

13. *The Fleet putting to sea after the review, July 20th*

Newspaper vendors
with their posters

Crowds outside the
War Office
on Tuesday,
August 4th

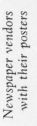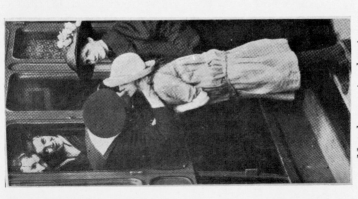

14. Naval reservists leaving
for Portsmouth

band of Teutons burst forth into 'Die Wacht am Rhein'; at which point an imperturbable London 'bobby' judged it wise to intervene with his gruff 'Pass along there, please! Pass along!'

The same night there was a great German rally in Gambrinus and much singing of German patriotic songs. Two men who gave an impressive display of the goose-step of the Prussian Guard up and down the hall were enthusiastically applauded. In the neighbouring streets the shouts of the newsboys caused a general rush out of doors. The pavements were thronged with shouting and gesticulating Teutons. Fraus and frauleins, shedding their accustomed dignity, danced gaily along the public ways. The young men embraced the maidens. The maidens smiled on the young men. There was a universal move towards the restaurants and clubs, where immense quantities of lager were poured down German throats to the success of German arms. The singing and dancing went on into the early hours of Sunday morning.

During the week-end, with the rapid development and spread of the crisis, the conflict of rival policies within the Government suddenly came to a head.

The hard core of the anti-war party in the Cabinet were Morley and Burns. They were the only ones in fact who at the last stood out against Grey's Entente policy which eventually imposed itself on all the rest. At the evening Cabinet of August 1st, when the two parties began to dicuss their differences freely and frankly, Burns took the lead in strongly opposing the interventionists. At this juncture it would appear that there were ten or eleven members of the Cabinet who were firmly opposed to Great Britain's entry into the war. The danger of a split was visibly drawing nearer. Runciman, with a troubled face, whispered to Morley as they were leaving the Cabinet Room, that he was very much afraid 'this is going to break us up tomorrow'.

When on the evening of August 1st the news reached London of Germany's declaration of war on Russia, Wickham Steed called on Count Benckendorff at the Russian Embassy and asked him whether there had been any hint of what Great Britain would do. Benckendorff answered in the negative.

I

'We have not been able to get the faintest indication of your Government's attitude', he declared, 'not so much as *that*', and he snapped his fingers with an expressive gestude. Sazanof (the Russian Foreign Minister) keeps telegraphing to me every few hours instructing me to beg Sir Edward Grey for some assurance of support, but Grey will not say a word or give any clue whatever to his thoughts. At St Petersburg, poor Buchanan (the British Ambassador) is sitting in his Embassy while fifty thousand Russians are singing 'Rule, Britannia' outside, and he knows no more than I do. What a position! No, I have got nothing, nothing—except a feeling, at the bottom of my heart, that Grey is straight. That is not much, but it is something.'[1]

In short, on August 1st, notwithstanding Germany's declaration of war against Russia, the British position remained unchanged. At this juncture Grey proposed to France and Germany that they should stand fast on their respective frontiers, without advancing, while Great Britain would remain neutral.

'If France', he told Cambon, 'cannot take advantage of this position, it is because she is bound by an alliance to which we are not parties, and of which we do not know the terms.' Grey said France would have to decide for herself at this stage without reckoning on assistance which, at the moment, he was not in a position to pledge. The Ambassador listened with growing indignation. He knew only too well that if the expected British assistance were not forthcoming it would probably mean both the ruin of his career and the destruction of his country as a great Power. He said in reply that he must refuse to transmit such a message to his Government. 'It would fill France with rage and indignation. My people would say that you had betrayed us!'

Soon after this the Ambassador, white with rage and nearly hysterical, staggered into Sir Arthur Nicolson's room. The latter hurried to his side and helped him to a chair.

'Ils vont nous lâcher', exclaimed the Frenchman, 'ils vont nous lâcher!' Nicolson thereupon went upstairs and angrily confronted his chief. Was it true, he demanded, that we had refused to stand by France in this her hour of greatest need? Grey only threw up his hands in despair and was silent. 'You will render us', said Nicolson violently, 'a by-word among nations!'

[1] H. Wickham Steed, *Through Thirty Years*, II, pp. 12-13.

Cambon then returned to the French Embassy, where he was visited by Wickham Steed. The latter asked him anxiously:

'Que faites-vous, M. Cambon?'

'J'attends de savoir', was the bitter reply, 'si le mot honneur doit être rayé du vocabulaire anglais.'

In the course of his visit to the Foreign Office, Cambon had spoken of the possibility of the German Fleet coming into the Channel to attack France.

Grey considered it improbable in the extreme that the Germans would run the risk of entering the Channel where they would be at our mercy if, finally, we should decide to intervene. He promised, however, to consult the Cabinet on this point; and at the next meeting, which took place on the following morning, he was authorized to inform Cambon that Great Britain was prepared to defend the coasts and shipping of France against enemy attack.

'There was really no news this morning [Asquith recorded in his journal]. Lloyd George, all for peace, is most sensible and statesmanlike for keeping the position still open. Grey declares that if an out-and-out and uncompromising policy of non-intervention is adopted, he will go. Winston very bellicose and demanding immediate mobilization. The main controversy pivots upon Belgium and its neutrality. We parted in fairly amicable mood, and are to sit again at eleven tomorrow, Sunday. I am still not quite hopeless about peace, though far from hopeful, but if it comes to war, I feel sure we shall have a split in the Cabinet.'[1]

Meanwhile in the Opposition camp things were beginning to move. General Wilson was as usual in conference with a number of leading Unionists, and the latter in turn were quickly passing on their information to the *Times* and *Morning Post*. On Saturday, August 1st, George Lloyd and Leo Maxse[2] interviewed, first, Count Benckendorff and, then, Paul Cambon. From them they learned of Grey's unwillingness to budge from the cautious position he had taken up and of his refusal to give them any pledge of support. It would appear from the discussion at the French

---

[1] Earl of Oxford and Asquith, *Memories and Reflections* (1928), II, pp. 7-8.
[2] The editor of the *National Review*.

Embassy that relations between the Ambassador and the Foreign Secretary were becoming strained to a far greater degree than one would perhaps deduce from Grey's version of these conversations. To Lloyd, Cambon unburdened himself without reserve.

'M. Cambon spoke of the situation as most critical and with great bitterness of the inaction of the British Government. He said: "It is true that you are under no written obligation and there is not a scrap of paper. But there is more. All our plans have been arranged in common. Our General Staffs have been consulted. You have seen all our schemes and preparations. Look at our Fleet! Our whole Fleet is in the Mediterranean in consequence of our arrangements with you, and our coasts are open to the enemy, *Vous nous avez livré.*" . . . Then, with a bitter cry, he exclaimed, "Honour! Does England know what honour is?" '[1]

'Where are your leaders?' the Ambassador next demanded. This was a decidedly awkward question for Lloyd, as most of the Conservative chieftains were on holiday in the country. (Not even the imminence of Armageddon, apparently, could change the agreeable usages of the English upper class.) But the interview galvanized the Opposition into energetic action. A telegram was dispatched forthwith to Lord Lansdowne at Bowood Park. Amery went down to Broadstairs to summon Austen Chamberlain; and Lloyd, who had already sounded Balfour, now drove off to Wargrave Hall in Berkshire where Bonar Law, Smith, and Carson were spending the week-end. He found that Smith and Carson had gone boating, while Bonar Law was playing tennis. The leader of the Opposition in fact refused to talk business until he had finished his set; and it was with some difficulty that Lloyd got him to return to town.

That night a meeting was hurriedly summoned at Lansdowne House, at which General Wilson expounded the military situation in western Europe to a distinguished party of leading Conservatives, which included Lord Lansdowne, Bonar Law, Balfour,[2] the Duke of Devonshire, and the Conservative Chief Whip.

[1] Austen Chamberlain, *Down the Years* (1935), p. 94.
[2] Balfour was a potent influence behind the scenes during these crucial days. He had been in close and continual touch with Winston Churchill.

Wilson, who was chafing at the Government's inaction, declared that mobilization orders ought already to have been issued, but that he had received no permission to take even preliminary steps. As a result of these deliberations, a letter was dispatched by car to 10 Downing Street, at noon on the following day, pledging the support of the Opposition leaders.

It was apparent by Sunday that our decision must soon be taken between neutrality and intervention. When the Cabinet met in the morning it was known that the Germans had invaded Luxemburg; in the evening the German ultimatum to Belgium was delivered.

The significance of these events was not lost abroad. The Russian Ambassador in Paris wired gleefully to St Petersburg that the German invasion of Luxemburg was looked upon very favourably in France, since it would inevitably evoke a protest from Great Britain and goad her into action. What would be even more effective for that purpose (added His Excellency cynically) would be the violation of Belgian neutrality.

The division in the Cabinet persisted throughout the first meeting on the Sunday; and Asquith recorded in his journal: 'We had a long Cabinet from eleven till nearly two, which very soon revealed that we are on the brink of a split. We agreed at last with some difficulty that Grey should be authorized to tell Cambon that our Fleet would not allow the German Fleet to make the Channel a base of hostile operations. . . . There is a strong party against any kind of intervention in any event. It will be a shocking thing if at such a moment we break up.'

The decision against allowing the German Fleet to operate in the Channel was not unanimous. Burns insisted that such a policy was tantamount to a declaration of war against Germany and refused to be a party to it. He accordingly resigned, though he was afterwards persuaded to postpone his resignation until the evening Cabinet.

On the issue as it had developed at this stage—the morning of August 2nd—the Cabinet was still, therefore, hopelessly divided on the subject of British intervention in the war. A majority of Ministers was, almost certainly, opposed to such a step. And not only the Cabinet, it appeared, but also the House of Commons and the nation were hopelessly divided. Asquith prudently resolved not to force the issue, and continued to wait upon events.

Early in the afternoon several of the Ministers, including Lloyd George and Samuel, went to luncheon at Lord Beauchamp's house in Belgrave Square, where the discussion was continued. Throughout these deliberations the Chancellor of the Exchequer maintained a detached, enigmatic, almost jocular approach to the problem which was confronting them. Neither the Prime Minister nor his colleagues had any idea what was going on inside Lloyd George's head. Much depended upon his ultimate decision. After luncheon Samuel returned to Downing Street; and Asquith's urgent inquiry was, 'What is Lloyd George going to do?' Samuel could not answer him with any certainty—but he said that he thought the Belgian issue would probably prove the decisive factor for nearly all the Ministers; whereupon the Prime Minister declared his intention of standing by Grey in any event.

Shortly after this Grey gave a written assurance to Cambon that the British Navy would protect the French coast against naval attack; but he added that he could give no promise of further assistance.

Morley passed the afternoon pondering the problem in the quiet of the Athenaeum. At last he made up his mind. He was frankly horrified at the imminent transmogrification of Campbell Bannerman's Cabinet into a Council of War; and he realized that for himself, at least, had come the parting of the ways. Rising from his chair, he left the club and made his way through the anxious crowds in Whitehall to Downing Street. During this walk he saw Ramsay Macdonald, Leader of the Labour Party, also bound for Westminster, and stopped. He asked him what line he was going to take. Macdonald replied that he would have nothing to do with war. 'Neither shall I', declared Morley; and added glumly that the prospect seemed very dark.

The evening Cabinet met at 6.30 p.m. All that day the German forces had been marching through Luxemburg and massing along the Belgian frontier. The Belgian issue held the centre of the stage. It was now agreed that it should be made evident that 'a substantial violation of the neutrality of that country would place us in a situation contemplated as possible by Mr Gladstone in 1870, when interference with Belgian independence was held

to compel us to take action.'[1] At this stage there began a significant swing towards intervention. The war party in the Cabinet
was visibly gaining ground. As the Ministers took their seats
Burns announced that he must go. When the Cabinet ended
Morley remarked quietly to Asquith that he was afraid that he,
too, must go.[2] Asquith looked him in the eye. 'One favour at any
rate', was his reply, 'I would ask you. Sleep on it.'[3] When the
Ministers emerged into Downing Street it was observed that
they were all looking deeply anxious and concerned.

[1] Q. Trevelyan, *Grey of Fallodon* (1937), p. 269.
[2] Simon and Beauchamp had also tendered their resignations, but were persuaded to withdraw them later.
[3] John Morley, *Memorandum on Resignation* (1928), p. 21.

CHAPTER 20

'Black Sunday'

The weather on Sunday, August 2nd, may be said once again to have symbolized the current international situation. It began with fine summer weather at dawn—but a few hours later the sky clouded over, and there was heavy rain. It continued gloomy and unsettled; and later there was a thunderstorm. Afterwards it cleared up for a while, and the sun shone brightly. Before nightfall, however, the clouds had rolled up again, and the day ended in a sombre, stormy sunset.

By order of the Archbishop of Canterbury special prayers for peace were offered this day in churches and chapels all over the country. These prayers frequently took the form of a solemn litany. The primate himself preached the afternoon sermon in Westminster Abbey, discoursing on the duty of the nation and the citizen. The Archbishop of York addressed a crowded congregation in York Minster in the morning. The gravity of the European situation and its lessons formed the subject of countless other sermons which were preached this Sunday. Preaching in Manchester Cathedral, the Dean declared that it was the duty of every Englishman, while hoping and praying for peace so long as peace was possible, to support the Government loyally if war was inevitable. 'A week ago,' observed the Vicar of St Matthew's, Torquay, 'little did we imagine the calamities which were to come so suddenly upon the Continent of Europe.' 'Those best able to judge', the Vicar of Wallington (Surrey) declared, 'said that we were in the face of the most terrible catastrophe in the memory of living man.' In not a few city and suburban churches, even as the congregations knelt and prayed for peace, the strident cries of the newspaper boys could be heard outside in the streets. The very quiet of the English Sabbath seemed charged with the ominous hush which precedes the storm. And even in little country churches, where the familiar sound and scents of high summer, drifting in through the open doors, usually made the

264

world's turmoils appear inexpressibly remote, the least imaginative could scarcely fail to note the measured pause which followed upon the versicle, 'Give peace in our time, O Lord', and the deep solemnity of the response, 'Because there is none other that fightest for us, but only Thou, O God'.

Even so, after the long years of peace and inviolable security in which generation after generation of our people had been lapped it was hard to realize the imminence of war. It was not only in secluded country hamlets, but also in quiet town squares and trim suburban avenues, that the inhabitants in their heart of hearts believed (as Sir William Harcourt had once remarked to Winston Churchill) that 'Nothing ever happens'.

It is, perhaps, not properly appreciated how short was the actual duration of the crisis and how quickly it flared up into war. Between the presentation of the Austrian ultimatum at Belgrade and the British declaration of war against Germany was an interval of only twelve days. The majority of the educated classes in this country, as has already been said, probably did not comprehend the gravity of the situation until about a week before the outbreak of hostilities; while the mass of the population only came to realize the imminence of the peril in the course of the last two or three days.

By Sunday the alarm was no longer confined to the *cognoscenti*. The man in the street was becoming increasingly anxious and concerned and was devouring the newspapers as never before. (The countryman, however, remained at least a couple of days behind him in awareness of the danger.) The *Daily Mail* came out with a midday special, with 'War Edition' inscribed in flaming red letters beside the title.

It is certain in the early part of the week-end public opinion —that is, in the nation as a whole—remained in a state of flux. Both the pro- and anti-interventionists in the Cabinet, Parliament, press, London, and the provinces commanded a numerous following; but the voice of neither party was, as yet, decisive. The great majority of the populace had still to make up their minds.

The neutralist party was strong in the industrial North. The great northern daily, the *Manchester Guardian*, opposed the war to the last possible moment. 'Neutrality the one policy', declared one of its headlines on August 1st—'The crime and folly of joining in'.[1] The neutralists were numerous in Birmingham and elsewhere in the Midlands, and also in the West Country. Even in the capital, which to all appearances was a stronghold of the war party, there were a large number of people who read and approved the neutralist sentiments expressed in the *Daily News*. As late as Sunday, the war was freely denounced in trains, buses, and other public vehicles. 'We place on record our conviction', observed the *Daily News* two days after war had actually been declared, 'that it was possible, and that it would have been just and prudent and statesmanlike, for England to have remained neutral.'

'It is safe to say', the *Nation* had declared on Saturday, 'that there has been no crisis in which the public opinion of the English people has been so definitely opposed to war as it is at this moment. The consternation in the world of German finance, the closing of almost every Stock Exchange in Europe, including that of London, are enough to explain the pacific spirit of the world of finance and commerce. . . . This spirit is reflected in the House of Commons, and it is everywhere recognized that a Minister who led this country into war would be responsible for a war as causeless and unpopular as any war in history.'

What had it got to do with England? That was the question that sprang to the lips of millions of ordinary men and women during the nationwide debate which raged over the week-end. There later on appeared a trenchant article in Horatio Bottomley's *John Bull* headed simply, 'To Hell with Serbia'. That really summed up the feelings of a good many people. 'Why', demanded the *Birmingham Gazette*, 'should we risk a century of really deadly enmity with Germany—for that is what it would mean whatever the immediate result of a European struggle—to intervene in a paying-off of old scores between France and Germany?' A very large following in the Free Churches was strongly opposed to the war. Innumerable sermons in Nonconformist chapels were preached against British intervention, followed by a spate of resolutions denouncing the very idea of our joining in

---

[1] On August 3rd the editor, Clement Scott, one of the most influential Liberals in the country, wired to Lloyd George: 'Feeling of intense exasperation among leading Liberals here at prospect of Government embarking on war; no man who is responsible can lead us again'.

the struggle. In the Established Church the anti-interventionist school was a great deal smaller and weaker; but, still, it existed.

It is interesting to note that a section of the English Catholics were tending at this stage to support what they evidently regarded as the Catholic side in the quarrel. 'Russia is the enemy', pronounced the *Universe*. 'The Muscovite Empire has constituted itself the protector of "the little Slav". . . . . We say then that the heart and mind of the British Empire ought to go out to Austria-Hungary and Germany in the cause of liberty, peace, and progress.'

Public opinion in a country like this is a vast and amorphous thing. At times the national temper will reveal itself in a manner that is quite unmistakable—but that is the exception rather than the rule. It is usually difficult, if not impossible, to assess the numerical strength of two conflicting schools of opinion; and in any case, numbers of themselves will not decide the issue. What really counted, during this crucial week-end, was that element of public opinion which was *politically effective*.

Here the more important daily and weekly papers, headed by the *Times*, played a major role in assisting the country to make up its mind.

Garvin's powerful leading article in the *Observer*, on August 2nd, was a potent factor in influencing public opinion in the circles that mattered. Garvin's leaders were regularly discussed and quoted in the mansions of Mayfair and Belgravia, in the clubs of Pall Mall, in country houses, in officers' messes, in cathedral closes, in the senior common rooms of the older universities, and in the upper levels of the middle and professional classes generally. The article in question, written in his usual terse and trenchant style, was one of the most important that he ever produced. It was a cogent and eloquent plea for our entering the war on the side of France and Russia. It began by emphasizing the extreme gravity of the situation and the magnitude of the issues involved:

'Which of us has not known once or twice in life the first dull hour of waking under a sense of appalling calamity? . . . Such a conscious moment in the life of the whole world has never been known; its memory will never be forgotten while the recollection of this generation endures, nor its record lost while a page of history remains. . . . It is not only the end of such a measure of safety as most nations have known for more than forty years. It is the doom of that general peace which has not been broken at one time from end to end of Europe since the climax of the Napoleonic wars a hundred years ago.'

Garvin went on to deal with the vital interests of this country in the balance of power and the independence of the Low Countries:

'Across the narrow waters our own vital issues are at stake— the existence of France and the independence of the Low Countries; the control of the opposite shores of the North Sea and its great ports so near to our own coasts; the very status of the Straits of Dover. Never even in the time of Napoleon was the danger of a European overturn so fraught with deadly peril for ourselves.'

He called for prompt and decisive action:

'Let us grasp these things without the loss of a single hour. Our duty is clear. We must do it with the whole of our energy. Since France mobilizes we must mobilize without loss of a day. We fight as every great people must fight for the collateral securities which are in this case of such a character that they are an indispensable part of our insular safety and our Imperial existence. . . . The main European question once raised swallows up all minor questions, like Aaron's serpent the rest. Upon that matter there is not the vestige of a doubt that our vital interests bind us to uphold France and to secure the neutral shores of the North Sea with instancy of decision and with the uttermost of our power.'

A view that had become pretty general among the British governing class was that war between Great Britain and Germany was in any case inevitable. 'They feel that it must come some time', Page declared, '—why not now and have it over?'

It would appear that as the crisis developed neutralist circles seriously underrated the strength of the war party. This was partly owing to the fact that the ministerialists had been in office for so many years that they were inclined to overlook the fact, in certain circumstances, the Conservatives would in all likelihood wax, and the Liberals wane, in power and influence. These circumstances were now arising. The attitude of the Opposition leaders was becoming more and more important. Though the Conservatives as a whole were nothing like so unanimous as the tone of their press would suggest, there can be no doubt that a significant proportion of them favoured Great Britain's entry into the war.

Throughout these crucial days, wherever groups of men were gathered together, the vital debate continued. In the home, in public transport, on cricket and tennis grounds, on quays and piers, in cabmen's shelters, in harbour offices, in village inns, and on benches in recreation grounds, railway stations, and on sea fronts, the talk went on and on. The rival policies were expounded with force and passion. However, the situation as it was, the mass of the population at the week-end were apparently still unconvinced by the arguments on either side. Some outstanding and overriding issue was demanded to determine their attitude to the impending struggle.

On Sunday the order went out for Naval Mobilization. The telegraph swiftly carried the order from end to end of the United Kingdom. In every seaport, town, and village in these islands telegraph boys, coastguards, policemen and others bore the fateful message to the reservists in the mercantile marine, fishing fleets, and every kind of civilian employment. Londoners, 'Geordies', Manxmen, Yorkshire 'tykes', West Countrymen, Scillonians, Channel Islanders, 'Taffies', 'Paddies', and 'Macs' forthwith donned their uniforms and departed for their depots. In Hull and Grimsby, and in the East Anglian fishing ports, large numbers of reservists received their official telegrams, and on Monday a trawler was dispatched to recall the fishing fleet in the North Sea. In Fleetwood the trawlermen, hurrying home to change their clothes and fetch their gear, reported in scores at the Customs. It has been estimated that of the Scottish drifter crews no less than sixty per cent were called up. In some of the smaller ports — Anstruther was one — the recall of so many reservists brought the summer fishing to an abrupt end.

Down in the West Country, the home of so many and flourishing a fishing community, the telegraph boys and policemen knocked at the doors of thousands of little homes huddled in tiers above the busy harbours. The word went swiftly round the boats and fishing lofts and benches by the harbour-side where the old men sat smoking and yarning in the sun; and presently all 'Fore Street' was in a ferment of excitement. Some of the reservists were away at sea. Others had to be roused out of their beds. Hurriedly they all shifted into uniform, while their wives and mothers—many of them in tears—helped them to pack their last things. Then, shouldering their kitbags, they were off. At Brixham the first notifications were delivered at four o'clock in the morning and by six all the men had received their orders. Soon they were toiling up the steep ascent with their kits on their way to the railway station. Nearly every family in Brixham was affected by the mobilization, and many of the smacks in the harbour were unable to put to sea for lack of crews. The annual regatta had to be abandoned. (A Brixham trawler entering Dunmore harbour in the south of Ireland was immediately boarded by the coastguard, and all the reservists taken out of her.) At Looe large numbers of men mustered by the quay and then marched off to the station headed by the town band. At Fowey, Polruan, and elsewhere large numbers of reservists departed for their depot amid scenes of unprecedented excitement. At Falmouth Naval Mobilization was proclaimed by the town crier; the reservists were speedily rounded up by the police and various volunteers, and some 200 of them got off by the evening train. Penzance swarmed with bluejackets; for three-quarters of the fishing fleets of Mounts Bay and St Ives had reservists on board. It was the same all the way up the Bristol Channel. 'I went home and found Appledore deserted', relates Captain W. J. Slade, the son of a local shipowner. 'All the sailors had gone to the Navy and Father had several ships left in different ports with no crews.'

Meanwhile another kind of mobilization was in progress. Germany, France, Russia, and other Continental Powers were hurriedly recalling their nationals. Soho was almost deserted in the afternoon. From the network of streets to the south of Soho

Square an apparently endless flow of foreigners of all nationalities passed down Charing Cross Road and through Trafalgar Square on their way to the railway stations. At Charing Cross and Victoria large numbers of travellers bound for the Continent waited for hours outside the barriers. Many hundreds of waiters, cooks, and other servants employed at hotels and restaurants throughout London, as well as hairdressers and musicians, were leaving or had already left England for their native land. During this and the following day French and Swiss chefs, and German and Austrian waiters, jostled British naval reservists in the crowded railway stations.

Across the Channel our partner in the *entente cordiale* anxiously waited for England to arrive at her decision. Though the French press affected confidence that all would be well and that the English would 'come in', the rulers of France were far from sharing that confidence. Cambon with consummate skill had succeeded in manoeuvring the British Government into a position which would make it extremely difficult for them to exercise that freedom of choice which, in theory, they possessed. But—supposing they took their stand simply on the written agreement of 1912? Suppose, after all, France were to be left in the lurch? As the British Cabinet hedged and hesitated and still continued to wait upon events, at the Quai d'Orsay anxiety increased. Were they never going to make up their minds, those islanders? Did they not realize that time was the all-important factor—that, unless here and now they took their stand by the side of their friends, the consequence, for France, might well be complete and irretrievable disaster?

In the evening, however, came the news of the imminent invasion of Belgium and of King Albert's appeal to our own King. Cambon telegraphed to his Government:

'The protection of Belgian neutrality is here considered so important that Great Britain will regard its violation by Germany as a *casus belli*. It is a specially British interest, and there is no doubt that the British Government, faithful to the traditions of its policy, will insist upon it, even if the business world —in which German influence is making tenacious efforts—exercises pressure to prevent the Government committing itself against Germany.'

Though, generally speaking, there was little outward sign of the widespread alarm that prevailed, the day might well have been named 'Black Sunday'. On all sides there was an insatiable appetite for news, and special editions of the morning and evening newspapers succeeded one another almost hourly. Newsboys combed the lanes and byways of every town and city, and crowds collected before the notice boards on view at the local newspaper offices. The holiday crowds paraded as usual on the promenades and in the public gardens; the children played on the sands, and the places of entertainment were well attended. But the underlying tension was significantly reflected in the omnipresent newspaper and newspaper poster; in the little knots of people which were continually forming to discuss the war news; and in a general restless anxiety to read and hear about the latest developments rather than settle down to the usual holiday diversions. And — more significant still — strong but repressed emotions began to break through the accustomed British phlegm. At Brighton, during a Sunday evening concert given on the Palace Pier, immediately the opening bar of the National Anthem was heard the large audience rose as one man, and heads were bared. After a series of patriotic pieces had been played, there was fervent and prolonged applause. At Worthing, Bournemouth, and other resorts similar demonstrations occurred.

All over the country on Sunday afternoon there was intense excitement when the mobilization orders were exhibited outside the post offices, and at the sight of the sailors themselves hurrying off to the railway stations. In most of the cities and larger towns the streets were thronged with all classes of people reading and discussing the news, crowding in front of the newspaper offices, and drifting aimlessly to and fro in a fever of excitement and suspense, until a late hour. But the highest tension of all was in London.

The immense crowds which gathered in the West End this day were restless and preoccupied. It was remarked by onlookers that there was no sign of 'maffiking'. From early in the morning until late at night the people eagerly bought up each successive edition of the newspapers as they appeared and assembled in groups to discuss the impending catastrophe. When the Ministers met at 10 Downing Street for the evening Cabinet, a large crowd waited, silent, patient, and orderly, outside in Whitehall.

A great peace demonstration had been arranged that afternoon in Trafalgar Square. But as soon as Ben Tillett had hauled himself up on to the plinth, a large crowd of anti-socialists began a noisy counter-demonstration which was presently joined by a large body of French reservists, waving tricolours, on their way to Victoria Station. The cheers which greeted each successive socialist speaker were almost drowned by an outburst of counter-cheers and booing. The strains of the 'Red Flag' mingled inharmoniously with those of 'God Save the King' and 'Rule, Britannia'. When Hyndman started to speak his voice was quite inaudible more than a dozen yards off; nor did the counter-demonstrators for an instant relax their efforts to shout him down. The hoisting of a red flag was the signal for a determined attempt on the part of the anti-neutralists to rush the platform and to seize the socialist banner, which the police only just managed to prevent. When the excitement was at its height a heavy shower of rain suddenly cleared the square. At the Admiralty Arch a second meeting was held—this one in support of intervention. A succession of warlike speeches were presently delivered and fervently cheered by the spectators.

The war fever spread from central London to quiet suburban streets and lanes several miles distant from the City proper. All day long there might be heard at frequent intervals the scud of flying feet and the shrill cries of newspaper boys shouting the latest news. Whereupon the dogs began to bark, windows were quickly thrown open, and masters, mistresses, maids, and children came running out of doors to buy a paper. Later in the day the clamour mingled with the sound of the evening church-bells— 'Germany marches into France! Germany marches into France!' As the congregations emerged into the sunlit streets after evening service the question was on everyone's lips, 'What will England do?'

Throughout the day there were large crowds gathered outside Buckingham Palace. From time to time cheers were raised for the King; but it was not until the news of the Naval Mobilization reached them that their patriotic fervour found relief in the singing of the National Anthem, 'Rule, Britannia', and the 'Marseillaise'.

That night there was a great Anglo-French demonstration outside the Palace. There was a crowd of about 5,000 people,

British and French, waving Union Jacks and tricolours and cheering for France and England alternately. 'God Save the King' and the 'Marseillaise' were sung with tremendous gusto, followed by round after round of cheers for the King and Queen. Shortly before ten o'clock the King and Queen came out on the balcony. At that a great shout went up from the French of 'Vive le Roi !' and 'Vive la Reine !' while the British broke into 'God Save the King', following this with the 'Marseillaise'. The King and Queen retired, and the crowd marched off in procession singing and cheering.

Sporadic outbursts of enthusiasm kept the West End in a ferment of excitement until late into the night. Just before eleven o'clock, when the crowd in Piccadilly Circus was at its densest, a party of young girls appeared on the roof of the Criterion Restaurant and unfurled a large Union Jack, which they draped over the parapet. This was the signal for a tremendous outburst of cheering, which went on until after midnight. Later still a procession, headed by a grey-bearded veteran, marched out from Piccadilly Circus, through the neighbouring streets, singing the 'Marseillaise'.

That same night the American Ambassador, who had lately rented a small farmhouse down in Ockham, Surrey, for his weekend quarters, recorded his impressions on returning from a stroll in the peaceful starlit countryside.

'The Grand Smash is come', wrote Page in his journal, ' . . . I walked out into the night a while ago. The stars are bright, the country quiet—as quiet as peace itself. Millions of men are in camp and on warships. Will they all have to fight and many of them die—to unentangle this network of treaties and alliances and to blow off huge debts with gunpowder so that the world may start again?'[1]

---

[1] B. J. Hendrick, *Life and Letters of Walter H. Page*, I, pp. 301, 303.

CHAPTER 21

The strangest Bank Holiday

Monday was the strangest Bank Holiday that Engand had ever known. With peace and war hanging in the balance, it was destined also to be the day of decision. The principal streets of the West End and City were thronged as never before on a Bank Holiday. A great many people who had intended to go away decided to stay in town after all; others hurried in from the suburbs and country in order to share in the excitement of the capital at this crucial moment of our history; many more who had had their plans for the day disrupted by the suspension of holiday traffic on certain lines remained at the railway stations to watch the departure of the reservists, and afterwards joined the throngs in the streets.

At first sight it appeared just like the normal Bank Holiday crowd—carefree, jolly, and gay. A careful observer, however, might have noticed that there was a strange exhilaration in the air, and that many of these folk, especially the men, were in the grip of a strong emotion. From time to time they seemed to lose all interest in the usual holiday pleasures, and would bury themselves in their newspapers, or stand about in little groups anxiously discussing the news. Most of these people forming the crowds 'up West' were apparently Londoners. Others, who had travelled up from the country that day, were noticeably less concerned at the turn of events, and were simply out to enjoy themselves.

Men in flannels and women in light summer frocks more suitable for the beaches than for the pavements of Westminster spent most of the day strolling about the Strand and Whitehall. The comings and goings of Cabinet Ministers and Ambassadors were awaited with breathless interest. Wherever there was a chance, in fact, of anything interesting or important to be seen large crowds quickly gathered. There was a brisk kerbside traffic in the rapidly succeeding editions of morning and evening newspapers, also in the miniature Union Jacks and tricolours now being hawked in the streets. It was noticeable that the gravity of the crisis had broken down the accustomed British reserve. Complete strangers spoke freely one to another, and news and views were eagerly exchanged. It is on record that bus and tram conductors became so interested in the all-absorbing topic of the day that they joined in the unending discussions that were going on among the passengers and often forgot to take their fares.

As on Sunday, at Charing Cross and Victoria large numbers of foreign reservists, on the way to rejoin their regiments, hurriedly bade farewell to their relations and friends before entraining for the Continent. The Frenchmen on leaving sang the 'Marseillaise' and cheered for France. They were cheered in return by the delighted holiday crowds. Naval reservists were still pouring into the capital from all over the country. Among them was a large contingent of trawlermen from our eastern and western fishing ports—tough-looking mariners with mahogany complexions, still wearing their dark blue jerseys and rough sea-going trousers. At Waterloo, where all the Bank Holiday excursions had been cancelled, a great crowd of holidaymakers thronged the departure platforms to cheer these seamen as they left in trainloads to join their depots. The scenes in the station that morning presented some extraordinary contrasts. On the one hand there were innumerable family parties—the children laden with buckets and spades for the beaches which they were not to visit. On the other there were all these hordes of naval ratings who had been so suddenly recalled to the Service from their various civilian avocations. There were unexampled scenes of ardour and enthusiasm as the holidaymakers gave vent to their country's traditional pride and confidence in the Fleet—and of pathos, too, as hundreds of these reservists bade farewell to their wives and children, very many of whom were in tears. From early morning till late at night, special train after special train rolled away out of the station on its journey to Portsmouth.

At the American Embassy pandemonium reigned. Even before breakfast time the offices were packed from wall to wall. Page and his staff were kept continuously on their feet till nearly two o'clock in the morning. That day more than 2,000 hapless United States citizens crowded into the Embassy in Grosvenor Square—

many of them in a state of near hysteria. 'Three thousand miles of ocean roll between you and them', Edmund Burke had said long ago in reference to the American colonists. All these throngs of respected, substantial citizens from the New World, thus suddenly entrapped in the toils of the European embroglio, desired nothing better than to get those three thousand miles of ocean between themselves and the greatest war in history at the earliest possible moment.

From morning till night they kept pouring into Grosvenor Square in such numbers that many of them were forced to queue outside on the pavement. The flight from the Continent had become almost a panic. The travellers arrived in this country for the most part without funds—men who had had to leave behind them expensive motor-cars, and women who had been glad to barter jewellery for a handful of sandwiches. Page and his secretaries continued to address them at intervals during the rest of the day, assuring them that they would all be safely sent home, if only they would be patient. Still, they were only partly mollified. Some of the more frantic callers waved British banknotes under the Ambassador's nose and demanded American currency, vowing that their Government and its agents ought to be shot. Others appeared to expect their passages home to be handed to them on the spot. Meanwhile shoals of letters and telegrams kept pouring into the Embassy. Page filled his offices with stenographers and carried on. For two whole days, he declared, it was 'bedlam turned loose'.

Many thousands of Londoners spent their Bank Holiday in the usual way. There were large numbers of people in the parks, in the Zoological Gardens, at Madame Tussaud's (where the latest exhibit was entitled 'The Crisis of Europe, with lifelike models of King George, the Emperor of Austria, King Peter of Serbia, and Other Reigning Sovereigns'), and at Earl's Court and the White City. The theatres, music-halls, and other places of entertainment were well attended. And there was cricket.

For the Bank Holiday match at Kennington Oval, Surrey v. Notts., there was a keen and appreciative attendance of about 17,000 people. The weather, particularly in the afternoon, was brilliant; and, in spite of the heavy rain that had fallen during the week-end, the wicket was in excellent order. Surrey won the toss and scored 472 for five wickets. This fine performance was due largely to Jack Hobbs' splendid innings of 226 runs—the highest total that he had as yet achieved.[1] But even at the Oval there was something in the atmosphere which suggested that a good many among that holiday crowd were thinking of graver matters than cricket. From where they sat on the balcony of the pavilion, members of the Surrey County Cricket Club and their guests could see, away across the vista of innumerable smoky rooftops, the flag flying over the Houses of Parliament, where even now, as they knew, Grey must be making his speech. The same reflection must surely have occurred to many on the crowded benches below, as their eyes wandered from the pitch to the flaring headlines in the paper spread out upon their knees, and from the paper back again to the pitch.

A favourite haunt of Londoners on a Bank Holiday was Hampstead Heath.

From the early morning of the 3rd immense crowds of holiday-makers had been gradually converging on the Heath. Up the road from the railway station and the tram terminus streamed a cheery, jovial, motley procession which was seemingly endless, of men, women, and children of all ages. Hundreds of thousands of working folk, released from toil and the drab round of every-day existence by this great national holiday, all of them intent—despite wars and rumours of wars—on enjoying themselves to their heart's delight, were making their way by train, tube, bus, or tram, and by wagonette, charabanc, cab, cart, pony-trap, float, or 'shank's mare', to the high, undulating open country which lay to the north of the capital. By about nine o'clock the fair was in full swing, and by noon the crowd had grown so great that one could scarcely see the grass at all for the people standing or sitting on it.

The setting of this annual Cockney carnival was superb. The southern side of Hampstead Heath commanded extensive views of central London, with the dome of St Paul's and the spires of many of Wren's finest masterpieces rising in the midst, and the

---

[1] Next day Hobbs was summoned to the office at the Oval. 'I have bad news for you', the Secretary informed him. 'The military authorities have commandeered the Oval' (Jack Hobbs, *My Cricket Memories*, p. 189).

serpentine windings of the Thames on its way to the North Sea
for more than twenty miles. From the summit of the Heath, up
by The Spaniards and Jack Straw's Castle, could be seen the roof-
tops of Harrow and Hendon, and the wooded hills beyond; and,
through gaps in these nearer heights, there were glimpses of the
distant Chilterns.

On their arrival upon the Heath the people gave themselves
up wholeheartedly to the enjoyment of the hour. The best of the
entertainment was free. There was always plenty to see and
to hear without the necessity of spending a penny. It was
almost like looking on at some colossal, non-stop, open-air
music-hall.

In 1914 there was still a distinctive coster speech, and a distinctive coster costume. On that day might be seen Harry and
Harriet in all their gala finery. Some of the men were wearing
their treasured 'pearlies' — greyish-coloured suits sewn with
myriads of pearly buttons. The women wore very large hats,
adorned with still larger 'fevvers'. Between parties and indivi-
duals there flowed unceasingly a quick-fire exchange of comment
and badinage spiced with the perky, cock-sparrow, gay, resilient,
indomitable humour of the true-born Cockney. (He was going to
need all that humour in the time that was coming.) The fun on
Hampstead Heath was quite uninhibited, uproarious, and full-
blooded; nobody stood on ceremony, and all were out to have a
good time; the pubs were open all day long, and the beer flowed
freely; there was naturally a good deal of drunkenness and horseplay, but hardly any hooliganism; apart from a few not especially
serious 'incidents', the holidaymakers, as a whole, and considering all things, were remarkably good-humoured and well-
behaved. The enormous Bank Holiday throng gave the police
little trouble.

The alarming antagonism between the classes, which was
partly the outcome of the savage party warfare of the last few
years, found no place in the revels on the Heath. A 'gent' strolling over from one of the larger houses in the vicinity to see the
fun was not regarded as an intruder, but rather as a welcome
visitor—the more so if he showed himself a 'sport' by knocking
down a coconut, or neatly ringing his prize in the hoop-la contest. Nor had the 'gent' the slightest objection to being greeted
with a cheerful shout of 'Where did yer get that 'at?' or—

admiringly—'What 'air!' The spectacle of the classes all jumbled together in a casual, carefree, cheery, jostling mob—each taking the other entirely for granted and regarding their foibles with good-humoured tolerance — was the legacy of an older and simpler England. It existed only on such occasions as this, and, on a smaller scale, fairly widely throughout the country, at certain village festivities.

On the other hand, the stricter kind of middle-class matron or spinster might well purse her lips at some of the goings-on on Bank Holiday Monday. For (though, generally speaking, nobody minded) the Heath on this occasion was certainly no Sunday School . . .

From the outskirts of the Heath by the Vale of Health the fair stretched up the hill to The Old Bull and Bush, Jack Straw's Castle, and The Spaniards road that ran along the ridge. On this part of the Heath a mushroom town of booths, huts, and tents had sprung up almost overnight. Here the crowd was at its densest, and here the fun was fast and furious. Here were the roundabouts, swingboats, shooting galleries, boxing booths, coco-nut shies ('Three shies a penny—roll, bowl, or pitch!', Aunt Sallies, hoop-las, peep-shows, waxworks, Punch and Judy shows, try-your-strength machines, contortionists, acrobats, and freak-shows (the Strong Man, the Fat Woman, the Boneless Wonder, and all the rest of them). Here were the vendors of cheap jewellery, tin trumpets, and drums, and of pork pies, pigs' trotters, cockles, mussels, whelks, oranges, bananas, tarts, ices, and other popular delicacies. Here were the famous tea gardens where generations of Cockneys had taken their pleasure. Here, too, were the donkeys, the ponies, the peripatetic photographers, and the gramophone operators. The crowded swing-boats rose and fell above the heads of the throng, while the roundabouts whirled round to the accompaniment of steam organs which blared forth, in unending succession, the popular tunes of today and yesterday, to which everyone within earshot whistled, hummed, sang, stamped, shouted, and howled the chorus—'Hold your hand out, naughty boy'—'Oh, oh, Antonio'—'Everybody's doing it'—'Alexander's Rag-Time Band'—'Itchy Coo'—'You made me love you'—'Tipperary'—and, of course, Florrie Forde's well-loved 'Down at The Old Bull and Bush', which was almost the national anthem of the Heath.

Come, come, come and make eyes at me,
Down at The Old Bull and Bush.
Come, come, have a port wine with me,
Down at The Old Bull and Bush.
Dear little German band—
La — la, la, la, la — la !
Just let me hold your hand, dear !

Above all, there was the dancing.

The girls as a rule were far better dancers than the youths. A frequent spectacle on the Heath, on August Bank Holiday, was four girls dancing together—two opposite two. Encouraged by the presence of a large and appreciative audience, these damsels, some of whom were remarkably gifted and graceful performers, gave of their best. In the grassy hollows of the Vale of Health, along the highway leading to The Spaniards, and in the leafy lane by The Old Bull and Bush, they danced with joy and abandon to the music of the piano-organ, melodeon, or steam-organ of the roundabouts. The spectacle of the costers dancing on Hampstead Heath on Bank Holiday has been vividly recalled by the late W. Macqueen-Pope:

'But despite all the Fun of the Fair, it was the dancing that mattered. In long lines they faced each other, women one side, men the other, young and old alike; the lines advanced upon each other, prancing and with heads down. When collision seemed inevitable they retreated, heads back, chests extended and knees working high in the air, the age-old dance of the true Londoner. And the climax came when the 'Arries and 'Arriets exchanged headgear. That was really the apex of the Carnival, the final expression of unconfined and unrestrained joy.'[1]

Another unforgettable feature of the old Bank Holiday revels was the skipping, which was scarcely less popular among the factory girls than the dancing. The skipping rope would be turned by men, who would also place a board on the ground for the use of customers. ('Now, then, lydies! Skip as long as yer likes for a penny!') There was, in addition, donkey and pony riding, kite flying on the breezy heights, and model yacht racing. Meanwhile many thousands of the holidaymakers had scat-

[1] Macqueen-Pope, *Twenty Shillings in the Pound*, pp. 368-9.

tered themselves, in little family parties, far beyond the limits of the fair. Away beyond The Spaniards road and Jack Straw's Castle, in brackeny hollows and bushy nooks, on sunny hill-slopes and in the shade of great old trees, they lay there picnicking, gossiping, sleeping, smoking, reading, or simply basking in the warm sunshine, while the blare of the steam-organs and the roar of the choruses, softened by distance, floated up to them from the fair.

At last, as the sun sank towards the western horizon, the stream of humanity began to flow towards the distant town. Though the singing and dancing was still going merrily on by The Old Bull and Bush, thousands of people were gradually making their way towards the railway station and the bus and tram routes. For a few blissful, carefree hours the multitude— especially the younger ones among them—had contrived to forget the dark shadow that was swiftly spreading over Europe and was now threatening to engulf this land. Even before they had gained the lights and pavements of the town the hoarse cries of the newspaper vendors stationed on the outskirts of the Heath recalled them to harsh reality.

'*Evening News!*' '*Star!*' '*Standard!*' '*Globe!*' '*Speshul!*' '*Invasion of France!*' '*Germany's Ultimatum to Belgium!*' '*England and the War!*' '*Pa - per!*'

Where the travelling facilities permitted, the holiday crowds spread themselves at large over the neighbouring coasts and countryside. But, wherever they went, near or far, it appeared that the War Cloud overshadowed them; and this despite the fact that the people were out to enjoy their holiday, war or no war—and that most of the larger holiday resorts were as crowded as ever they had been.

Before noon some twenty special trains from London had each disgorged a load of several hundred passengers at Brighton Station. A ceaseless stream of humanity now surged steadily down Queen's Road to the front. Soon an immense throng had covered the promenades, the upper and lower esplanades, and the foreshore—the crowds on the beach between the two piers were so dense that one could scarcely see the shingle. The Palace

Pier was, perhaps, the leading centre of attraction. The converging streams of strollers on the front lost no time in filling its spacious promenade deck, which was brilliantly illuminated by the bright sunshine and ablaze with gay bunting. Throughout the day holidaymakers lounged in deck-chairs in the sun and breeze; bathers disported themselves in the tumbling surf; children played on the sands and paddled, or amused themselves at the automatic machines; steamers and sailing yachts glided to and fro on the sunlit, sparkling sea.

Large crowds awaited their turn on the little electric railway which ran along the top of the beach as far as Black Rock to the eastward (it formerly ran, on piles, to the neighbouring village of Rottingdean) and afforded an excellent view of Brighton front.

From the shingle near the Aquarium, where a certain well-laden sailing yacht was about to shove off, there came the familiar cry:

'Any more for the *Skylark*?'

The *Skylark* was more than just a sailing yacht: she was an institution. Indeed, it was impossible to imagine Brighton beach without her. Every morning and afternoon ('Wind, weather, and other Circumstances permitting') she would put out for 'a jolly sail' in the Channel. Her present master and owner, Cap'n Collins, was the son of a famous Brightonian, Cap'n Fred Collins, whose sturdy, thickset figure, crowned by a glazed black straw-hat, had been familiar to generations of visitors. It is said that in his time he had taken out well over a million passengers. The captain had died, greatly revered, nearly two years earlier—like Daniel Peggotty and many another good seaman, old Fred Collins, after a long illness, 'went out with the tide'. Thousands of English youngsters had made their first acquaintance with the sea, and with *mal de mer*, on board the old *Skylark*. On this particular day they were likely to have experience of both—for, after Sunday's south-westerly gale, there was a lively sea running.

Still, the War Cloud overshadowed the scene.

The people were enjoying themselves, it is true, but this was not as other Bank Holidays. The emotional reaction was quite abnormal whenever the bands on the Palace Pier and elsewhere played patriotic airs. (It was the same all over England.) Flags were another portent. Not since Coronation year had there been so many of them. Down on the beach an enterprising Italian ice-cream vendor had adorned his stall with a couple of large Union Jacks and was thereby attracting crowds of customers.

For another thing, there were the newspapers. As on the two previous days, the number of newspaper readers in the crowds was quite unprecedented. On ordinary holiday occasions the newspaper was simply carried under one's arm and glanced at casually and intermittently, whenever one had a moment to spare. Not so today. In the train coming down, on the beach, on the pier, on board the yachts and steamers even, and on the homeward journey, the newspaper was an irresistible lure which drew all eyes. It was the outward and visible sign of the War Crisis. The secret dread and foreboding which lay at the back of everyone's mind were revealed by the avidity with which the special editions were bought up as soon as they appeared. Brighton that day was alive with posters. They seemed to be everywhere. There were the posters of the national morning and evening papers—all colours of the rainbow; the yellow posters of the local *Sussex Daily News,* the black and pink posters of the *Evening Argus.* As the day wore on there was a periodical surge and pulsation in the drifting holiday crowds as the swarms of newsboys came pouring out of Robert Street with their bundles of papers and raced for the principal thoroughfares, the sea front, and the piers. 'Evening Argus!' 'Latest news . . . special!' Most significant of all was the grave expression on the faces of the upper classes as, sitting about the Brunswick Lawns and along the King's Road, and outside such places as the Bedford and the Royal Crescent Hotels, they anxiously digested their newspapers—page by page, column by column—with almost feverish intentness. This is what they read that day in the first leader of the *Times*:

'The die is cast. The great European struggle which the nations have so long struggled to avert has begun. Germany declared war upon Russia on Saturday evening, and yesterday her troops entered Luxemburg and crossed the French frontier in Lorraine without any declaration at all. It is idle to dwell upon events such as these. They speak for themseves in a fashion which all can understand. They mean that Europe is to be the scene of the most terrible war that she has witnessed since the fall of the Roman Empire.'

There was much the same preoccupation with the crisis at most of the other holiday resorts.

In the Isle of Thanet the thousands of holidaymakers who emerged from the crowded trains looked unwontedly serious and subdued. On the journey down they had been studying the latest developments with their neighbours; and what they had learned thereby was not conducive to a happy and carefree holiday. It was significant that, whereas the crowds who flocked to the St Lawrence ground that morning to see the Kent v. Sussex match with which the Canterbury Week opened talked of nothing but cricket, on the return journey in the evening they talked of nothing but the war. At Eastbourne there seemed to be the usual influx of visitors and in the well-tended gardens of the hotels and villas along the front there was a brilliant show of flowers. The sands and promenade were crowded, and smaller parties of holidaymakers followed the chalky lanes and tracks over the Downs leading to Beachy Head. But the presence of the War Cloud was reflected in the continual anxiety for the latest news and the chastened demeanour of the visitors. (At a firework display in Devonshire Park that evening the crown of the pyrotechnic feast was an elaborate set piece representing Great Britain and her colonies. This part of the display evoked a tremendous burst of cheering, followed by the singing of 'Rule, Britannia' to the accompaniment of the orchestra.) At Worthing, owing to the cancellation of excursions on two other lines, there was a record number of visitors. On the sands cricket and other games were played as usual, the children went for rides in goat-carts and on Shetland ponies, and many bathed and paddled. But here again crowds collected outside the newspaper offices, and in the Steyne Gardens, frequented by the elderly and retired as well as by the nannies and their charges, newspapers were to be seen on all sides. At Littlehampton also there was a record influx of visitors. The sands were crowded, and most people seemed to be enjoying themselves. But the usual effervescent gaiety was lacking, and the war news was the sole topic of conversation.

In other parts of the country the chastening effect of the war news was also apparent. At Whitby there was a record influx of holidaymakers—but it was noticed that there were almost as many anxious countenances as happy ones to be seen on the front, particularly among the older people. Southend drew its usual huge Bank Holiday throng; but the holiday mood was damped, and the crowds were less effusive than of old. At Weston-super-Mare the influx of visitors was well below the average, and there was a general feeling of anxiety and gloom engendered by the development of the crisis. The one absorbing topic of conversation on the beaches, front, restaurants, and public gardens was the war; and the question everyone was asking his or her neighbour was, 'Will England be brought in?'

The least imaginative could not fail to be impressed by the warlike preparations which accompanied the 'Precautionary Period' that were now going on on many parts of the coast. Dover was quiet, but very much on the alert. The dockyard and all piers and quays were patrolled day and night. Soldiers with fixed bayonets were guarding the railway line; under Shakespeare's Cliff a party of men, with their rifles stacked beside their tent, were lying on the sands watching the sea through binoculars; everything was in readiness for placing the boom across the harbour. On this day Lord Kitchener was suddenly summoned from his cabin on board the Calais steamer (he was on his way to take up an appointment in Egypt) and ordered to return at once to London, where his services were urgently required. At coastguard stations around the coast small boys eagerly watched the coastguards, armed with revolvers, setting out on their rounds. Throughout the night searchlights swept the approaches to the great naval ports and other important harbours.

After the passage of half a century, the recollection by many folk of that fateful first Monday in August is chiefly one of brilliant sunshine, billowing clouds, fresh breezes, and sparkling waves; of summer frocks and sunshades, straw hats and flannels, sailor-suits and pigtails; of white and brown sails gleaming in the sun, and hoops bowling and kites flying.

To those who were then children all the alarum and excitement that seemed to be in the air that day were by no means unwelcome. On their way down to the seaside they would crowd at the windows of their compartment to stare at some passing train which was filled with men in uniform. At all the larger stations they would catch sight of groups of bluejackets or territorials standing about the platforms. Except for the older ones among them, who could remember the imposing procession of troops which had marched through London at the coronation of King George V, most of these youngsters had never seen so many soldiers and sailors before in all their lives. Another thing they would remember was the extraordinary preoccupation of their elders in the newspapers, and also the intense excitement when the band on the pier or esplanade played 'God Save the King', or the 'Marseillaise', or that slow and solemn, rather sad melody, which somebody told them was the Russian Imperial Hymn.

For a time the enjoyment of such a fine summer's day and of the familiar round of holiday pleasures might lull the people into fleeting forgetfulness and *joie de vivre*. But all day long, from early morning till dusk, mingling with the swash of waves on the shingle beach, with the lighthearted laughter and chatter on the pier, with the rousing strains of a military band, with the rollicking chorus of a pierrot show or the high-pitched, nasal dialogue of Punch and Judy, with the staccato thud of tennis balls, and with the plaintive cries of the herring-gulls wheeling and circling above the ebbing tide—was to be heard the far-off, muted, but strangely insistent shouting of the newspaper vendors. And everywhere were to be seen posters with their bodeful tidings inscribed in great red and black type.

CHAPTER 22

A famous speech

It was at this stage that the principal and decisive factor in determining the policy of Great Britain came dramatically to the fore. Whatever were the rights and wrongs of the *entente* with France and Russia, there could be no possible doubt regarding our special interest in the independence and integrity of the Low Countries. It was apparent that the domination of that vital region by a great military and naval Power would at once revive the menace to our island security which was the abiding concern of the rulers of this country from the days of Queen Elizabeth to our own. In defence of this long-standing interest we had repeatedly taken up arms against a Continental aggressor. For this same reason Belgium had been neutralized in 1839, and Gladstone's Government had peremptorily warned off France and Prussia in 1870.

It is somewhat surprising, in the circumstances, that the matter of Belgian neutrality was not considered by the Cabinet until as late as July 30th. On that day, after carefully reviewing the obligations of Great Britain with respect to Belgian neutrality, the Cabinet arrived at the conclusion that the issue, if, indeed, it arose, would be one of policy rather than of legal obligation.

Another remarkable aspect of the case is that it was not considered by the House of Commons simply as a historic British interest—as it was by their predecessors in 1815, in 1793, in 1743, in 1701, and in even earlier times—but as a matter of honour and chivalry: something which resembled, perhaps, the *motio valida* that had inspired the First Crusade, something which was essentially emotional in its appeal, exciting a spontaneous, passionate, and unquestioning indignation that had no parallel in our annals since the Bulgarian atrocities of the mid-Victorian age.

A possible explanation of this may be looked for in the altered composition of the House of Commons. Prior to the crucial election of 1906, which had resulted in a political landslide, both Houses of Parliament had been largely drawn from families having an inbred and traditional interest in foreign affairs. In the ensuing decade this was no longer the case. Certain members of the Cabinet, high officials of the Foreign Office and Admiralty, historians, and the like might be sufficiently alive to the realities of the European situation: but certainly not the average M.P., and still less the average well-to-do citizen of that era.

The consequence was that when the Belgian issue presently became of overriding importance it was presented to the public in a guise undreamed of by their forebears.

The eyes of Ministers now turned anxiously on the ancient cockpit of Europe. Signs were not lacking of Germany's intention to break into the Low Countries. The huge military camps along the Belgian frontier, the intricate system of strategic railways on this side of Germany, the endless miles of sidings, and the enormous depots there, could have but one meaning. One thing was certain: if the Germans marched, nothing could save Liège. It must fall in a very few days—perhaps in a few hours.

During the night of August 2nd-3rd August the Germans continued their remorseless advance towards the Belgian frontier. Public opinion, which throughout this fateful week-end had seemed to hang in the balance, received a decisive shock. Would Belgium resist? If she did not and contented herself with a mere formal protest, and then suffered the Germans to pass through her territory, it would make the ultimate decision of the British Cabinet vastly more difficult.

The current now set strongly towards intervention.

'Will England declare war today?' inquired the *Daily Chronicle*. 'The mailed fist strikes!' the *Daily Mail* announced in heavy black headlines; and added, 'We shall have to uphold the honour of England by demeanour and deed'. The *Times*, in similar vein, exhorted the Government to stand firmly by the Entente. 'Now they have but to do their plain duty as patriotic statesmen to be the leaders of a movement of the national spirit such as no living man has known.'

On the same day the London correspondent of the Paris *Figaro*, who, like so many of his countrymen, was almost beside himself with anxiety, rang up a friend in the *Daily Mail* office.

K

'Have you any news?' he inquired despairingly. 'Oh, are you going to the help of France? I know the whole British nation is with us, but this rotten "wait and see" Government of yours, when will they move?' [1]

The sudden rise of warlike ardour was significantly reflected in the bellicose tone of the *Daily Telegraph*—a paper which had hitherto maintained a far more detached and objective approach to the problem than the *Times* and certain other Opposition journals. The invasion of Luxemburg was hailed as a challenge which could not and ought not to be ignored. 'At last the suspense is at an end, and we believe that every Briton with the stuff of manhood in him will hear the news with relief. Since Germany will have it, she shall have it, and that in full measure.' The invasion of Luxemburg led on to the vital issue of the Low Countries. Here the interventionists stood on firm ground.

'Today we are bracing ourselves for the fray. Germany is rendering our neutrality impossible. If there was one cardinal precept of our foreign policy', observed the *Glasgow Herald*, 'it was the independence and integrity of the Netherlands'.

It was the Belgian issue which finally decided Lloyd George's attitude to the matter. Throughout Sunday morning, together with Burns, Morley, and Simon, he had appeared to be leaning towards neutrality. On the other hand, just as Charles II had been resolved never to set out on his travels again, so Lloyd George (not unmindful of his experiences during the Boer War) now informed another member of the Cabinet that he had had enough of 'standing out against a war inflamed populace'. Then on Sunday evening came the German ultimatum to Belgium, followed by King Albert's appeal to King George V on Monday morning. At that Lloyd George came down firmly on the side of war—a decision which once and for all destroyed the hopes of the neutralists. 'Mr Lloyd George', was Lord Beaverbrook's pungent comment, 'alone had the genius to play Charles James Fox, and he declined the role.'

For Great Britain Monday, August 3rd, was destined to be the day of final and fateful decision. Everything, in fact, on this

[1] Tom Clarke, *My Northcliffe Diary*, pp. 63-4.

momentous day united to heighten the dramatic effect — the glorious bursts of brilliant sunshine alternating with the heavily overcast skies, the remarkable *greenness* of the trees in the streets and parks so late in the year, the immense Bank Holiday crowds strolling about the West End, the occasional glimpse of marching troops, the shrill cries of the newspaper boys as they announced each successive edition, and, last but not least, the unmistakable sense of crisis in the air. The imminent threat to Belgium lay heavy upon the national consciousness. Suddenly there had come news of the German ultimatum to Brussels, and of King Albert's appeal to our own King. And now, this very afternoon, Parliament would have to make its decision.

Early on Monday morning Bonar Law and Lansdowne came to see the Prime Minister in Downing Street. They were in general agreement with Asquith, but laid great stress upon Belgian neutrality.

The war party in the Cabinet was much strengthened by the promised support of the Opposition leaders—also by the surging tide of popular indignation over the threat to Belgium. By this time the majority of Ministers regarded war as inevitable.

That morning, when Morley entered the Cabinet Room for the last time, he informed Lloyd George that he had resigned. The latter appeared surprised and dismayed. 'But if you go', he observed rather naïvely, 'it will put us who don't go, in a great hole.' Lloyd George then spoke of the threat to Belgium, which, he said, had caused him to change his mind with regard to British neutrality. Morley in reply expressed his strong aversion to the whole Entente policy and the ruinous consequences which must follow in its train.

On his arrival the Prime Minister briefly outlined the situation to the Cabinet and declared that he would stand by Grey. But all danger of a split had vanished. As a result of Burns' and Morley's resignation, there no longer existed an anti-war group in the Government. Before the Ministers separated that morning, the majority of them had expressed their approval of the general outline of the statement which Grey was to make in the House of Commons in the afternoon.

It was two o'clock before Grey arrived back in his room at the Foreign Office. There he had a hurried interview with Prince Lichnowsky, who had come to implore him, should the Germans

in fact march through Belgium, not to make it a *casus belli*.
Grey, of course, could give him no such assurance.

Meanwhile outside in the streets the tension was steadily
rising. Warlike passions were mounting here in London as well
as in the capitals of the Continent. The angry murmur of the
crowds in Whitehall demonstrating for war against Germany
could be heard by the Ministers sitting in the Cabinet Room. So
dense was the throng which gathered at the end of Downing
Street during the morning Cabinet that the Ministers' cars could
scarcely get out. Throughout the day the people continued to
gaze at the unpretentious, brown-brick front of No. 10—the
official residence of the First Lord of the Treasury and Prime
Minister of Great Britain since Sir Robert Walpole had taken
possession of the place nearly two centuries before. Hour after
hour they waited. The arrivals and departures of high officials
like Sir Arthur Nicolson of the Foreign Office and of Prince
Lichnowsky and other members of the Corps Diplomatique were
watched with almost passionate interest. When the First Lord
left Downing Street after the morning Cabinet to drive to
Buckingham Palace he received a rapturous welcome from the
crowds. Churchill beamed on the cheering throngs as if he had
not a care in the world. Some journalists leaving the House of
Commons in a taxi-cab were mistaken for M.P.s and also
enthusiastically cheered. Even youngsters had succumbed to the
patriotic fervour of the occasion; and there was as much good-
humoured applause as amusement when, about midday, a troop
of raggety urchins, carrying a Union Jack and a Royal Standard,
and beating a martial tattoo on tin cans, marched with determined mien all the way up Whitehall.

Throughout the day the crowds continued to grow. A dense
mass filled Trafalgar Square. Whitehall became impassable for
traffic, and in the afternoon the police were hard put to it to
clear a passage for Asquith and Lloyd George who were walking
to the House of Commons to hear the Foreign Secretary's eagerly
awaited speech. A large number of people, especially the
decorous and sober middle-aged element, appeared anxious and
preoccupied. But the gravity of the occasion could not wholly
extinguish the Bank Holiday spirit, as, from time to time, various
well-known figures were recognized and heartily cheered.
Thunderous applause greeted the arrival of the First Lord of the

Admiralty, accompanied by one of the Opposition leaders,[1] in Palace Yard. Winston Churchill, who was smoking one of his favourite cigars, raised his hat in response to the tumultous cheers of the multitudes surging around them as the two men entered the House.

The afternoon saw a marked quickening of the war ferment. This was the result partly of the rapid march of events abroad, and partly of the dramatic scenes that were being enacted here in the metropolis. Even while Sir Edward Grey was making his great speech to the Commons, large columns of troops were marching past the Palace of Westminster; and the cheers of the vast crowd could be heard in the Chamber.

St James's Park and Green Park were full of families picnicking. Fathers and mothers sat about on the greensward, chatting or dozing, and children were playing games and fishing for tiddlers, when the sound of martial music was heard from the nearby Wellington Barracks. Immediately fathers collected their offspring and mothers snatched up baskets and bags and other belongings; and there was a general stampede in the direction of the Palace. As the Guards, accompanied by their band playing a lively march, with the Colours carried in the centre, emerged into the road, the effect was electrifying. Motor-cars, taxis, vans, and other traffic were at once held up. Then, as the Guards swung past the eager crowds and entered the courtyard of the Palace, countless heads were bared, hats thrown into the air, handkerchiefs waved, and a tremendous cheer went up.

Hour after hour the crowds waited patiently outside the railings, standing about the adjacent roadways and around the Victoria Memorial; some of them gazing silently towards the Palace, and others discussing, in subdued tones, the latest news from abroad. Occasionally the sun came out between the heavy clouds and blazed down upon the scarlet ranks of the geraniums in their beds among the trim green lawns. When presently the figure of a child, the young Prince John, was seen at one of the Palace windows, cheer after cheer went up from the people assembled below: whereupon the little boy, clearly delighted, waved his handkerchief in response. At half-past four the King and Queen drove out in an open carriage. They were accorded a

[1] F. E. Smith.

rapturous reception all the way along the Mall and back by way of Pall Mall.

So the hours went by.

On the afternoon of the 3rd the House was densely packed as it had not been since the introduction of Gladstone's Home Rule Bill in 1886. Long before the Speaker took the chair the House was full. The press was so great that, with every inch of space upon the long green benches and in the side galleries completely occupied, chairs had to be placed across the gangway. The Peers, Spiritual and Temporal, were overcrowded in their small gallery —the diminutive figure of Field-Marshal Lord Roberts, the much-loved 'Bobs', being almost buried beneath his larger neighbours. In the Press Gallery sat the Archbishop of Canterbury and the Lord Chief Justice. In the Diplomatic Gallery Count Benckendorff, wan and weary, with expressionless mien awaited the decision upon which the destiny of Europe largely depended. The public and other galleries were crammed in like manner. Before the arrival of the Ministers, members conversed in under-tones. The atmosphere was charged to the highest degree with breathless expectancy and suspense. Outside in Parliament Square the vast crowd waited in the brilliant sunshine; and away across the narrow seas the Governments and High Commands of the Great Powers waited also.

A great cheer went up when Asquith, with grave and impassive face, walked slowly to his place beside the Foreign Secretary; and members drew forward in their seats as, shortly afterwards, Grey rose and stood by the dispatch box.

The terrible strain of those last few days had left its mark upon Grey. His clear-cut, aquiline features were pale and drawn with anxiety. He spoke in calm, measured tones, quietly and fluently, almost conversationally, and with impressive earnestness; and only on occasion the level tones seemed very slightly to tremble.

'Last week I stated that we were working for peace not only for this country, but to preserve the peace of Europe. Today events move so rapidly that it is exceedingly difficult to state with technical accuracy the actual state of affairs, but it is clear that the peace of Europe cannot be preserved. Russia and Germany, at any rate, have declared war upon each other.'

For about half an hour Grey spoke of our understanding with France and all that that entailed. As he developed this theme, the occasional bursts of applause, which at first had come from a few scattered groups in the House, gradually spread, and at last became general.

'For many years we have had a long-standing friendship with France. . . . But how far that friendship entails obligation—it has been a friendship between the nations and ratified by the nations—how far that entails an obligation, let every man look into his own heart, and his own feelings, and construe the extent of the obligation for himself.'

He went on to refer to the inauguration, in 1912, of the new naval dispositions whereby our main Fleet was concentrated in the North Sea, while that of France was transferred to the Mediterranean. He dealt at some length with this important new factor in our relations with the Republic; after which, raising his voice and speaking with sudden emphasis, he turned to the possibility of a German attack upon the shores of France:

'The French coasts are absolutely undefended. The French Fleet is in the Mediterranean, and has for some years been concentrated there because of the feeling of confidence and friendship which has existed between the two countries. My own feeling is that if a foreign Fleet, engaged in a war which France has not sought, and in which she had not been the aggressor, came down the English Channel and bombarded and battered the undefended coasts of France, we could not stand aside, and see this going on practically within sight of our eyes, with our arms folded, looking on dispassionately, doing nothing. I believe that would be the feeling of this country.'

The shouts of applause which swept through the crowded Chamber at this pronouncement appeared to be practically unanimous. It was manifestly the feeling of a considerable proportion of members. Two prominent Irishmen, Willie Redmond and Arthur Lynch, leaped on the bench and stood cheering frantically and waving their order papers. The solid mass of Unionist members ranged behind the Opposition front bench shouted, roared, and yelled their approbation. Only a small minority of ministerialists, chiefly Radical and Labour stalwarts, sat silent and unresponsive.

In the second half of his speech Grey dealt with the neutrality of Belgium. He referred to the engagements of 1839 and 1870, guaranteeing the independence and integrity of that kingdom, and he read out to the House the appeal which the King of the Belgians had just made to our own King. Here the reaction of the members became even more pronounced. The cheers grew louder and fiercer. It was evident that Grey was carrying the House with him at every step. As he spoke of the bid which the German Government had made for our neutrality in the war, his voice rang with indignation.

'We were sounded in the course of last week as to whether, if a guarantee were given that, after the war, Belgian integrity would be preserved, that would content us. We replied that we could not bargain away whatever interests or obligations we had in Belgian neutrality.'

He quoted with telling effect from a speech delivered in 1870 by Gladstone, in this same Chamber, appealing to the principle of public right and public law in Europe:

'We have an interest in the independence of Belgium which is wider than that which we may have in the literal operation of the guarantee. It is found in the answer to the question whether, under the circumstances of the case, this country, endowed as it is with influence and power, would quietly stand by and witness the perpetration of the direst crime that ever stained the pages of history, and thus become participators in the sin.'

Again the full-throated cheering, again the stamp of feet. As Grey enlarged upon this theme of Belgian neutrality, the fervour and enthusiasm of the crowded assembly rose ever higher. No longer was there room for doubt whether the policy of the

Government had the approval of the House. The tumultuous, passionate cheering which broke out again and again showed, beyond question, which way their sympathies lay. The parliamentary reporter of the *Westminster Gazette*, gazing down from the Press Gallery, noted that the Irish Nationalists appeared to be no less enthusiastic than the Unionists. Grey's speech drew to its close:

'The most awful responsibility is resting upon the Government in deciding what to advise the House of Commons to do. We have disclosed the issue, the information which we have, and made clear to the House, I trust, that we are prepared to face that situation, and that should it develop, as probably it may develop, we will face it. We have worked for peace up to the last moment, and beyond the last moment. How hard, how persistently, and how earnestly we strove for peace last week the House will see from the papers that will be before it. . . .

'I have now put the vital facts before the House, and if, as seems not improbable, we are forced, and rapidly forced, to take our stand upon these issues, then I believe, when the country realizes what is at stake, what the real issues are, the magnitude of the impending dangers in the West of Europe, which I have endeavoured to describe to the House, we shall be supported throughout, not only by the House of Commons, but by the determination, the resolution, the courage, and the endurance of the whole country.'

As the Foreign Secretary sat down, Bonar Law as Leader of the Opposition rose to pledge the support of his Party.

'The Government already know, but I give them now the assurance on behalf of the Party of which I am Leader in this House, that in whatever steps they think it necessary to take for the honour and security of this country, they can rely on the unhesitating support of the Opposition.'

Then came a dramatic and totally unexpected interposition. At the top of the gangway, John Redmond, the Leader of the Irish Party, rose to address the House. The Unionists listened at first with bewilderment, and then with amazed approval and delight. For, as he spoke, it became apparent that, for perhaps the first time in our history, England's danger was not to be Ireland's opportunity. By this magnanimous and courageous act Redmond rendered a service of almost incalculable value to the cause of the Entente.[1] A storm of enthusiastic applause swept across the crowded benches.

'I say to the Government that they may tomorrow withdraw every one of their troops from Ireland. I say that the coast of Ireland will be defended from foreign invasion by her armed sons, and for this purpose armed Nationalist Catholics in the South will be only too glad to join arms with the armed Protestant Ulstermen in the North. Is it too much to hope that out of this situation there may spring a result which will be good, not merely for the Empire, but good for the future welfare and integrity of the Irish nation?'

Finally, Ramsay Macdonald spoke for the small—but by no means inconsiderable—minority who still resisted our entry into the war. Not a few of these were sincere and convinced pacifists and members of the Society of Friends, which has always been opposed to war. Even in the Labour Party, however, it was soon found that a clear majority favoured the war; and, shortly after, Macdonald resigned the leadership.

After the last of the Party Leaders had spoken, the sitting was suspended for two hours. Before it reassembled, news of the highest importance reached the Government from the Belgian Legation in London.

While Grey was speaking Wickham Steed was with Sir Arthur Nicolson at the Foreign Office. The latter asked him how he thought 'it would go'.

' "If you mean Grey's speech," I answered, "it will go excellently. He has only to tell the truth and he will have the House and the country with him."

[1] In consequence of this gesture, and as a tribute to John Redmond and the Irish people, Churchill insisted on naming the latest dreadnought battleship, H.M.S. _Erin_.

' "I wish I felt as sure as you", Sir Arthur Nicolson replied. "There is a good deal of active opposition and the crisis has come so rapidly that the country does not know what it is all about."

'He discussed the situation until a secretary came into the room with a strip of paper from the tape machine.

' "They have cheered him, sir", he said.

' "Thank goodness!" ejaculated Sir Arthur, in a tone of intense relief.

'Soon after four o'clock, Lord Onslow, Sir Arthur Nicolson's private secretary, burst into the room. He had come straight from the House of Commons.

' "He has had a tremendous success, sir", he said. "The whole House was with him."

'Sir Arthur Nicolson sank back into a chair in the attitude of a man from whose shoulders a crushing burden of anxiety had been lifted.

' "Thank God!" he said fervently. "Now the course is clear, but it will be a terrible business." ' [1]

At about seven o'clock the Foreign Secretary returned to the House of Commons to disclose some information which had not been in his possession when he made his speech in the afternoon. It was to the following effect:

'Germany sent yesterday evening at seven o'clock a note proposing to Belgium friendly neutrality, covering free passage on Belgian territory, and promising maintenance of independence of the kingdom and possession at the conclusion of peace, and threatening, in case of refusal, to treat Belgium as an enemy. A time limit of twelve hours was fixed for the reply. The Belgians have answered that an attack on their neutrality would be a flagrant violation of the rights of nations, and that to accept the German proposal would be to sacrifice the honour of a nation. Conscious of its duty, Belgium is firmly resolved to repel aggression by all possible means.'

As has already been said, a certain number of members on the Ministerialist side of the House did not share in the general enthusiasm. Later in the evening, E. D. Morel, Josiah Wedgwood,

[1] H. Wickham Steed, *Through Thirty Years*, II, pp. 26-7.

Keir Hardie, and a number of others rose to speak against British intervention in the war. But the effect of these protests was small (Balfour in fact described this interlude as 'the mere drugs and lees of debate') and in one or two cases the member was practically shouted down.

The House then rose after one of the most moving and memorable occasions in all its long history. That night the news of Grey's great speech was all over London; and, on the following day, it was all over the country.

The growing threat to Belgium, combined with this historic oration of August 3rd, had an almost magical effect upon public opinion throughout the British Isles. From this time on the neutralist movement was doomed. Grey's speech may fairly be said to rank with the finest performance of William Pitt the Younger in the war against the French Revolution. It was altogether remarkable for its fairness, restraint, and absence of emotion. At the one point where the chain of reasoning was manifestly weak, he appealed unerringly to the Englishman's innate sense of justice and fair play. It was remarkable, too, in that it was the only speech made in Europe in which a Foreign Minister fairly and squarely set out the whole complex situation to his country's elected representatives, leaving to them the final decision. And it was completely successful. At the eleventh hour Grey had made good the semi-secret understanding with France by ranging his fellow-countrymen solidly on the side of the Entente.

'In that autumn,' observes Trevelyan, 'when all round the globe men and peoples judged as spectators or took sides as actors in the most awful conflict in history, Grey stood in the world's mind as the representative of England's case. To him was largely due the impression that right was on our side.'[1]

The overwhelming reception accorded to Grey's speech marked the consummation of the Entente policy to which he had devoted so many years of patient toil and effort. It hardened the national resolve and steeled the hearts of countless men and women for the imminent conflict. It was beyond question the greatest hour of Grey's life and the summit of his career.

As they were leaving the House of Commons, Churchill asked Grey:

[1] G. M. Trevelyan, *Grey of Fallodon* (1937), p. 267.

'What happens now?'

'Now', was the reply, 'we shall send them an ultimatum to stop the invasion of Belgium within twenty-four hours.'

Late that evening Spender visited Grey at his room in the Foreign Office. The two men stood by the window overlooking the lawns and groves of St James's Park. The sunset had faded in the western sky; it was getting on for dusk, and the lamps were being lit along the Mall. Grey turned to his friend with the pregnant words: 'The lamps are going out all over Europe; we shall not see them lit again in our lifetime'.

The impending invasion of Belgium had effectively accomplished Cambon's purpose: it finally forced Great Britain to enter the war on the side of France. Long afterwards, the French Ambassador described this period of agonized suspense and doubt as the darkest hour of his life. Disaster and ruin stared him in the face. However, it had all ended happily. *La perfide Albion* had turned up trumps after all. Meeting General Wilson in Sir Arthur Nicolson's room at the Foreign Office, Cambon thankfully held out both hands to that ardent Francophile. Their dreams had come true at last. The Entente was about to become an alliance. 'So different from the day before yesterday', the General recorded in his diary. Cambon telegraphed the good news to Paris.

That night a large crowd assembled outside the French Embassy — singing, shouting, and cheering for France! The Ambassador listened to the uproar with mixed feelings. He was an elderly man and the ordeal of the last few days had taxed his strength severely. Though he appreciated these tokens of friendship on the part of the Londoners, he was desperately in need of a night's rest. The demonstrations did not end until well after midnight.

The scenes of enthusiasm enacted in the capital were altogether unprecedented within living memory. The appearance of the Foreign Secretary and the First Lord, as they left the House that afternoon, was greeted by the spectators in Parliament Square with an outburst of terrific applause; and when presently Asquith was seen in Downing Street the crowds acclaimed him with extraordinary fervour. The Government, in truth, had never been so popular in time of peace as they were just now, with the country on the brink of war. As Redmond, too, left the House he received an ovation from the London crowds to which he was scarcely accustomed. Lord Roberts also was recognized and loudly cheered. When Parliament adjourned a procession of young men marched singing through Whitehall, Trafalgar Square, and Piccadilly. As the hours went by, the demonstrations became noisier and more general. Parties of young men went by in taxi-cabs joyfully chanting the 'Marseillaise'. The number of Union Jacks and tricolours to be seen among the crowds had vastly increased.

Processions carrying the flags of Britain and France marched continually up and down the Mall, singing and cheering. Large crowds gathered outside the closed gates of the Palace, where, in response to a terrific outburst of cheering, the King and Queen, the Prince of Wales, and Princess Mary all appeared on the balcony overlooking the forecourt. When the Royal Party retired the crowds showed no signs of dispersing, but remained outside the railings, in an ecstasy of patriotic fervour, chanting warlike songs and clamouring for the King. Afterwards they all sang 'We want King George' to the tune of the Westminster chimes. The singing and cheering grew louder and louder—and finally, shortly after nine o'clock, the King and Queen and the Prince of Wales again appeared, this time on the balcony outside the dining-room, to receive another tumultuous welcome. The Sovereigns remained bowing for several minutes, and the Prince of Wales waved his hand. Some time later the enormous concourse dispersed in processions which almost blocked some of the principal streets of the West End.

CHAPTER 23

The last hours of peace

On Tuesday morning the Bank Holiday aspect of the streets had gone. Men in naval and military uniform were everywhere to be seen, each carrying his service kit. It was a notable day for the Royal Fleet Reserve. By dozens and scores they arrived at the railway stations, bade farewell to their families by the gates, and passed down the platforms. During the morning train after train left the termini with the inscription 'For seamen only' posted on the carriages. Late in the day the Admiralty announced that the mobilization of the Royal Navy was in all respects complete, and that the entire Navy was on a war footing.

If, understandably, there was not the same degree of throbbing tension and excitement in the suburbs as there was in central London, there was still the same tendency for groups and crowds of people to gather in the local High Street; to stare at the official notice boards, to buy up each edition of the newspapers as they appeared, and to wave flags and to sing patriotic choruses. Each scrap of fresh intelligence was pounced upon and eagerly discussed. In the suburbs there was also the same nightmare feeling of unreality about the appalling situation that had so suddenly developed and the same difficulty in grasping the full implication of happenings on the Continent. 'The aspect of affairs has changed with such startling suddenness', the *Wimbledon Borough News* declared, 'that it is almost impossible to believe that it can be real, and one feels that one must wake up presently to find that all has been a hideous dream and that life is quiet and serene once more.'

Nearly every town and city in the kingdom was by now, in greater or lesser degree, in the grip of the war ferment. Even in the former strongholds of the peace movement neutralist sentiment was weakening and wavering. In the industrial North many a substantial businessman was pursing his lips and shaking his head over the headlines in the *Manchester Guardian* and confiding to his neighbour in train or bus that the old stalwart seemed somehow to be losing touch. As the legions of mill-hands clattered over the stone setts to and from their work that day, their talk was all of war, war, war.

It was the same in another fastness of Liberalism—the West Country. War was recognized as inevitable. The issue had to be faced. 'It is', declared the *Western Morning News*, 'no longer possible to hope that England can remain at peace for more than a few hours.'

On top of the existing dislocation of finance, commerce, and industry, there arose another cause for public anxiety. For some days past the prices of provisions had been rising. The price of butter and eggs had increased by nearly fifty per cent; that of sugar was rising astronomically. Tuesday saw the start of something like a general food panic. In many places, notwithstanding official reassurances and urgent newspaper appeals, there was a rush by local housewives to lay in stocks of foodstuffs against the shortages they feared; in almost every grocer's shop in some districts the shelves were practically stripped, and not a few shops were actually forced to close. The well-to-do not infrequently arrived in motor-cars and taxi-cabs, provided themselves with sacks, buckets, and bins, and laid in enough flour and bacon to last their households for several months. It was some days before the panic gradually subsided.

From the trend of countless conversations that day, Tuesday, August 4th, in trains, tubes, trams, and buses; in clubs, offices, shops, factories, mills, works, yards, and depots; in hotels, restaurants, and country inns; around coffee-stalls and buffet counters; in urban squares and on village greens: it was apparent that a nationwide conversion had been effected. No longer did there exist any influential body of leaders, or any significant mass of the population, still opposed to war. The anti-war caucus in the Cabinet had disappeared; the neutralist movement throughout the whole country had been rendered virtually impotent. The spate of resolutions and manifestoes denouncing Great Britain's entry into the war had signally failed to influence public opinion to any material degree. Most pathetically futile of all the anti-war demonstrations was a great Women's Meeting arranged for the evening of the 4th, which solemnly proceeded to 'deplore the abandonment of peaceful negotiations, the failure to settle the present international differences by conciliation or arbitration, the outbreak of war in Europe, as an unparalleled disaster'. The German declaration of war against France, the invasion of Luxemburg, and the imminent threat to Belgium—combined with the abiding impression of Sir Edward Grey's great speech—had, almost overnight, wrought this astonishing change in public opinion.

'The menace of Germany—The Neutrality of Belgium', proclaimed the headlines in the *Times*. 'Here at home and in the far off Dominions', declared that journal, 'the sure instinct of our peoples teaches them that the ruin of France or of the Low Countries would be the prelude to our own. We can no more tolerate a German hegemony in Europe than we can tolerate the hegemony of any other Power.' The *Daily Telegraph* took a similar line with 'Hands off Belgium—Violated Treaties'. 'A straight lead at last', announced the *Morning Post*, and observed thankfully, 'Substantially, England is now a united nation'. 'We are bound', declared the *Daily Mail*, 'as Sir Edward Grey stated, by pledges in the case of Belgium. We are going to stand by those pledges. . . . Orders have been given to back Sir Edward Grey's words with deeds. The Navy is mobilized; the British Army is mobilizing.'

In the vital matter of the Low Countries, the Liberal press, no less than the Conservative, pronounced decisively against Germany. For the threatened violation of Belgian neutrality represented a moral issue of a kind to which British Liberalism had habitually responded. The *Manchester Guardian* still remained uncompromisingly opposed to the war, and referred acidly to 'Sir Edward Grey's strange blunder'. But not so most of the others. 'Germany', stated the *Daily Chronicle*, 'has therefore, we fear, committed herself not only to war with France and Russia, but to an entirely unprovoked war on Belgium, made with full knowledge that Great Britain is pledged by treaty to defend Belgium, and also that she regards Belgium as a British interest.' 'It would seem, therefore', summed up the *Daily News* soberly, 'that if we are not yet at war with Germany, war is a matter of hours, and the Government has taken measures in anticipation

BRAVO, BELGIUM!

of conflict.' The *Birmingham Gazette*—hitherto a determined
opponent of intervention — referred with admiration to Sir
Edward Grey's 'frank and honest recital'. In the North and
Midlands, as well as in London and the southern counties, the
Belgian issue was a potent factor in arousing public opinion.

Belgium, in short, was the answer to all our doubts and difficulties. It won over certain wavering Conservative M.P.s to the cause of intervention, and it provided a convenient way out for dissident dissenters as well as for the Catholic *Universe*. 'By her action', declared the *Methodist Times*, 'Germany has put herself in the wrong with the whole civilized world, and incurred the heaviest moral responsibility for the ensuing conflict.' 'Everybody will agree', concurred the *United Methodist*, 'that we must fulfil our obligations as to the maintenance of Belgian neutrality.' The *Universe*, which, it will be remembered, had been strongly championing the cause of Austria-Hungary and the venerable Francis Joseph, executed a remarkable *volte-face*. Hailing Sir Edward Grey as 'the lofty and inspired voice of the National Conscience', the *Universe* proclaimed that 'the crime against civilization and humanity in the invasion of Belgium was in itself alone an irresistible challenge to our honour, and proclaims our quarrel just'. The pronouncement of another well-known Catholic journal, the *Tablet*, succinctly expresses the sentiment which was rapidly uniting the entire country behind Asquith and Grey. 'For the sake of this little people, fighting for its freedom against desperate odds, England will go out by land and by sea. So she will vindicate the honour of her sacred word and there is no nobler cause for which any man may die.'

Foreign observers received much the same impression of British unity. 'There is absolutely no doubt that British sentiment is for war', declared the *New York Herald*. 'The appeals of the pacifists get no hearing. Not one man in a hundred in London seemingly wants the nation to remain neutral.'

Across the Channel, the French newspapers were enthusiastic and French statesmen profoundly relieved at Grey's pronouncement and the reaction of the British Parliament. 'C'est fait', the *Figaro* declared. 'L'Angleterre s'est prononcée.'

Events now moved rapidly. During the morning of the 4th it became known to the Government that the Germans had crossed the Belgian frontier and were advancing on Liège. The news was swiftly spread by special editions of the newspapers; and a wave of indignation swept over London.

'I think the effect produced by Grey's speech has not died down', Asquith recorded in his diary. ' . . . We had an interesting Cabinet, as we got the news that the Germans had entered Belgium and had announced that if necessary they would push their way through by force of arms. This simplifies matters. So we sent the Germans an ultimatum to expire at midnight requesting them to give a like assurance with the French that they would respect Belgian neutrality.'[1]

That afternoon when the Prime Minister, accompanied by his wife and daughter, drove down to the House of Commons, their progress was marked by loud and continuous cheering, a general waving of hats and sticks, and shouts of 'Good old Asquith!' The appearance of the First Lord ('Good old Winston!') and Mrs Churchill was the signal for another and equally enthusiastic demonstration.

At three o'clock the Prime Minister rose to inform the House that the German Government had stated, through their Ambassador in London, that their reason for disregarding Belgian neutrality was for the purpose of forestalling a French attack across Belgium; that it was a question of life or death for Germany to prevent the French advance, and that Germany would, under no pretext whatever, annex Belgian territory.

'We cannot', declared Asquith gravely, 'regard this as in any sense a satisfactory communication. We have, in reply to it, repeated the request that we made last week to the German Government, that they should give us the same assurance in regard to Belgian neutrality, as was given to us and to Belgium by France last week. We have asked that a reply to that request . . . should be given before midnight.'

Amid a great outburst of cheering the Prime Minister rose and walked slowly down the floor of the House.

At half-past three a score of newspaper boys ran shouting down the Strand: 'British ultimatum to Germany! England at war by midnight!' The crowded streets were seething with excitement. Under the noses of the sentries at Horse Guards, four extremely stout Frenchmen, waving miniature Union Jacks and tricolours, started to dance round and round in a ring like children.

Half an hour before the American Ambassador had received

[1] Earl of Oxford and Asquith, *Memories and Reflections* (1928), II, p. 20.

news of the invasion of Belgium from Grey at the Foreign Office. The British Foreign Secretary greeted Page gravely. Then, sitting down beside him, he came straight to the point.

'The neutrality of Belgium', declared Grey, 'is assured by treaty. Germany is a signatory power to that treaty. It is upon such solemn compacts as this that civilization rests.'

He went on to say that Great Britain would be for ever contemptible if she should sit by and see that treaty violated; that her position would be gone if Germany were thus permanently to dominate Europe; and that he had accordingly invited the Ambassador to come to him to tell him that, a few hours earlier, the Cabinet had dispatched an ultimatum to Germany—warning her that, if the assault on Belgium's neutrality were not immediately called off, Great Britain would declare war.

'Do you expect Germany to accept it?' asked Page.

Grey shook his head.

'No', he responded. 'Of course everybody knows that there will be war.'

After that the Ambassador took his departure.

'I came away', Page later related, 'with a sort of stunned sense of the impending ruin of half the world.'[1]

During the same afternoon an important discussion took place in Berlin.

Sir Edward Goschen, the British Ambassador, called on von Jagow, the German Foreign Minister, to inquire whether the German Government would undertake to respect the neutrality of Belgium. Von Jagow at once replied that the answer must be 'No', as the German Army had already crossed the frontier into Belgium some hours before. Von Jagow declared that they had been forced to advance into France by the quickest and easiest route, in order to achieve an early decision. It was a matter of life or death for them, he went on to explain, as they could not have advanced by any other route without encountering very formidable opposition, entailing great loss of time. This would have enabled the Russians to bring up their troops in time to Germany's eastern frontier. Rapidity of action was Germany's great advantage, while that of Russia was her inexhaustible reserves of men.

Some hours later Goschen again visited the German Foreign

[1] B. J. Hendrick, *Life and Letters of Walter H. Page*, III, pp. 313-15.

Ministry and informed von Jagow that, unless the Imperial Government could give an assurance that by midnight they would halt their advance into Belgium, he had been instructed to demand his passports. . . . Goschen added that he would like to go and see the Chancellor, as it might be the last time he would have an opportunity of seeing him. Von Jagow begged him to do so. Goschen later reported:

'I found the Chancellor very agitated. His Excellency at once began a long harangue, which lasted for about twenty minutes. He said that the step taken by His Majesty's Government was terrible to a degree; just for a word—"neutrality", a word which in war-time had so often been disregarded—just for a scrap of paper Great Britain was going to make war on a kindred nation who desired nothing better than to be friends with her. All his efforts in that direction had been rendered useless by this last terrible step, and the policy to which, as I knew, he had devoted himself since his accession to office had tumbled down like a house of cards. What we had done was unthinkable; it was like striking a man from behind while he was fighting for his life against two assailants. He held Great Britain responsible for all the terrible events that might happen.'

About the same time the editor of the *Westminster Gazette* was walking with Winston Churchill across the Horse Guards Parade on the way from Downing Street to the Admiralty. The First Lord's lively imagination was already at work envisaging the opening moves of the great struggle as he glanced upwards at the tall wireless masts erected over the roof of the Admiralty.

'At midnight', he told Spender, 'we shall be at war, at war! Think of it, if you can—the Fleet absolutely ready, with instructions for every ship, and the word going out from that tower at midnight.'[1]

Already the slender aerials high above were taking in messages of fateful import flashed from many hundreds of miles to the southward: where, throughout the long summer's day, two British battle-cruisers, the *Indomitable* and *Indefatigable*, were shearing through the dark blue waters of the Mediterranean in the track of the *Goeben*. To his young son Louis, then a cadet at

[1] J. A. Spender, *Life, Journalism, and Politics* (1927), II, p. 15.

Osborne, the First Sea Lord spoke hopefully of the speedy destruction of the German battle-cruiser. At about 5 p.m. he reminded Churchill that there was still time to sink the *Goeben* before dark . . . But the First Lord's hands were tied by a Cabinet decision: no act of war could be permitted until the expiration of the ultimatum to Germany at midnight. In the silence of the War Room, where Churchill sat waiting, 'one could hear the clock tick'. Years later, he was to recall the crescendo of excitement and expectancy as the evening advanced. 'The windows of the Admiralty were thrown wide open in the warm night air. Under the roof where Nelson had received his orders were gathered a small group of Admirals and Captains and a cluster of clerks, pencil in hand, waiting.[1]

Once again great crowds were drifting about the West End. They stood in Whitehall and outside Palace Yard, watching the coming and going of Ministers and high officials, listening to the deep-toned chimes of Big Ben as they marked the passage of the last few hours of peace; while above their heads the stiff green leaves of the plane trees hung motionless in the dusk.

As on the previous evenings, there was a spontaneous move towards Buckingham Palace, and much singing and cheering. At eight o'clock the King and Queen came out on the balcony over the central arch and stood, bareheaded, looking down on the multitude. Behind them were Princess Mary, all in white, and one of the young Princes. For some ten minutes the Royal group stood there, motionless, while a great roar of acclamation came up from below—until finally, waving a farewell, they drew back again through the window.

All day long the rattle of the reaping machine was heard in the cornfields under Chanctonbury Ring. It was fine harvest weather—warm and sunny, with a light south-westerly wind which scarcely stirred the tree-tops. Long before midday the air above the ranked sheaves was shimmering in the heat. Occasionally one of the men paused to wipe the sweat from his brows with a sun-browned forearm, exchanged a word or two with his neighbour, and then resumed his toil. The cows grazing in the

[1] W. S. Churchill, *The World Crisis*, I, p. 229.

park sought the shade of the spreading oaks and chestnuts. Presently the men sat down to eat their luncheons in the neighbouring rickyard, where a barrel of beer awaited them. The usual tales were told, the same sort of chaff went round—and yet, somehow, there was a difference. Though scarcely a cloud drifted across the vast azure dome of the sky, there was a feeling of unrest in the atmosphere. The news, by all accounts, was getting worse, and there was talk of the reservists being called up. But, as always, the harvest came first.

The day wore on, and the men toiled on, hour after hour, at the shocking up. It was hard, dusty, thirsty work, and there were continual visits to the barrel of beer which stood out here in the field as well as in the rickyard. Little parties of children, lately released from school for the summer holidays, strayed about the stubble, swung on gates, or begged a ride in one of the long, blue-and-red-painted, Sussex wagons. Up at Hill Barn that afternoon Charlie, the shepherd, was busy trimming lambs; his uncle, old Tom, the one-armed shepherd, was up on the hill with the tegs. From time to time the gruff voice of the carter could be heard exhorting his horses as they turned into the lane.

The westering sun shone on the great beech-grove clump high above on Chanctonbury Hill, on the smooth folds of the Downs stretching away on either side into the blue, misty distance, on the broad expanse of golden corn, and on the old grey walls and gables of Wiston House. All was peace and serenity. Soon after two the cows were turned into the lane to Big Barn, where Ted, the cowman, and his wife were getting ready for milking. Beside the sunny stable wall, near the old coachhouse which had seen so many harvest homes and other festive gatherings, one or two cats lay sleeping. Swallows twittered under the eaves. Sometimes a breeze brought the faint baa-ing of sheep from the distant flock; the rooks cawed in the elm-tops around the churchyard, wood-pigeons crooned in the ash plantations, and there was a drowsy hum of bees.

As the evening approached, the shadows cast by the tall Lombardy poplars grew longer. The ewe flock which had been grazing on the slopes above slowly descended the long grass track leading down from Chanctonbury Ring to the fold by Owlscroft. After sundown the air grew cooler. Rabbits crept out from under the hedgerows to frolic in the meadows, and bats began to wheel to and fro along Mouse Lane. Over the Downs gleamed the evening star. Still the heavy toil in the cornfields continued. Blue wood-smoke was going up from cottage chimneys as suppers were cooked, and women stood chatting in doorways. Children were called in to bed. Lamps were lit. At last it was too dark to see, and the long day's work ended. The tired men slung their jackets over their shoulders and set off homeward. All around in the deepening dusk could be heard the rumble of wagon wheels as the last loads of sheaves were carried to the rickyards.

Along the white roads of France, lined by tall poplar trees, stretching away endlessly across the northern plains, clouds of fine greyish dust were rising in the blazing August sunshine as regiment after regiment marched steadily towards the point of danger. All day long the movement of troops continued. Batteries of field artillery, accompanied by interminable convoys of munition wagons drawn by horses, rumbled slowly in the wake of the infantry. On railway lines leading to the north-eastern frontier train after train swept by loaded with soldiers; a number of the carriages bore the slogan, scrawled in chalk, *Special excursion for Berlin*.

Germany had declared war on France at 6.45 p.m. on the previous day. Next morning the German advance columns broke into the Grand Duchy of Luxemburg on their way to march through Belgium to the invasion of France.

The German General Staff, staking everything upon a lightning turning march westward, in overpowering force, across the plains of Belgium and northern France, expected to envelop and destroy the French Field Army in one swift, decisive, and final campaign.

The German War Plan was the work of General von Schlieffen, who was their Chief of Staff from 1890 to 1905, when he was succeeded by General von Moltke. The crux of the Plan was to concentrate their mass of attack on the German right flank wheeling through Belgium into northern France.[1] It was provided in the Plan that a force of at least seventeen army corps

---

[1] The speedy seizure of Liège and the opening of the four railway lines which passed through it were essential to the success of the German War Plan.

was to attack and envelop the French left flank north of Paris. Seven corps were to pass westward of and around Paris, and take the French Army in the rear. According to the Schlieffen time-table, France would be forced out of the war within six weeks; and the German Army would then be free to deal with Russia.

Throughout August 3rd the small Belgian Army, which had mobilized on the last day of July, had been feverishly preparing to meet the danger. Troops were rushed up to the northern frontier, the roads that led from Germany were systematically broken up and barricaded with tree-trunks, and the railway tunnels and many of the bridges over the Meuse were hurriedly destroyed.

Early the following morning six German columns under General von Emmich, preceded by von Marwitz's cavalry corps, crossed the Belgian frontier near Gemmenich. Presently horrified peasants, toiling in the harvest fields, beheld the sun glinting on the endless lines of helmets and rifle-barrels as the invading hordes rolled steadily onward to the strains of 'Deutschland über Alles' and 'Die Wacht am Rhein'. The horse-drawn field artillery rumbled after them. Motor-cars laden with staff officers swept past the marching ranks. The German cavalry patrols spread out swiftly over the surrounding countryside, ruthlessly trampling the corn underfoot. Near the Dutch frontier, fierce fighting broke out before the fortress of Visé, which controlled the lines of march of the German 1st and 2nd Army. By nightfall they had succeeded in crossing the Meuse to the north of the town. A patrol of Uhlans rode instantly for Liège, which, girdled by a ring of strong forts, barred the gateway into Belgium from Germany. General von Ludendorff, the Deputy Chief of Staff, passed his first night on foreign soil at the modest inn opposite the railway station at Hervé. Within the walls of Liège the Belgian garrison anxiously awaited the assault, which they knew would soon be launched with overwhelming force.

On the evening of Monday, August 3rd, up in the spacious, land-locked anchorage in the Orkney Islands, the bugles sounded 'Sunset'. The ensigns came slowly down from their staffs, as on board the anchored ships, in obedience to the Navy's ritual, the men stood rigidly to attention.

Since their arrival in Scapa Flow on July 31st the Fleet had watched and waited in suspense. On August 2nd the Poldhu wireless announced that Germany had declared war on Russia the evening before. 'If that is true the end can't be long in coming', a young officer wrote in his diary. 'I put it for the day after tomorrow.'

Far across the Pentland Firth rose the dark crags of Dunnet Head and Duncansby Head, and, further still, the faint blue peaks of Morven. To the northward lay the principal island of the Orkney group, Mainland, with the cathedral of St Magnus rising high above the grey roof-tops of Kirkwall; with its hundreds of little, white-walled crofts, brown peat-stacks, tidy, well-tilled fields, and heather-clad heights. On the south-eastern side of the Flow were the low-lying islands of Burray and South Ronaldsay; and on the south-western side, the mountainous island of Hoy with its reddish cliffs glowing in the evening sunlight, and, in the Sound between Hoy and South Ronaldsay, the low green isle of Flotta.

The great ships were moored in order. There was the flagship, the *Iron Duke*. There were the four Battle Squadrons: *Marlborough, Colossus, Hercules, Neptune, St Vincent, Vanguard, Superb,* and *Collingwood; King George V, Centurion, Ajax, Audacious, Orion, Monarch, Conqueror,* and *Thunderer; King Edward VII, Hindustan, Britannia, Africa, Hibernia, Commonwealth, Zealandia,* and *Dominion; Dreadnought* and *Temeraire.* There was the 1st Battle Cruiser Squadron: *Lion, Princess Royal, Queen Mary,* and *New Zealand.* There were the 2nd and 3rd Cruiser Squadrons and the 1st and 2nd Light Cruiser Squadrons.

On Sunday the order was given to rid the ships of all superfluous woodwork. Doors were accordingly dismantled and thrown overboard, followed by most of the cabin furniture— tables, chairs, chests of drawers, etc.; and most of the ships' boats were sent ashore. 'We are enveloped in fog', wrote Beatty to his wife, 'with our nets out ready for most things. We spent all yesterday getting rid of superfluities, and still preparing.' On Monday night the battle cruisers and the armoured cruisers were ordered to reconnoitre the Shetlands in consequence of a report — subsequently found to be groundless — that the Germans might be attempting to land on those islands. On Tuesday morning Sir John Jellicoe was ordered to take over command of the Fleet which, an hour before noon, put to sea and stood to the eastward.

Twelve hours later a wireless message in cypher was received from the Admiralty. It was the long-awaited War Telegram: *Commence hostilities against Germany.*

CHAPTER 24

' *War by midnight* '

As the warm summer dusk deepened into darkness, after the last of the waterfowl in the willow-encircled lake had gone to roost, and as the long tiers of brilliantly lighted windows of the Admiralty and Foreign Office gleamed through the intervening foliage, there was a sound of ceaseless hurrying footsteps along the trim gravel walks of St James's Park: for there were more wayfarers abroad just then than was usual at that late hour. Presently the current of traffic, both here in the Park and also in Birdcage Walk and the Mall, set increasingly towards the Palace.

Throughout the whole of the evening the principal streets of the West End were thronged with excited crowds of people eagerly awaiting the news that war had been declared. The British ultimatum to Germany was due to expire in this country at 11 p.m.: for Central European Time is one hour ahead of G.M.T. Wild reports of German acts of aggression which never occurred were quickly spread by successive editions of the evening newspapers. Motor-cars adorned with French and British colours, moving cautiously through the throng, were loudly cheered. Bands of men and women were marching up and down, singing patriotic songs and waving flags. At the head of one of the largest of these processions there was proudly borne an Irish flag—a golden harp on a green field: for, owing to Redmond's speech on the previous day, Ireland and the Irish had suddenly become very popular with the London crowds. From time to time soldiers in scarlet or khaki appeared and seamen with kitbags slung over their shoulders. This added a further touch of colour and drama to the occasion. Many people stopped them and insisted on shaking hands with them.

While the excitement and suspense were at their height J. B. Booth and Edgar Wallace, then on the staff of *Town Topics*, stood for a moment on the pavement at the Shaftesbury Avenue corner of Piccadilly Circus, waiting to cross over, on their way

317

to dine at the Café Royal. The traffic roared past them in a steady stream until the policeman on point duty raised his hand, when a large motor-car, filled with young men and girls in evening dress, all cheering and waving flags, slowed down at the crossing.

Edgar Wallace, who had himself served in the Army, had his eyes on a ribbon on the constable's tunic.

'South Africa?' he asked, and the man nodded.

'They're making a terrible fuss about a terrible thing, sir.'

That night the brasserie and grill-room of the Café Royal were crowded and uproarious above the average. The tall mirrors between the opposing caryatids that rose to the gaudily painted ceiling reflected the flushed and excited countenances of the diners leaning forward on the red plush settees as they discussed unendingly the one topic of the hour. The great European war which had been so often and so confidently predicted within these very walls had come at last. Only a few brief hours separated them from Armageddon. Nothing short of a miracle could avert it. Before midnight England would be at war ! It was inconceivable, it was appalling, *but it was happening!* At intervals were heard bursts of lusty cheering in the streets outside, and the roar of patriotic choruses. The tension in the overheated, smoke-laden atmosphere steadily increased, and the babel of contending voices grew louder. Presently :

'German waiters were standing on the marble tables singing the "Marseillaise" with great gusto. The impromptu choir was conducted by Ashley Dukes, then dramatic critic of the *New Age*. A few more enthusiastic young men stood around the tables encouraging the German waiters, who lustily exhorted the citizens of the French Republic to unfurl their banners, form their battalions, and march, march, march.'[1]

Most of the noise on that hectic August night at the old Café was in fact made by the younger set—the various 'arty' groups and their models, the *New Age* coterie, and the like. But at other tables, where sat the journalists and theatrical folk conversing in low tones of newspapers going out of business and of theatres closing down, there was noticeably less gaiety: for them the future was grim and forbidding.

[1] Deghy and Waterhouse, *Café Royal* (1955), p. 134.

Some time later Herman Finck strolled over to Booth, and the two men set off up Shaftesbury Avenue to the Palace Theatre, where the night's performance of *The Passing Show* was about to begin. Booth watched the revue for an hour or so from the back of the stalls, and then went round to Finck's room. It was crowded, as usual, with actors, artists, musicians, and writers of all sorts and conditions. There also the mood was one of gloom and foreboding. 'I think', Booth wrote in retrospect, 'there was not a man there who did not realize that we were at the deathbed of the old pleasant order of things; that life, as we had known it, lived it, and loved it, was at an end for ever.'[1]

Soon after nine o'clock Asquith and several of his senior colleagues met in the Cabinet Room in 10 Downing Street. The day had been full of conflicting rumours and reports; but no sign had come from Germany, nor any word from Sir Edward Goschen. Then suddenly news arrived of a message from the German Foreign Ministry to their Embassy in London, which had been intercepted by the War Office, informing Prince Lichnowsky that the British Ambassador in Berlin had asked for his passports at 7 p.m. and declared war. (It was later discovered that Goschen's own telegram to the Foreign Office had been held up by the German authorities.) The Admiralty was thereupon ordered to warn the Fleet and our coastal defences were put on their guard against a possible surprise attack. Otherwise it was decided that nothing should be done until the expiration of the ultimatum. War was now a foregone conclusion. The Ministers sat round the long green table in that historic chamber where, each in his day, Chatham, Shelburne, Pitt, Fox, Castlereagh, Canning, Wellington, Palmerston, Disraeli, Gladstone and Salisbury had pondered and deliberated, under the great portrait of Sir Robert Walpole. Slowly the minutes passed. To the end of their lives these Ministers would remember that agonizing pause before the sands ran out, and the irrevocable deed had been done.

'As the hour approached a deep and tense solemnity fell on

[1] J. B. Booth, *The Days We Knew* (1943), p. 2.

the room. No one spoke. It was like awaiting the signal for the pulling of a lever which would hurl millions to their doom—with just a chance that a reprieve might arrive in time. Our eyes wandered anxiously from the clock to the door, and from the door to the clock, and little was said.

' "Boom !" The deep notes of Big Ben rang out into the night the first strokes in Britain's most fateful hour since she arose out of the deep. A shuddering silence fell upon the room. Every face was suddenly contracted in a painful intensity. "Doom ! Doom ! Doom !" to the last stroke. The big clock echoed in our ears like the hammer of destiny . . . '[1]

Shortly after Winston Churchill arrived, buoyant and self-assured, from the Admiralty. He informed his colleagues that the War Telegram had just been dispatched to the Fleet. Soon afterwards the Ministers dispersed.

Away across the Parks, Cambon arrived back in the French Embassy at Albert Gate from the Foreign Office about half an hour before the British ultimatum to Germany was due to expire. On his way up to bed the old Ambassador stopped to talk with a few of his secretaries. Silence fell on them as the clock struck eleven. 'Gentlemen !' exclaimed Cambon. 'England has declared war.'

The theatres were emptying now, and taxi-cabs filled with loads of cheering, shouting, flag-waving youngsters added themselves to the joyous throng. Hitherto the ringleaders in these increasingly rowdy demonstrations had belonged to the younger generation; but, as time went on, the patriotic ferment began to work upon their elders also; and later a good many of the middle-aged people, who earlier in the evening had preserved an admirably calm and orderly demeanour, proceeded to let themselves go.

Shortly after 11 o'clock the news that Great Britain had declared war on Germany spread like wildfire through the enormous crowds in Piccadilly and Whitehall. A great roaring cheer of defiance arose from the huge gathering in Trafalgar Square.

[1] David Lloyd George, *Memoirs*, I, p. 71.

Young men hoisted themselves up on the roofs of passing taxi-cabs and rode around, scarlet-faced, in the wildest spirits, singing and cheering at the tops of their voices. Innumerable Union Jacks and tricolours fluttered in the air. Carriages and taxi-cabs pulled up, and ladies and gentlemen in evening dress got out and fraternized with the commonalty. Processions were formed, and marched solemnly round the base of Nelson's column. A party of Frenchwomen danced a lively *cancan* to the strains of an accordion. Men lounging on the backs of Landseer's lions alternately cheered and refreshed themselves with pots of beer handed up to them from their friends below.

The German Embassy in Carlton House Terrace was besieged by an angry crowd, which first contented itself with hissing and groaning, and presently took to stone-throwing. After a number of windows had been smashed, a telephone call was sent out for assistance. A strong force of foot and mounted police thereupon arrived from Cannon Row police station, and, not without difficulty, finally succeeded in restoring order.

The warlike demonstrations of that sultry August night culminated in a dramatic scene outside Buckingham Palace. To the delight of the huge crowds who were assembled there the King and Queen again showed themselves on the balcony for a short time after dinner. Again and again there arose roar after roar of full-throated applause, followed by the singing of 'God Save the King', 'Rule, Britannia' and the 'Marseillaise'.

The King and Queen at last retired through the window; but the enormous crowd remained—tens of thousands of people, their numbers continually increasing as more and more, drawn by the sound of those great rolling cheers, converged from all directions on Buckingham Palace. Hawkers carrying trays filled with favours moved to and fro among the throng, crying, 'Don't forget your colours! Don't forget your colours!' Lord Lonsdale, a well-known sporting figure of the day, stood looking on in the company of one of his coster protégés. All ages, all ranks, and most callings were represented in that vast concourse. Procession after procession of young men marched in from the neighbouring streets. And still the crowds went on increasing until they filled the whole space around the Victoria Memorial.

Presently word was passed round by the police that silence

was necessary, as the King was in council. For a while the tumult subsided, except for a few spasmodic outbursts of cheering; and there ensued a throbbing, low-pitched hum of excited argument and discussion until a lady came out of the Palace and announced that war had been declared. At that the cheering burst out afresh, culminating in a terrific roar of applause that might have been heard across St James's Park at the German Embassy. There were continual calls for the King, interspersed with the singing of 'For he's a jolly good fellow' and 'We won't go home till we see him'—the sentiment was immensely popular, and the words were chanted over and over again. Motor-cars gaily decorated with flags and streamers, crowded inside and out, drove round and round the Victoria Memorial in processional order—men and women standing up on the roofs waving flags and cheering vociferously, until they were at last brought to a standstill by the pressure of the throngs assembled outside the Palace.

Suddenly there came a cry, 'There they are!' — and to a tremendous roar of applause, King George and Queen Mary, for the last time on that historic night, appeared on the balcony. Presently the young Prince of Wales, who could be seen standing shyly in the background, came forward on a motion from his father and stood beside them. For several minutes the Royal Party remained on the balcony, bowing their acknowledgments to the madly excited multitudes, then finally retired amidst a thunderous salvo of applause; while on the steps below, scarcely recognized in all the uproar, stood a little group of Ministers, including Sir Edward Grey and Winston Churchill. Children were hoisted up on the shoulders of their parents to behold such a scene of frenzied and sustained enthusiasm as none of those who were present were ever likely to forget. All around was packed a seething mass of wildly applauding spectators, many of whom had climbed up on to the Victoria Memorial; walking sticks and umbrellas were waved in the air, hats raised in salute; men and women stood side by side on the roofs of the stationary taxi-cabs, cheering, cheering, cheering . . .

Once again the opening bars of the National Anthem crashed out. Tens of thousands of voices were lifted up, in fervent, ecstatic accord, extolling the Monarch who stood, silent and still, on the balcony above; while a glorious moon rose high above the tree-tops, shining down on the obsequies of the old order.

INDEX